# Palgrave Advances in Luxury

**Series Editors**
Paurav Shukla
Southampton Business School
University of Southampton
Southampton, UK

Jaywant Singh
Kingston Business School
Kingston University
Kingston Upon Thames, UK

The field of luxury studies increasingly encompasses a variety of perspectives not just limited to marketing and brand management. In recent times, a host of novel and topical issues on luxury such as sustainability, counterfeiting, emulation and consumption trends have gained prominence which draw on the fields of entrepreneurship, sociology, psychology and operations.

Examining international trends from China, Asia, Europe, North America and the MENA region, *Palgrave Advances in Luxury* is the first series dedicated to this complex issue. Including multiple perspectives whilst being very much grounded in business, its aim is to offer an integrated picture of the management environment in which luxury operates. It explores the newer debates relating to luxury consumption such as the signals used in expressing luxury, the socially divisive nature of luxury and the socio-economic segmentation that it brings. Filling a significant gap in our knowledge of this field, the series will help readers comprehend the significant management challenges unique to this construct.

More information about this series at
http://www.palgrave.com/gp/series/15396

Isabel Cantista · Teresa Sádaba
Editors

# Understanding Luxury Fashion

From Emotions to Brand Building

*Editors*
Isabel Cantista
Lusíada University of Porto
Porto, Portugal

Teresa Sádaba
ISEM Fashion Business School
Madrid, Spain

ISSN 2662-1061          ISSN 2662-107X   (electronic)
Palgrave Advances in Luxury
ISBN 978-3-030-25653-1     ISBN 978-3-030-25654-8   (eBook)
https://doi.org/10.1007/978-3-030-25654-8

Cover illustration: MirageC/Moment/Getty Images

This Palgrave Macmillan imprint is published by the registered company Springer Nature Switzerland AG
The registered company address is: Gewerbestrasse 11, 6330 Cham, Switzerland

*To our Students who share with us the passion for a better Fashion and a better World.*
*To our families who fill our hearts with Joy. Thank you for being there, no matter what.*

# Foreword

*Understanding Luxury Fashion: From Emotions to Brand Building* is not an option in the contemporary world of fashion. It is a necessity due to the outstanding development of luxury products and services in the field of Fashion.

In this book, edited by Isabel Cantista and Teresa Sabada, both teaching at University, the luxury dimension in Fashion is explored through ten chapters, mixing theory and case studies, with an international approach.

What is particularly interesting is the choice made by the editors to highlight the preeminence of the immaterial perspective on material and tangible aspects. This immaterial dimension is key and deals with the "aspirational" needs related to personal values and the "positional" needs, which are more external and social.

This approach leads to a transdisciplinary framework, combining philosophy, psychology, sociology and history, enabling a comprehensive and deep analysis of the phenomenon of luxury fashion.

However, the current challenges are not ignored, when it comes to the impact of digital technologies and sustainability through the whole fashion value chain. The growing importance of China and Chinese consumers in luxury fashion, all over the world, is also underlined.

Dr. Dominique Jacomet
Professor & Dean
Institut Français de la Mode
Paris, France

# Contents

# Notes on Contributors

**Cesare Amatulli** is Associate Professor of Marketing at the University of Bari, Italy. He has been Visiting Professor at LUISS University, Italy, and Visiting Researcher at the Ross School of Business, USA, and at the University of Hertfordshire, UK. He has published in major international peer-reviewed academic journals, such as *Journal of Consumer Research, European Journal of Marketing, Psychology & Marketing* and *Journal of Business Research*.

**Liz Barnes** is a Professor of Fashion Marketing at Manchester Metropolitan University, UK. Her research interests focus on the concept of 'fast fashion' in relation to supply chain management, omnichannel retail, fashion marketing communications and the fashion retail environment. She is an Editorial Advisory Board member of the *Journal of Fashion Marketing and Management* and Deputy Chair of the Academy of Marketing's Fashion Marketing and Consumption SIG. Liz has held a number of senior posts at higher education institutions in the UK and is currently Head of the School of Fashion at Manchester Metropolitan University.

**Isabel Cantista** is Associate Professor of Marketing and Innovation at Universidade Lusíada, Porto, Portugal and a Visiting Professor at ISEM—Fashion Business School, in Madrid. Isabel conducts research projects on fashion innovation and marketing, having published so far several books. She has been invited to be a Key Speaker by organisations like COTANCE—European Confederation of the Leather Industry, or IAF—International Apparel Federation World Conference. In 2008, Isabel created the GFC-Global Fashion Conference®. This international conference aims to bring together academia and industry contributing to the building of knowledge and the sharing of positive experiences with the scope of promoting a sustainable model of development for fashion business.

**Lindsey Carey** is a Senior Lecturer in Consumer Behaviour and Research Methods from Glasgow Caledonian University where she also leads the international development of partnerships. Lindsey's teaching expertise lies within the discipline of Marketing. She is involved with research in the area of ethical behaviour and sustainability. Another area of interest of Lindsey is in educational research and the impact of mobility on student experience. She is an external examiner, a reviewer for academic journals, member of the scientific committee of a conference and currently a consumer expert for the Mail on Sunday (Scotland).

**Ambrogia Cereda** is a Researcher in Sociology of culture and communication at e-Campus Università Telematica Novedrate, Italy. Ambrogia helds a Ph.D. in Sociology and Methodology of Social Research at the Università Cattolica del Sacro Cuore of Milan, where she collaborates with ModaCult, Centre for the study of fashion and cultural production. Ambrogia was involved in research projects on consumption, design and fashion-advertisement. Her main research interest lies in the sociology of the body, with a special concern for the issues related to body image, identity and gender. She is currently developing research in the field of emotion studies.

**François H. Courvoisier** is Ph.D. in economics, graduated from the University of Neuchâtel, Switzerland. François is a Professor at the

University of Applied Sciences Western Switzerland, where he teaches marketing in the Haute Ecole de Gestion Arc.

In 2010, he has co-founded the Institute of Watch Marketing: he manages research projects, events and publications for the watch brands, their partners and suppliers.

He has published manuals in marketing and written several articles on watch marketing in scientific journals and in the specialised watch press. He is co-author of ten books specialised in watch marketing published at LEP (Editions Loisirs & Pédagogie).

**Matteo De Angelis** is Associate Professor of Marketing at Luiss University. He got his Ph.D. in Management at the University of Bologna in 2008. He has been Visiting Scholar at Northwestern University in 2007 and Visiting Professor at the University of Wisconsin-Milwaukee from 2009 to 2012. His articles have appeared in such top journals as *Journal of Marketing Research, Journal of Consumer Research, International Journal of Research in Marketing, Journal of Business Ethics, Psychological Science, Journal of the Academy of Marketing Science* and *Journal of Business Research*. He is author of the book *Sustainable Luxury Brands* edited by Palgrave Macmillan.

**Virginie De Barnier** is a tenured professor at Aix-Marseille Graduate School of Management in France. She also serves as the Dean of this school and is a member of several Aix-Marseille University boards since 2013. She holds degrees in both marketing (Ph.D., M.B.A. and Master's degree) and psychology (Master's Degree). Her research interests include studying the links between psychology and marketing. She studies luxury brand management, brand personality and communication. Her work has been presented at many international conferences. She wrote several books and chapters in books and supervises numerous Ph.D. students working on luxury branding issues.

**Carmela Donato** is a post-doc research fellow at Luiss University, Italy. She got her Ph.D. in Economic and Business Administration at University of Calabria (IT) and a Research Master in Business Administration (Marketing profile) at Rijksuniversiteit University of Groningen (NL). Her research has been published in national and international peer-reviewed academic journals such as *Psychology & Marketing*, moreover her research has been presented in major international marketing conferences such as European Marketing Academy Conference, Association Consumer Research and Academy of Marketing Science.

**Catherine Glover** is a Senior Lecturer in Fashion Communication at Northumbria University, UK. She has an industry background working in luxury public relations, design journalism and arts publishing and teaches these specialisms. Her research interests are transnational brand storytelling and how social and brand communities enact story processes that engage and activate grassroots action. Glover has particularly published work looking at the luxury brand Rapha, fashionable cycling and transmitted cultural flows, and reported for many years on the fashion, design and architecture scene in the UK for a Japanese avant-garde audience.

**Eugenia Josa** has a Bachelor's Degree in Landscape Architecture from the University of Navarra and an Executive M.B.A. in Fashion Business Management from ISEM Fashion Business School. She holds a Ph.D. from the University of Navarra, where her research focused on the design of fashion stores. His doctoral thesis is titled: *The Architecture of the Store. The Cases of Javier Carvajal for Loewe*. She has presented papers in international conferences and has written a chapter "The Store in the Digital Environment" for the book *Fashion in the Digital Environment*. At ISEM she is responsible for lecturing and conducting activities within the topic of Creativity.

**Marta Mendonça** is Professor of Philosophy at Universidade NOVA de Lisboa, Portugal. Marta holds a Ph.D. from this University with a thesis on *The Doctrine of Modalities in the Philosophy of Gottfried Wilhelm Leibniz* (2001). Her main fields of interest are Modalities, Early Modern Philosophy, Philosophy of Nature and Bioethics. She is author of numerous articles on these topics and visiting professor in different Universities in Portugal, Spain, Brazil, Chile and the United Kingdom. She coordinates a research project on "Comprehension, Explanation and Language" at the CHAM—Center for the

Humanities, research unit of NOVA School of Social Sciences and Humanities.

**Patsy Perry** is a Senior Lecturer in Fashion Marketing at The University of Manchester, UK. She has published academic journal articles and book chapters from her research on corporate social responsibility and sustainability in fashion, luxury consumption and marketing, and fashion supply chain management. She is an Associate Editor of the *Journal of Fashion Marketing and Management* and has appeared on TV, radio and in the press on the topic of fast fashion sustainability and online fashion retail. She is a Fellow of the Higher Education Academy and has experience of international teaching at academic institutions in Europe and China.

**Claire Roederer** is an Associate Professor of Marketing at EM Strasbourg Business School in France. Graduated from ESCP Europe Paris, she received her Ph.D. in Marketing from the University of Bourgogne (Dijon-France). Her research focuses on experiential consumption, experiential marketing and customer experience. She launched the Customer Experience Chair at EM Strasbourg in 2017 to promote academic research on customer experience. She has published several academic articles and case studies on the topic and written "Marketing and Experiential Consumption" (2013) (Ems Management & Société) and "Experiential Marketing: Toward a Marketing of Cocreation" (2015) with M. Filser (Vuibert, Paris).

**Elyette Roux** was a tenured professor at Aix-Marseille Graduate School of Management in France. She served many years as the director of the CERGAM research centre. Her research interests include brand management, consumers' relations to brands and luxury brands. Hers book, co-written with the French philosopher Gilles Lipovetsky, *The Eternal Luxury*, published in paperback and translated into several languages, made her work worldwide known. She supervised many Ph.D. theses and participated to many Ph.D. and HDR juries. She contributed to what she liked to call "the co-construction of knowledge".

**Teresa Sádaba** has been professor of Political Communications and Legal and Political Institutions at the School of Communication of the University of Navarra, where she collaborated in the launch of the Master in Political and Corporate Communications. Teresa is also Professor at the Graduate School of Political Management at George Washington University.

Teresa is currently the Dean of ISEM Fashion Business School of the University of Navarra, having launched the doctorate in Applied Creativity. Her research has focused on the theory of Framing, on which she has published numerous articles and two books. She has been a research scholar at different universities.

**Kirsten Scott** is Programme Leader for M.A. Fashion Design Womenswear at Istituto Marangoni in London. Her work as a fashion, textile and accessory designer and lecturer is multidisciplinary and process-led. She completed a Ph.D. in Constructed Textiles at the Royal College of Art in 2012 and has worked for leading international brands. As a passionate maker, Kirsten's practice asks questions about the meaning and value of the hand made and the human in future, sustainable, luxury fashion; her focus as a researcher has become increasingly holistic and multidisciplinary, concerned with fashion's potential in benign design.

**Aileen Stewart** is a lecturer at Glasgow Caledonian University within the School of Business and Society, in Scotland (UK). She received her bachelor's degree in 'Clothing' from Heriot Watt University, School of Textiles and Design and a master's degree in International Fashion Marketing from Glasgow Caledonian University. Her current research interests are luxury fashion brand extensions, consumer buyer behaviour of fashion and Consumer Brand Relationship (CBR).

**María Villanueva** holds a Ph.D. in Architecture from the University of Navarra, where she graduated with Honors in the Final Project and won the Luis Moya Blanco Fin de Carrera Award. She lectures at the School of Architecture, the Faculty of Communication and ISEM Fashion Business School in the University of Navarra.

María focuses her research on the history and theory of design. She has presented her work in international conferences and published book chapters and articles in indexed journals like *PPA, Res Mobilis,*

*Constelaciones, Estoa.* She has been a visiting scholar at universities like the Getty Research Institute in Los Angeles and the GSAPP Columbia University in New York.

**Tiantian Ye** undertook an MPhil under the supervision of Patsy Perry and Liz Barnes at The University of Manchester on the conceptualisation of luxury fashion in China, decoding the China's dynamic and fast-changing consumption landscape through insights of the nation's social ideologies and cultural heritage. He is an experienced fashion and culture writer, contributing to several national media outlets. He is currently developing branding strategy and curatorial projects for an emerging design hotel brand reinventing the poetic Chinese fine living concept and raising awareness of ethical tourism. He is the co-founder of Haoji Creative Lab, a Chinese design exhibition curation agency.

# List of Figures

# List of Tables

# List of Boxes

# Part I

## Introduction

# 1

# Understanding Luxury Fashion: Origins and Contemporary Issues

Isabel Cantista and Teresa Sádaba

Luxury has been reflected on for more than twenty-five centuries, from Plato to Epicure, from Luther to Mandeville and Veblen, as mentioned by Lipovetsky and Roux (2012). And the allure of luxury has never faded; on the contrary, its appeal has intensified in contemporary society.

On the other hand, the connections between luxury and fashion are profound. In the beginning, fashion coincided with luxury (Belfanti 2011), being available only to some and was the object of detailed regulation through sumptuary laws[1] (Beebe 2010; Belfanti 2009) which

---

[1]Beebe (2010, p. 812) defines a "society's sumptuary code as its system of consumption practices, akin to a language (or at least a set of dialects), by which individuals in the society signal through

---

I. Cantista (✉)
Lusíada University of Porto, Porto, Portugal
e-mail: icantista@por.ulusiada.pt

T. Sádaba
ISEM Fashion Business School, University of Navarra, Madrid, Spain
e-mail: Teresa.sadaba@isem.es

© The Author(s) 2020                                                                                  3
I. Cantista and T. Sádaba (eds.), *Understanding Luxury Fashion*,
Palgrave Advances in Luxury, https://doi.org/10.1007/978-3-030-25654-8_1

defined who could use certain garments, colours and fabrics in an effort to govern appearances, with the aim that these reflected a defined social order and hierarchy. But in the more modern era, new paths have been forged with fashion becoming more democratic. Yet, the reference to luxury has never been forgotten (Jacomet 2016). And for this reason, it is important to reflect on luxury.

The work of Lipovetsky and Roux (2012) briefly portrays the evolution of luxury and its meaning over the course of time. Luxury begins as a luxury-gift, which distracts man from his natural inclinations towards a sense of ownership or the conservation of what is of immediate utility to him. To give and reciprocate generously is a way of subordinating the individual element to the global scheme of things, ensuring the predominance of relationships between men over the relationship between men and things. In this way, and through the ostentatious donation of presents and their recompense with other presents of comparable value, primitive society makes an effort to consolidate a network of relationships and to establish peace treaties. It can thus be affirmed that primitive magnificence is revealed as being at the service of a superior social rationale: the desire for peace.

Luxury also serves as a means of guaranteeing a relationship of alliance between the living and the dead, between men and gods, a means of attracting the protection and benevolence of the gods or beings and spiritual forces, to men.

And when social organisation becomes more complex—through social, religious and political transformations—gifts then become monuments, grand sculptures, splendid palaces with beautiful decorations, and sumptuousness becomes linked not only to principles of inequality and power relationships, but also to ideas of inalterability and permanence, and to the desire for eternity.

---

their consumption their differences from and similarities to others. Laws that seek to control and preserve this code are sumptuary laws". The sumptuary laws originated in Republican Imperial Rome.

From the end of the Middle Ages, the aristocracy divested of its former military prerogatives, surrounded by the court and dependent on royal power, transformed itself by adopting luxurious lifestyles that were more decorative and sometimes characterised by their superficiality. Nevertheless, the Renaissance was also a period for the flourishing of the arts. Kings and princes wanted to be the protectors of artists and musicians and to surround themselves with works of art, to hear beautiful pieces of music and take care with their presentation. The growing wealth of merchants and bankers leads to the emergence of the bourgeoisie and luxury becomes a sphere accessible to the fortunes amassed through work, talent and merit, a sphere that thus opens to social mobility. The nobility and rich bourgeoisie equally seek to surround themselves by works of art: patronage, collections and the ownership of works of art become instruments of prestige in the world of the social elites. The collective and the sacred are replaced by a more personal and more aesthetic relationship, a more subjective aspiration to a more beautiful life that is more refined and more emotive. Until the sixteenth century (Belfanti 2009, 2011) luxury and fashion coincide. From the sixteenth century onwards, everything changes.

According to Belfanti (2009), the sixteenth century is the "turning point". Changes in clothing and accessories already start to become more frequent in the fourteenth century, but the expression of one's own taste in clothing was still to a great extent limited to the narrow circle of the social elite, with the careful strategy of appearance defined precisely by one's social class.

In this century there was not a generalized increase in purchasing power (Belfanti 2009, p. 272). On the contrary, the price of food increased such that it made the poor even poorer and landowners even wealthier. Meanwhile, there was an increase in the number of middle class and upper-class people whose success originated in the world of work. This increase led to an inflation of sumptuary laws in Europe, with examples of this (Beebe 2010; Belfanti 2009) also to be seen in other parts of the world, from Japan to the United States, in an attempt to maintain the status quo. Anyone who did not dress according to the strict definitions was put on trial and punished.

In the preamble to the proclamation issued in 1588 by the queen of England Elizabeth I, quoted by Belfanti (2009, p. 268), the sovereign deplores "the confusion of degrees of all estates, amongst whom diversity of apparel hath been always a special and laudable mark." The comments about the social confusion generated by this, are nevertheless, generalized. Belfanti (2009, p. 269) refers to, among others, comments made in 1583 by the English Puritan Philip Stubbles who wrote "it is verie hard to knowe who is noble, who is worshipfull, who is a gentleman, who is not…this is a great confusion and a general disorder." But the answer could have been given to him by an anonymous writer who, as early as 1565, wrote to the Governor of Milan saying "if it is said it is decorous for a city the ability to distinguish by dress at first sight the commoners from the nobles and the greater nobles from the others, one might answer that this means nothing (…) if there were not freedom of dress, it would be a good thing to introduce it if for no other reason than that men might have the motivation to be known one as being better than another not for their dress but for their virtuous acts (…) as though nobility depends on clothes, or nobles know no other way of making themselves known".

The reasons behind the great increase in the sumptuary laws are political and economic and are not limited to a mere strategic game of appearances and, yet, they did not succeed in halting history. It is impossible to erase the ambition of human beings to become greater, and to have more, in what we can express as the extended self as proposed by Belk (1988).

The emergence of Fashion as a typical element of European society can thus be associated with a series of social situations, such as life in the court, the life of the aristocracy, the development of cities and the rise of the bourgeoisie and, namely, the affirmation of the individual to whom freedom of choice is a legitimate and inalienable right.

Nevertheless, we also would like to draw attention to many similarities between the consumption of luxury in the West and the East, with some historians even affirming that fashion was a Chinese invention from the Tang Dynasty (618–907) because of the Empress Yang Kuei-fei, whose style influenced tastes in Europe of the Middle Ages. However, even though fashion might have been born in China, it has to be recognised that it neither had the social nor economic conditions for this to affirm itself as a system or as a cultural institution of modernity.

According to Belfanti (2011, p. 211) while in India, China and Japan, fashion was identified with luxury and its influence came from a "trickle-down" effect, in Europe, the greater availability of a supply of Fashion products and accessories at more reduced prices led to many examples of a "trickle-up" effect.

In the West, Fashion attracted the attention of intellectuals, promoted the emergence of literature specialised in this area which aided the diffusion of its proposals and created a sophisticated and shared Culture of Fashion.

The passion for luxury and, as a consequence, for luxury fashion, is profoundly connected to the perspective of the other. In his reflections, Lipovetsky and Roux (2012, p. 63) refers to the desire to be admired, to be recognised by the other. He even affirms that in a time of unbridled individualism, luxury fashion contributes to the affirmation of individuality, expressing a need to stand out from the masses, to be different from the others, to feel like an exceptional being while simultaneously being immersed in the medium of others, with this distinction being justified precisely because of this immersion. In these times of relentless mass production, giant cities and globalisation, luxury fashion fulfils this function in an exemplary way.

In economic terms GDP per capita has reached levels never before witnessed in the world[2]; there have never been so many billionaires in the world, while the luxury segment can be divided into at least 16 sub-segments.[3] Because of this all, luxury products and services have multiplied in the world of Fashion. Luxury is everywhere and for its impact on many lives, not only the lives of consumers, but also the many lives dedicated to the production and selling of products and services of luxury fashion in the world, it deserves attention.

---

[2]The Conference Board Total Economy Database: McKinsey Global Institute analysis, 2016.
[3]Armando Branchini, "True Luxury Global Consumer Segmentation", Porto Luxury Brands Summit, Porto, 8 May 2015.

This book has an international approach, seeking to contribute to a deeper and richer understanding of the phenomenon of luxury fashion and brings together texts from different areas of study.

From all those perspectives, we want to focus luxury fashion in its human essence. And this is too the essence of the book: to approach luxury studies from a human, spiritual perspective more than a material one.

The structure of the book thus follows a logic that considers first, the framework for this analysis with a more philosophical approach and then, it goes through two main aspects in the relationship between luxury and the human being.

On the one hand, the emotional perspective: the aspirational sense and inclinations towards being more. On the other hand, the social perspective, our need of others, for belonging. And in both aspects detaining ourselves into contemporary expressions of luxury fashion.

Then, the book finishes with three chapters on different case studies, where those previous aspects are confirmed.

In this sense, the reader of this book is invited to discover luxury in a very distinctive manner; contributions in the book make us think about a comprehensive concept of luxury, exceeding limited tangible, material approaches. Contemporary material expressions are analysed starting from the aspects referred to above.

In this project we focussed on aspects which define as their horizon a future involving sustainable values, the presence and impact of digital technology and the growing importance of China in the world. And we did this with the aim of contributing to a debate that will shape the future.

The framework for the book is established in the chapter by Marta Mendonça and from a philosophical perspective, the origin of luxury and its relationship with human beings is explored. It is referred to by various authors, among them Voltaire, who questions "why luxury is a necessity in the lives of humans". And it is explained how culture, the "human world", provides the conditions so that the dynamics of tastes and desires materialise in different ways and thus furnishes humans with the realisation of their aspirations to luxury.

With regard to emotions, Ambrogia Cereda invites us to discover the transformation of consumer culture through the lens of "glamour", as defined by Gundle and Castelli (2006) the search for an enchanting and dreamlike experience with goods and services. This auratic dimension attached to places and things is understood in terms of luxuriousness, exists in the mind of the consumers and is linked to their interpretation of the symbolic world attached to the wide range of luxury goods.

Virginie de Barnier and Elyette Roux present a comparative study of values and emotions between Chinese and Brazilian consumers of luxury. This study, connecting psychology with consumerism, explores the existence of negative sentiments associated with the consumption of luxury goods, namely the phenomenon of shame and guilt. By comparatively analysing Chinese and Brazilian consumers, there is an identification of a greater degree of feelings of shame among Chinese consumers and a greater degree of guilt among their Brazilian counterparts. It also throws light on compensation phenomena that emerge and which lead to a sense of the need to recompense society, from their own considerable wealth, in a rebalancing of emotion and reason. This study is not only interesting in the sense of helping understand the market and consumer feelings, but also by way of what it can offer in terms of encouraging brands to contribute to the creation of more positive emotions in this market.

In the chapter written by Kirsten Scott, the Barkcloth Research Network is presented. This network of researchers was created in 2016 and has the objective of analysing the potential of the Ugandan barkcloth a non-woven, fibrous textile produced from the wild fig tree since at least the thirteenth century. Through artisanal productions processes, the potential of this fabric has been explored, taking on contemporary approaches to design, with its durability figuring importantly among its various qualities. They link this production with well-being, progressing from a material analysis to a deeper, more emotional one.

In the next section of the book—considering luxury as a social element—the first chapter is the proposal of Donato, De Angelis and Amatulli. They examined the Corporate Social Responsibility (CSR) initiatives of four Italian luxury fashion companies: Brunello Cuccinelli, Giorgio Armani, Prada and Fendi. The study illustrates how the values of sustainability contribute to "illuminating the positive contributions of these brands to the communities and societies in which they operate." Furthermore, the study demonstrates how the clients who buy luxury products for their inherent quality and not because of what they symbolise as status symbols—these being the most common clients in mature markets (Western Europe and the U.S.A.)—are particularly receptive to the similarly discreet communication of these values.

Focussing on the theme of perfume, the contribution of Aileen Stewart and Lindsey Carey links the consumption of perfume with the social networks of millennials. Millennials are that young generation, who are tech savvy, informed, with disposable time and income and who offer brands the promise of a future. From among the conclusions of this study, we highlight the value attributed by millennials to offline communication and how their use of perfume is more influenced by the communities they belong to and their lifestyle, rather than by celebrities with prestigious names.

Also from the society perspective, the chapter by Patsy Perry, Liz Barnes and Tiantian Ye illustrates how China became the largest luxury market in volume, representing in terms of value, the third largest market, after the U.S.A. and the E.U. Due to its vastness, China represents a world of diverse realities and the authors of the chapter bring our attention to this aspect and how it is a fallacy to attempt a linear and simplistic analysis of the Chinese market. But in this study, carried out through interviews with consumers of luxury in China, a trend is identified in terms of the fusion of traditional Chinese values with Western values, in a creative reinvention that influences the attitudes of Chinese consumers of luxury and opens the way to the development of further studies.

In the case study section, three case studies illustrate important aspects of the strategy of positioning and communication of luxury brands. The virtual communities created through social networks, the collaborative projects between architects and brands and the ability to involve consumers through storytelling and community-building are among the themes explored.

François Courvoisier and Claire Roederer present a case study, of how through social networks, particularly Instagram, the Omega watch brand launched, in collaboration with the watch enthusiast Robert-Jan

Broer and his watch community Fratellowatches.com, created in 1994, an event—Speedy Tuesday—which combines characteristics of viral marketing and tribal marketing. In two consecutive years, Omega launched on just one day, a limited collection for those passionate about the brand. The results vastly surpassed expectations.

And in the chapter by Eugenia Josa, María Villanueva and Isabel Cantista the relationship between architecture and fashion brands is explored through the lens of a case study, the analysis of the decades-long collaboration between the architect Javier Carvajal and the Spanish luxury brand Loewe. It is suggested that the cultural values that are shared and that materialise through projects for stores, contribute to so much more than simply communicating a visual identity in one of its expressions: visual merchandising. This case study illustrates how the Loewe brand projected itself as a modern brand, which sets store by its Spanish roots and its tradition of high-quality craftsmanship. The brand's identity in cultural terms is emphasised and a new model of dialogue between architecture and luxury brands is proposed.

Catherine Glover, in her chapter, through a critical textual analysis, explores how the Rapha brand, connected to the world of cycling, has managed to affirm itself as a luxury brand. Storytelling and community building have been the engine that determined the image of this sport brand and this was established by charting specific socio-cultural indicators, refined qualities and materialised story strands. The chapter shows how the stories use themes of luxurious adventure, rarefied travel and a philosophy of leisure through a rich textual and visual story content. This investigation is an interesting example of how the idea of luxury infiltrates twenty-first century marketing and quest for global wellness.

# Bibliography

Beebe, Barton. 2010. "Intellectual Property Law and the Sumptuary Code." *Harvard Law Review* 123 (4): 810–888.

Belfanti, Carlo Marco. 2009. "The Civilization of Fashion: At the Origins of a Western Social Institutions." *Journal of Social History* 43 (Winter): 261–283.

Belfanti, Carlo Marco. 2011. "Mode et Luxe à l' Époque Moderne: 'une grande divergence' entre Occident et Orient." In *Le Luxe – Essais sur la fabrique de l'ostentation*, edited by Olivier Assouly, 199–212. Paris: IFM/REGARD.

Belk, Russel W. 1988. "Possessions and the Extended Self." *Journal of Consumer Research* 15 (2): 139–168.

Gundle, Stephen, and Clino T. Castelli. 2006. *The Glamour System*. Basingstoke: Palgrave Macmillan.

Jacomet, Dominique. 2016. "The Globalisation of the Fashion Industry: Opportunities for European Companies?" In *Fashion Spaces—Geographical, Physical and Virtual*, edited by Isabel Cantista, 17–28. Coimbra: Conjuntura Actual Editora.

Lipovetsky, Gilles, and Elyette Roux. 2012. *O Luxo Eterno – Da Idade do Sagrado ao Tempo das Marcas*. Lisboa: Edições 70 (first published by Éditions Gallimard, 2003 Le Luxe Éternel. De l'àge du sacré au temps des marques).

# 2

# Understanding Luxury: A Philosophical Perspective

Marta Mendonça

## Introduction

Luxury is a multidisciplinary theme of study and reflection. A brief assessment of the most recent literature on the theme appears to focus on the economic, psychological and cultural thematics of luxury.[1] Much is written about the economy of luxury, about the economic impact of the so-called 'luxury' market, etc.; we deepen our understanding of the psychological motivations that lead us to be attracted to luxury and what might reinforce or inhibit such motivations; the marketing of luxury is developed and we attempt to understand the differentiating nuances of luxury. From a historical perspective, the emphasis is mainly on the culturally contextualised nature of luxury (Berry 1994). Obviously, luxurious objects or, more generally, the experience of luxury changes with time and differs between cultural contexts, just as it varies over the course of our lifetimes.

M. Mendonça (✉)
Universidade Nova de Lisboa, Lisbon, Portugal
e-mail: mmendonca@fcsh.unl.pt

© The Author(s) 2020
I. Cantista and T. Sádaba (eds.), *Understanding Luxury Fashion*,
Palgrave Advances in Luxury, https://doi.org/10.1007/978-3-030-25654-8_2

The anthropological and ethical considerations around the topic of luxury seem to have received less attention, in contrast to what we have seen in the past.[2] We have deepened our understanding of the more obvious underlying mechanisms of the phenomenon of luxury, but we are less interested in its meaning and *raison d'être*. What does the phenomenon of luxury tell us about ourselves? What does it reveal about our way of positioning ourselves before nature and how do we make use of luxury to fulfil our needs?

This affirmation does not annul the validity of another interesting observation. The term 'luxury' is quite frequent in the scientific literature that does not focus on the phenomenon of luxury in itself. It typically appears associated with 'need'; we ask ourselves if certain resources, certain medical techniques, certain educational environments or other such things, are "a luxury or a necessity." The term thus takes on a modal meaning, referring to something disposable or possibly even superfluous. Nevertheless, this is accompanied by a positive connotation; luxury is presented as something valuable and beneficial, despite not being available to all and despite the fact that it cannot be claimed as a right by all.

The anthropological and philosophical reflection on luxury is in itself, like philosophy as a whole, the object of this dichotomy; we frequently ask ourselves if "philosophy is a luxury or a necessity." It is thus also valid to ask whether *thinking about luxury*, about its nature and its meaning, is *a luxury or a necessity*.

In the following pages the countless technical dimensions of the phenomenon of luxury will not be dealt with; we are solely interested in briefly reflecting on its presence in human life and on what the complex reality of luxury reveals about our very being and the way we relate to the world.

## A Specifically Human Phenomenon

Whatever our assessment of this phenomenon, of what defines it, of what the experience of luxury consists of, etc., perhaps one common denominator can be found in all perspectives: that the phenomenon of luxury is *exclusively human*. Regardless of what we identify as luxurious, luxury only seems to manifest itself in the lives of human beings, taking a great variety of forms. This means that luxury provides a possible window onto human reality and its singularity. Exploring the dichotomy established, one should ask—alluding to Voltaire—not whether something is a luxury or a necessity but, rather, *why luxury is a necessity in the lives of humans.*

The more or less general consensus about the humanness of the experience of luxury and its universal nature does not waive the need for a minimal reflection on what luxury, as such, consists of. After all, the phenomenon of luxury is not the only one that we recognise as being exclusively human. This task is anything but easy; if we glance through the specialised literature on the subject, we soon realise that the defining notes are highly diverse and variable (Hyeong-Yeon 2003, I, Chapter 1). The range of notes is incredibly vast. There are those who associate luxury with excellence, exclusivity, simplicity, elegance, etc. Others prefer to define it negatively, as the opposite of vulgarity. While many—possibly the majority—insist on the expensive character of what they consider to be luxurious, others regard authentic luxury as something priceless, that cannot strictly be bought; it is often seen as something free, a peculiar form of excess and surprise which accompanies certain, possibly even day-to-day, experiences—such as having time for a good conversation or for reading a book, contemplating a landscape or going for a walk, etc.—thus being accessible to a vast number of people. Clearly, not all these notes exclude each other, but they certainly do not exhaust the definitions of the experience of luxury.

This fact, despite making a reflection on luxury particularly difficult, is unsurprising and, to a certain extent, predictable. Being a specifically human phenomenon, the experience of luxury is directly connected to the experience of freedom, and it is precisely this exercise of freedom that makes it possible. It therefore comes as no surprise that it can only be codified with great difficulty. The linking of luxury to freedom explains why it is so difficult to provide a comprehensive description of its distinguishing characteristics. We find it easier to think that luxury refers so closely to personal life that it can only be truly defined or identified on a case-by-case basis, with reference to each individual and their unique context. For the parents of a very young child, an uninterrupted night's sleep is a 'luxury'; for a student, the first afternoon at an outdoor café after the exam period is desired as a 'luxury'; for Viktor Frankl, an Auschwitz prisoner, to be able to have an 'inner conversation' with his wife who was imprisoned in a different concentration camp, was also a 'luxury' that could not be stolen from him, not even in those conditions of extreme precariousness (Frankl 2000, pp. 48–50); for an immigrant who has just arrived at his new destination, to be able to speak his own language is also a 'luxury'. The examples are infinite and refer to the circumstances of our personal lives and the spheres of liberty enjoyed within them. In all of these cases, we regard a luxury as something that makes a certain life experience particularly pleasant, softenens a given experience of life, makes life less harsh and enables us to escape from the often laboursome or tiring environment of daily existence. This is the reason why the phenomenon of luxury has such close affinities with celebration, and why our ability to celebrate is one of the most culturally disseminated forms of luxury in the lives of humans (Pieper 1963, Chapters 1 and 2).

Having established this, the common use of the term leads us to some notes connected with the experience of luxury. The term seems to contain both a *quantitative* dimension, associated with the idea of excess ('a luxury of details') and a *qualitative* dimension associated with the idea of refinement ('to have luxurious tastes'). Luxury therefore seems to always make some kind of reference to a measure—which is exceeded in luxury—and tends to be presented as something relative, be it historically, individually or socially; this is also why—as is well known—novelties begin as luxuries and then stop being seen as such. As a result, culture and history, understood as spheres of growth and appropriation of possibilities, comprise the framework in which luxury is possible and evolves.

The idea of a measure is important. In the human experience of luxury, there is a contrast between what is 'necessary' and what is 'superfluous', which operates in many dimensions of human existence and that goes well beyond what we tend to consider as luxurious; it is the contrast between our quotidian and what diverges from it, between work and celebration, between effort and rest, between the indispensable and the possible, etc. Contained in the idea of luxury, in the exceeding of the measure, is the possibility and the desire to evade the multiple forms of limitations that life, in one way or another, is subject to. And, yet, the idea of the measure is crucial; we do not think about life as a celebration, but we seek celebration at the heart of life. What makes evasion so valuable is that it is not a permanent state. In this sense, luxury is always as such 'an extra', something which we concede to ourselves, but which we do not savour permanently.

Considering the difficulties inherent to the effort of focussing on the luxurious object, it may be preferable to consider human beings instead, in order to understand what there is in them that simultaneously permits and requires the experience of luxury. While it may be true that the experience of luxury is a specifically human experience—exclusive to human beings and universal in the world of humans—it is worthwhile trying to understand why human beings have this natural relationship with the 'superfluous', a relationship that is so intrinsic to our nature that it drives us to seek the superfluous almost as if it were a necessity. Otherwise, only with great difficulty could we acknowledge the universality of the phenomenon of luxury.

Despite its enigmatic appearance, this possibility is not contradictory. Plato recognised it with great acuity in *Protagoras* (320 c–322 d) and reflected on its ambivalent meaning in Book II of *Republic* (372 e). In the first case, by dealing precisely with the question of what distinguishes us from other living beings, Plato presented the human being as an animal made for luxury, that is, as an animal—the only one—for whom the superfluous becomes a necessity (322 a). In *Republic* he considers what implications this unique nature of human beings has on the constitution of society. He observes, for example, that the city of men has to be "a city of luxury" (372 e), where the things deemed as necessary do not simply include housing, clothes or footwear, but also all the combinations of colours, gold, ivory, etc. (373 a). As a result of this, cities are constrained to develop, and to include new professions or reinforce existing ones (372 c–373 d).

The two observations are both immensely pertinent and complementary. Thanks to the first one, we discover ourselves as beings that exceed a strictly biological dimension. Thanks to the second, we discover that this new dimension of existence enables, although it does not guarantee, human fulfilment. By permitting excellence we are also exposed to the risk of failure. It is thus understood that the phenomenon of luxury always ends up being an object of ethical consideration.

Through this Platonic analysis, what makes humans beings beings for luxury is that they are constituted in such a way that what might be considered sufficient for the satisfaction of biological needs is also felt by human beings to be insufficient. And what makes the phenomenon of luxury an object for ethical consideration is that the relationship with the supra-biological is enabled by, and managed through, freedom; such relationship summons and binds freedom. In other words, there are many kinds of excess and not all of them are capable of guaranteeing what is sought through them: to live in conformity with our condition. Let us briefly consider each of these aspects.

## The Human Being as a Being Made for Luxury

In his presentation of the human condition, Plato presents human beings as an absolutely unique synthesis of biology (albeit poorly adapted) and of a not strictly biological inventive resourcefulness—*logos*. This unpredictable synthesis of biology and intelligence reveals itself—Plato argues—as a synthesis that is a simultaneously triumphant and distinguishing synthesis in human beings. *Logos* enables the biological viability of human beings (we are not biologically well adapted beings and consequently we are obliged to invent responses in order to ensure survival), and it simultaneously allows us—and obliges us—to transcend our own biology. Equipped by our intelligence to ensure our own survival, this capacity has led far beyond mere biology, allowing us to 'live well', that is, to aspire to the 'superfluous'. This means that, as a result of their rational nature, human beings are able to ensure their own survival, while at the same time discovering other aspirations within themselves, other needs, which extend far beyond biological needs, also seeking to fulfil such aspirations.

This is the reason why, when compared to other living beings, human beings emerge as animals made for luxury, made for the superfluous. They are animals for whom the mere satisfaction of biological needs is not enough, but who have aspirations that are not strictly biological—to truth, good, beauty, freedom, etc.—aspirations of meaning, ultimately. Thus, although it might be obvious that biological needs are absolutely crucial conditions for all human existence, if nothing more is offered to humans than the possibility of fulfilling these needs, if all else is denied, they feel they are being treated inhumanely.

Acknowledging these aspirations, one can affirm that the need to discover the meaning of life and to attribute meaning to their own activity somehow summarises what Plato intended when he presented human beings as beings made for luxury; for them, the superfluous (biologically speaking) is indispensable (in the human sense).

That which has been referred to negatively (when speaking of a need for meaning), can also be stated in a positive manner. Intelligence is not merely a resource developed in order to compensate for weak instinctive prowess, thus making human life biologically viable; rather, it is a sign of the excellence and singularity of humans. Culture—in its multiple dimensions—is the most obvious material expression of that excellence and singularity. It is also because of this that culture so clearly reveals the characteristics of human freedom and creativity, which human intelligence provides the crucial foundations for. To consider human beings as beings made for luxury is, fundamentally, to maintain that they are cultural beings by nature. Because our natural way of acting is always creative—inventive—the world of human beings is a world of culture and the superfluous or luxurious (in the radical anthropological sense) is intrinsic to human life, thus broadening the horizons and possibilities of human experience.

All cultures, including the most ancient, eloquently illustrate the affirmation above. In highly vulnerable contexts, in often extreme environments, human beings never simply limit themselves to satisfying their need for protection, food, defence, etc. Neither do they do this in a uniform way. They invent their own responses while invariably seeking beauty, decoration, the adornment of the human body and of the objects they produce, imbuing these very physical objects with the hallmarks of their being and of their individual actions. As far as can be assuaged, this quest for the superfluous—which here takes the form of beauty—is contemporary with those human actions which seek to ensure survival and respond to needs.

The omnipresence of this dimension of beauty in human life cannot be rationally seen as merely accidental. It presents itself as an essential dimension of our being, whose function is more closely related to what we refer to as the 'human world' than to the mere satisfaction of basic needs, although, as mentioned, it aims at fulfilling the latter.

A path is therefore opened to understanding the anthropologically radical nature of such omnipresent phenomena in contemporary culture as fashion and luxury, understood in the modern sense. Typically, human behaviour reveals the creativity intrinsic to that inventive resource we refer to as intelligence. Therefore, men and women are not merely samples of the human race; they are unique realizations of what it means to be human. As a result, life for them is also more than just an event; it is also a task, essentially executed through freedom and creativity.

By living life for themselves, human beings are naturally driven to express themselves and to express their own sensibilities. This is done either by freely adopting models and examples of things they identify with (enabling the phenomenon of fashion), or by seeking a distinguishing element, the unprecedented, the exclusive (giving rise to luxury, in its modern sense). In both cases, what humans are really aspiring to is luxury in the Platonic sense.

## Luxury and Freedom

We maintain—according to the Platonic suggestion of *Protagoras*—that luxury plays a role in the constitution of the human experience and that it is an element that emerges from our unique condition among other living beings. The human being is a being that is naturally engaged by luxury. Simultaneously, culture—which we refer to as the 'human world'—provides the conditions of possibility of this unique status, as well as its most obvious expression. It is now appropriate to highlight the ambivalent character of this relationship. The possibility of living life for oneself, the possibility of managing one's own life based on freedom, makes the human being the most excellent among all animals, but does not guarantee that life will be lived in this way. Life is a task that cannot be delegated, but the success of this enterprise is not guaranteed from the outset. Furthermore, given that personal fulfilment lies, to a large extent, in the hands of each human being—much more so than in circumstances—human fulfilment is somehow always threatened from within by the potential for failure.

To emphasise the relationship between luxury and freedom is also inevitably to link it to ethics. In effect, if it is thanks to *logos* and freedom that each human being is and experiences his/herself as a being for luxury, this means that the experience of luxury is inextricable from the ethical dimension of human existence which arises precisely because of this dual dimension of rationality and freedom. Daily life constantly reminds us of this fact; we position ourselves before the superfluous—the not strictly biological—as before an unlimited horizon, which interacts with freedom and obliges us to choose. Although we may be obliged to steer our lives through our freedom, we understand that this steering is not merely mechanical; on the contrary, it requires the daily management of desires and possibilities: on the one hand, thanks to the dynamics inherent to freedom, the qualitative dimension of tastes and desires presents itself as a limitless territory, both presently and habitually, both on an individual and on a community level; while on the other hand, this limitless freedom—that of possibilities—exists in parallel to the limitations of each life and the limitations imposed by our biological condition. Although we might aspire to everything, we are inevitably confined by the choices we make.

This ambivalence—that freedom is the source of unlimited desires yet only allows finite fulfilment—is revealed in a particularly eloquent manner through our relationship with luxury, i.e., it reveals itself both in our *manner* of aspiring to the superfluous and through those *objects* which we value as superfluous and that bring us fulfilment. It was this ambivalent dimension that Plato had in mind when he pointed out, for example, that certain professions need to be present in the *Republic*, understood as the 'city of luxury', or need to be reinforced, precisely because the human being is given to excess.

Plato illustrates his idea with the medical profession: in a "city of lux-ury" we should consider the need for a greater number of doctors, and should do so because our relationship with the superfluous is not always appropriate and may even be incorrect or harmful. An exam-ple of this is the desire to not simply "eat well", but to "overeat", harming our own health (373 d).[3]

The reality that Plato's observation indicates is the same one that we have considered before. Upon contemplating the possibility of a "city of luxury", as opposed to what Plato refers to as a "healthy city" (372 e), he seeks to highlight the fact that human life cannot be restricted to the cycle of natural causation. In the city, human life cannot be limited to the cycle "live to work, work to eat, eat to live". Although this would be satisfactory for a "city of pigs" (372 d), it does not adequately describe a city of human beings. Undoubtedly, most human beings need to work in order to eat, but human beings do not work solely to eat, just as they do not eat simply to live. In other words, the human city is a "city of luxury" and luxury is always, even in its most discreet manifes-tations, a form of evasion from mere necessity, or, to use Plato's para-doxical expression, a way of having "superfluous needs" (373 b). Both the wealthy person who surrounds himself by gold or ivory or the poor person who paints his home in his preferred colour are indulging in a luxury. By doing this they are affirming that they—and not merely bio-logical nature—determine the most significant spheres of their actions and it is they who define the specifically human horizon on which their lives run their course.

This independence encompasses multiple dimensions of human exist-ence and extends well beyond our possessive relationship with things. Suffice to remember that one of the most eloquent manifestations of luxury—and one which has received more attention from Philosophy—concerns one's control over time; human life is not simply absorbed by work and the production of things. Celebrations, public holidays and leisure are universal expressions of luxury because they are ways of freely appropriating our time, that is, our lives. Understood in this broader and more radical sense, luxury reveals the nature of our transcendence over the remaining reality of the natural world; it emphasises the fact that we are not merely limited to the utilitarian, that we aspire to a non-instrumental experience of time and that we always somehow live for this latter and radical goal. Thus, a purely economic perspective of luxury—that reduces it to a relationship of possession of 'luxurious' objects—is probably unable to capture the more profound significance of this phenomenon and even less able to explain its powers of attraction in human culture and life.

To summarise, freedom from natural causation, that we be agents rather than mere links in a causal chain of needs, desires and responses, expresses our excellence and reveals our not purely biological condition. However, at the same time, it exposes us to the risk of not honouring it and deviating from it. Only a being capable of aspiring to the superfluous is able to fulfil him/herself humanly, but also only a being of this kind runs the risk of frustrating his/her own fulfilment.

## The Ambivalence of the Superfluous—The Ethical Dimension of Luxury

We insist that what makes humans beings for luxury is what simultaneously makes them free beings and, therefore, ethical subjects. Human beings distinguish themselves by not being limited to a physical causality, but by being genuine authors of their own acts, *agents* in the true sense. It is this protagonism in our response to needs—the fact that they are satisfied through creativity—that makes us animals that can 'live well', that are not simply limited to the imperatives of survival. But this possibility is also experienced as a burden and as a task; life does not occur within us or in spite of us, as if we were mere links in a causal chain in which we truly do not intervene. Rather, as we have seen, it is a unique prerogative that is always experienced as a challenge, a risk and a compromise. In one way or another, we all know that it does not suffice to be in the world to live humanly; life is experienced as a task and it is always experienced through freedom, be it because we aim for excellence—inscribed in our being as a possibility—be it because we relinquish it.

A look at human culture is enough for us to become aware of the ambivalence that defines our unique nature: human beings are capable of great feats, of magnificent gestures and also of inhumane behaviour. No other being is capable of taking its nature thus far, yet no other is as capable as human beings of betraying its own nature.

Plato addressed this ambiguity of freedom, as mentioned previously, by affirming the need to furnish cities with certain professions that aim at limiting the disorder which freedom contains within it as a possibility. The city needs police, doctors, etc., because the use we make of life, of resources, etc., is liable to excesses and these must be kept within a reasonable limit for the good both of man and society.

Now, the possibility of excess—to overeat, to use freedom in a way harmful to others, etc.—is directly associated with luxury in the anthropologically radical sense that we have previously mentioned because, like luxury, it is associated with the exercise of freedom. Luxury is also experienced as an *excess*, as liberation from daily life and as the possibility of living in environments that are not strictly required by our physical dimension and which far surpass it: rest, contemplation, decoration, a bunch of flowers, a party, a jewel, a unique product, etc. However, we can now see that not all excesses are authentic luxuries—true luxuries, we could say—because not all the uses we make of the superfluous fulfil us in the same way and not all of them humanise us.

In its extreme complexity, the human quest for excellence occurs alongside a need to inscribe it within a daily sphere of commitment, effort, work, need and sharing. The superfluous, as we have already affirmed, only offers complete fulfilment when it is not part of the quotidian, when it offers an escape from this daily life which one will return to on the following day or month. The possibility of buying all the jewels that exist makes them uninteresting—prosaic. Similarly, the permanent possibility of doing nothing does not tend to turn life into a continuous party; rather, it darkens the day like a shadow, bringing tedium, making time empty and unbearable.

The fact that human beings need the superfluous does not mean that all the ways of aspiring to the superfluous are liberating, neither does it mean that the multiple forms that the superfluous assumes always reflect human greatness. Because of this, since time immemorial, philosophy has reflected on our relationship with goods and pondered the ethical dimension of property and luxury. And it has addressed this relationship not only in terms of justice, but also in terms of self-possession, which the Greeks referred to as temperance or moderation (*sophrosyne*). Luxury can be an expression of freedom and it can also be an expression of a lack of freedom. In the former case, man experiences his relationship with goods from a position of freedom and is truly master of what he owns; in the second case, on the contrary, things are what possess man and through freedom man surrenders to things and is possessed by them in such a way that he cannot live without these goods.

The dietary excesses that Plato referred to are precisely one example of this lack of self-possession, which arises out of freedom but diminishes it, because it ends up creating dependence and restricting the horizons of the exercise of freedom. This may also be the way we deal with other forms of luxury, now understood in the modern sense: exclusive pieces, costly products accessible to very few, etc. This would mean that we had transformed our fulfilment into a form of possession—and ostentation—and not a way of being; that we had linked our status—the way in which we wish to be distinguished and recognised—to *having* and not to *being*.

Clearly, this attitude is not an inevitable one. To insist that there are immoral uses of luxury does not mean that luxury is immoral. Luxury is a need in our nature, but not all the manifestations of this need are humane and legitimate manifestations of it. Sometimes, this is a question of justice, because by indulging in abundance beyond our needs, we deprive others of essentials; at other times, because what we might become, as people, can be determined by what we have identified as our luxury. As a result, we might limit ourselves to less noble forms of luxury, that is, our fixation on these forms of luxury might prevent us from recognising and desiring greater ones, inscribed in human nature as genuine requirements. If this occurs—given that choosing certain luxuries is associated with the relinquishing of others—we may fail to fulfil our true selves, i.e., as animals that aspire to the superfluous in the multiple forms that this can assume.

We have highlighted two aspects of the experience of luxury that particularly draw our attention. On the one hand, thanks to *logos*, while human beings inventively satisfy their biological needs, they live radically as beings that transcend the purely biological level and aspire to 'live well', i.e., they seek, as a (human) necessity, multiple forms of the superfluous or *luxury* (in a biological sense). On the other hand—and this is inevitably connected to the superfluous, precisely because it is superfluous—humans are seen to steer their lives through their freedom, i.e., they themselves take charge of their own human fulfilment. Through this dual approach, luxury is always an indicator of humanity; whether luxury is seen as a factor in human fulfilment will depend on the way we interpret the breadth of the concept of luxury and the way we freely attach ourselves to its expressions.

## Conclusion

The phenomenon of luxury is profoundly complex and its analysis is inevitably interdisciplinary in nature. The preceding reflections proposed a focus on two aspects of luxury that are relatively consensual: that luxury can only be observed in the human world and that it is a reality or phenomenon that is absolutely universal.

The recognition of these two characteristics—the *exclusivity* and the *universality* of the phenomenon in the human world—led us to seek an understanding of what the reference to superfluity—embedded in the phenomenon of luxury—reveals to us about human beings and their way of relating to their own lives and things. First of all, we observed that the experience of luxury is directly related to the experience of freedom and, thus, it is just as difficult to codify as freedom itself. We then observed that the experience of luxury is defined—be it qualitatively or quantitatively—with reference to a measure. This measure establishes the frontier between what is necessary and superfluous, and between what is indispensable and possible. This reference to the measurement, which is surpassed by luxury, explains how the adjective 'luxurious' can be applied to both what can be acquired, and to what is priceless and is experienced as an escape from daily life, with regard to its laborious or constrictive nature. Radically, luxury is apprehended more clearly through contrasts, experienced as 'an extra', as something desirable but in which we neither are nor can be permanently installed.

In consonance with some analyses by Plato, we highlighted two aspects of the experience of luxury that particularly attract our attention. On the one hand, human beings—due to *logos*—while inventively satisfying their biological needs, simultaneously perceive themselves as beings that transcend the purely biological dimension, aspiring to 'live well', that is, as beings that seek, as a (human) need, multiple forms of the superfluous or of *luxury* (in a biological sense). On the other hand, this inevitable connection to the superfluous, precisely because it is superfluous, reveals that human beings conduct their own lives grounded on freedom, that is, they guide their own human fulfilment by themselves. Through this dual approach, luxury is always an *indicator of humanity.*

The last part of the text explores—following another suggestion by Plato—the ambivalent character of the human relationship with luxury, understood in this manner. Being, in itself, a sign of excellence, our aspiration to the superfluous nevertheless contains the risk of failure in how we fulfil this need. The fact that human beings are beings with a need for the superfluous is no guarantee that all the ways of aspiring to the superfluous are equally liberating, nor does it mean that all the forms that the superfluous assumes reflect human grandeur equally. The way in which we apprehend the entire breadth of its content and the way in which we freely attach ourselves to its multiple variations also determine the degree to which luxury is a *factor in human fulfilment.* This is—just as life itself—a task destined to be performed by each human being.

# Notes

1. Literature on the subject is highly abundant; cf., for example, Calefato and Adams (2014), McNeil and Riello (2016) and Turunen (2017).
2. One just has to recall the lively discussion between Rousseau and Voltaire, in the mid-eighteenth century, about the origins and meaning of luxury: Rousseau maintains that luxury, the Arts, etc., are opposed to

virtue (Rousseau 1750), Voltaire links them directly to humanity's progress: «Si l'on entend par luxe tout ce qui est au-delà du nécessaire, le luxe est une suite naturelle des progrès de l'espèce humaine; et, pour raisonner conséquemment, tout ennemi du luxe doit croire avec Rousseau que l'état de bonheur et de vertu pour l'homme est celui, non de sauvage, mais d'orang-outang» (Voltaire 1836, p. 42).

3. The same could be said about other excesses—not the desire for evasion, but indulging in uninterrupted evasion; not the desire for celebration, but the refusal to work, etc.—which also require reinforcement when planning the operation of the city.

# References

Berry, Christopher. 1994. *The Idea of Luxury: A Conceptual and Historical Investigation*. New York: Cambridge University Press.

Calefato, Patrizia, and Lisa Adams. 2014. *Luxury: Fashion, Lifestyle and Excess.* London and New York: Bloomsbury Academic.

Frankl, Viktor. 2000. *Man's Search for Meaning*. Boston: Beacon Press.

Hyeong-Yeon, Jeon. 2003. *Analyse des sites web de marques de luxe*. Thèse, Université Lumière – Lyon 2. http://theses.univ-lyon2.fr/documents/lyon2/2003/jeon_hy/download. Accessed on 20 March 2018.

McNeil, Peter, and Giorgio Riello. 2016. *Luxury, a Rich History*. New York: Oxford University Press.

Pieper, Josep. 1963. *Zustimung zur Welt. Eine Theorie des Festes*. Munich: Kösel-Verlag.

Rousseau, Jean-Jacques. 1750. *Discours sur les sciences et les arts*. Genève [i.e. Paris]: Noël-Jacques Pissot.

Turunen, Linda. 2017. *Interpretations of Luxury: Exploring the Consumer Perspective*. Cham, Switzerland: Springer.

Voltaire. 1836. *Le Dictionnaire philosophique*, in *Oeuvres de Voltaire*. Tome VIII. Paris: Furne.

# Part II
## Understanding Luxury and Emotions

# 3

# From Mere Luxury to Unique Lifestyle: The Transformation of Taste in the 'Age of Glamour'

Ambrogia Cereda

## Luxury and Society: Evolution of a Paradoxical Relation

Famous fashion designer Karl Lagerfeld provocatively assessed in a commercial: "It's all about taste. If you're cheap, nothing helps". Might it be an apparent way of legitimating his collaboration with the fast fashion brand H&M, or a revealing insight in the evolution of nowadays market, he has pointed out a crucial factor in the contemporary approach to luxury.

Luxury has a long and charming history. Starting from the Egyptian era to the present, within luxury goods notions of need and desire are intertwined as crystallizations of specific moments in the chronicles of humanity. Objects and facilities thus give physical shape to a system of sociocultural conditions and standards of aesthetic perception, which

A. Cereda (✉)
Center for the Study of Fashion and Cultural Production (ModaCult),
Università Cattolica del Sacro Cuore, Milan, Italy
e-mail: ambrogia.cereda@unicatt.it

© The Author(s) 2020
I. Cantista and T. Sádaba (eds.), *Understanding Luxury Fashion*,
Palgrave Advances in Luxury, https://doi.org/10.1007/978-3-030-25654-8_3

31

can be better understood, if reconstructed in episodic perspective (Berry 1994). The evolution of the idea of luxury seems indeed to regularly tackle a variety of issues, ranging from the innocence of the desire for certain typologies of allegedly refined goods to the relational connotation of the concept, generally paired with the notion of need/necessity.

While in the past centuries luxury appeared as an issue regarding only the élites and the wealthy ones who could show their status and social positioning by means of specific symbols of conspicuous consumption (see Veblen 1912). Beginning from the twentieth century, the luxury world has started to lose part of its the exclusivity and total isolation, and it has opened the doors to an increasing number of ordinary consumers from the upper middle class who are not wealthy but want to enjoy a short trip in the universe of luxury, they are the so-called "excursionists" (Dubois and Laurent 1995), who represent a source of luxury growth even if, different form their wealthy peers, they "cannot buy lofts or penthouses, or even Chanel suits, but they might occasionally buy a small product from a prestigious brand for themselves, friends, or some important contact. This development drives the queues of tourists waiting outside the Louis Vuitton or Gucci flagship stores in capital cities" (Kapferer 2015, p. 26).

What is depicted by Kapferer as a phase of the transformation of luxury from niche to mass phenomenon, also represents part of the results of a long process of enchantment and instillation of desires started with the growth of the city as a new realm in which specific zones developed dedicated to consumption and entertainment and on which glamour could flourish a new form of (imaginative) behaviour.

> Glamour is excessive and abundant and it strikes the imagination by bypassing the commonly accepted bourgeois sense of moderation and measure. It is not elaborate style so much as a popularization of style that everyone can understand. It mixes the appeals of class and sleaze in a way that produces unsettling effects that, for its audiences, are predominantly pleasurable. (Gundle 2008, p. 24)

Those areas could generally be found next to the centres "of wealth and power and they quickly acquired an allure as tourist sights, places of style and opulence, and home to all that was modern and fashionable" and the "ultimate purpose of such grandiose efforts was to endow commodities with an aura, a mystery or an appeal that went beyond their use-value" (Gundle and Castelli 2006, p. 10). As cities expanded, and the thirst for luxury increased, they also became the point of reference for cultural change (Dewald 1996, p. 133) and for finding events, entertainment and more, so that new ways emerged for old and new elites of asserting their social and cultural leadership. In the same time, against the background of the metropolitan life role-playing and fantasy could become key elements of an individual's social behaviour (Gundle and Castelli 2006, p. 29).

In the urban context the possibility to access luxury in some form has increasingly expanded, mainly due to the incorporation of that exclusive world into the spheres of industrial and consumer society. Such transformation has not only affected but has also blurred the boundaries between goods as well as it has reversed the relationship between luxury and rarity, that is now deeply embedded in the typical mechanisms of imitation and competition of late modern societies: "[G]rowth and absorption have influenced current views on the concept of luxury, and the idiosyncratic nature of luxury has been influenced by the rules of competition of industrial economy and society" (Turunen 2018, p. 16). That relationship is far from being irrelevant and needs to be reframed, as the main goal of luxury brand management reveals in Kapferer's view (2015, p. 32), "unlike any other sector, for luxury, growth creates ambivalence, because the expanded market penetration dilutes perceived exclusivity. By starving the market, managers can drive prices up and earn excess margins, which can be reinvested in creating brand prestige. Thus, luxury brand management is highly specific and turns traditional marketing principles upside down", the crucial factor for the existence of luxury products and brands is thus fundamentally to create an excess of demand without satisfying it.

The ambivalence pointed out by the observers like Kapferer seems to find its roots in the very history of the industrial society, where a new idea of luxury emerges in opposition to the previous one: the bourgeois idea of luxury, deeply different from its antecedent, the aristocratic one, and defined by instinctual factors and lack of measure (Campbell 1987, p. 8).

The new bourgeois' conception is characterized by an internal drive, emotion and passion to be contrasted with the aristocrat's aloofness and control. If the key of desire appears as a useful tool for managing the perception of luxury among the consumers in the eyes of luxury brand managers, at the same time it seems to appeal to the main feature of the typical middle class mentality.

As Campbell (1987, pp. 35–38) puts it, this distinctive emotional condition is at the basis of a desiring or yearning predisposition that fuelled aspirations and dreams of the bourgeoisie, and that was characterised by insatiability, an apparently unlimited pursuit of wants. Also due to the fact that middleclass people "had neither heritage nor breeding to draw on, they set about winning this by fashioning a lifestyle of great ostentation. Massive palaces, ultra-refined interiors, enormous yachts, grand summer houses, glittering parties, elegant weddings, and international travel became the key markers of status of the super-rich" (Gundle 2008, p. 122).

Besides, while the aristocrat's hedonism was intended for the satisfaction of specific pleasures, the bourgeois idea of pleasure was more abstract and free-floating, emotional and psychological in nature. In this framework, imagination turns up with a crucial role and transforms the satisfaction of wants into a pleasurable activity in itself: "Individuals employ their imaginative and creative powers to construct mental images which they consume for the intrinsic pleasure they provide, a practice best described as day-dreaming or fantasizing" (Campbell 1987, p. 77).

This "Modern autonomous imaginative hedonism", as Campbell calls it, represents a kind of mentality that is also central to the development of the idea of "glamour" (Gundle and Castelli 2006). Glamour indeed was born in that same ambivalent context in which the bourgeoisie was contesting many of the hereditary privileges of the aristocracy and in which society was becoming more open than before. Nevertheless, even if the traditional aristocracy was losing part of its power, it was still defining many features of the desirable lifestyle: style, beauty, fashion, luxury, and even fame have been under its monopoly for centuries (Gundle 2008, p. 19). Hence, the aristocracy seems to have never loosen its hold on the concept of luxury and, more importantly, it seems to have preserved its place in the collective imagery as a point of reference for the expression of one's lifestyle in the public space. As a class "it conserved social and cultural influence by offering a template for the new men and women who now came to the fore, made fortunes, or occupied the public limelight" (ibidem).

Luxury and glamour thus start to have many aspects in common, first of all their aristocratic heritage and the connotation of *extraordinarity*.

> Glamour was about the way in which the most visually striking manifestations of aristocratic privilege were taken over and reinvented by newly emergent people, groups, and institutions. This occurred in several realms including the political sphere, the modern city, consumption and lifestyles, and theatre. Commodity culture provided a key channel for this process of appropriation which did not simply take the form of imitation. (Gundle 2008, p. 19)

As consumer culture evolves, in late modern societies, luxury is increasingly shifted to the dimension of the imagery and turned into a lifestyle and a connotation of products (Amatulli 2009), that first proliferated in the discourse of advertising, promotion of events, food, houses, and apparel as the last escapes from an all too ordinary life (Berry 1994). Luxury is offered as an option to stylize one's life, that consumers can embrace completely or only partly, as Mazzalovo and Chevalier (2012, p. 5) suggest: "Truly luxurious lifestyles are present, more than ever, in any modern communication. They are often promoted by intermediate luxury brands, which offer countless possibilities to the middle class to take part symbolically, partially or virtually, in this world".

Finding a way to enjoy exclusive pleasures is conveyed in the media as a crucial way of changing a life in which almost every kind of experience can be easily reached, bought, and consumed via apps and shared on social networks. As Kapferer maintains luxury has gained enormous visibility even though social issues of hunger and poverty are not encountering solutions on a global scale,

> yet airports all over the world are transforming into luxury commercial centers, in which the luxury brand names are the same from one capital

city to the next, and they appear as well in urban department stores and malls. Despite the growth of e-commerce and the Internet, such luxury stores remain destinations for travelers who spend hours walking the aisles, discovering consumption at its best and experiencing a world of privilege where everyone can dream. (Kapferer 2015, p. 26)

Adding on that, we can observe that contemporary consumers have increasingly become experienced about many kinds of products as they are sometimes portrayed as skilled actors (Fabris 2010), who feel somewhat blasé about the auratic dimension attached to the goods they are expected to consume or are merely waiting for the option that suits them best. What matters in their everyday experience is the practice of re-appropriation of goods, appreciation, and communication that include elements of resistance and innovation (Warde 2005), in fact their practices of consumption are often a combination of motives and expectations which need to be investigated thoroughly but are inevitably influenced by factors of social position and market offers. The consumer society deals with goods that are continually reformulated in increasingly beautiful and interesting ways aiming at revealing and supporting an identity or, better said, temporary identifications which are useful to secure the fleeting and fragmented self of the postmodern actors, their possibilities of self-presentation and the representations of themselves within the world (Bovone 2014, p. 65).

In this perspective, luxury goods are available for self-narration in many forms, distributed on the two levels of the global chessboard, where wealthy consumers can find a place next to middle class consumers in order to receive social recognition, success, and increase one's own prestige (Mazzalovo and Chevalier 2012, p. 5):

The global luxury chessboard is therefore distributed on two levels, if not more; on the one hand, true luxury, which few people can afford, increases its hold on the market. The growth in the number of wealthy consumers (especially in the BRIC [Brazil, Russia, India, China] countries), combined with a bigger supply, plus investments in the luxury industries that have been yielding higher returns on investment than ordinary brands, have led to wide visibility of luxurious lifestyles. The press and the media in general contribute actively by exposing the lives of the rich and famous. On the other hand, intermediate luxury brands, by applying their logic of volume of production and communication, ensure the democratization of luxury. They multiply the opportunities for consumers of the middle class to be in contact with the possible imaginary worlds they offer. What is more naturally human than to aspire to signs of social recognition, success, comfort, and prestige?

This scenario seems to recall the one of the advanced industrialization in which all goods could undergo a process of "auratization", if they were relying heavily on the ideas that were associated with the promise of magical transformation or instant escape from the constraints of everyday life, and could be inserted into sales contexts that disguised their primary purpose and could engender temporary feelings of pleasure and luxury (Gundle and Castelli 2006, p. 10).

Nowadays' consumers appear as ostensibly continuing their search for forms of excitement or diversion, for identification or self-expression, also to avoid a return to the obnoxious vision of a well-organized and planned life as heralded in the modernity (Campbell 1994). Ranging from gourmet food and wine to lavish weekends at prestige resorts, the variety of possibilities for the appropriate deluxe experience seems to be expanding every day, drawing with itself a plethora of new issues about what luxury is going to be, most of all in the form of "self-illusory, imaginative hedonism that found a practical outlet in the distractions and shopping of the late nineteenth century and after [...]. The daydreaming to which novelists had become so expert in catering was sustained and further stimulated in the new temples of consumption" (Gundle and Castelli 2006, p. 10).

Inside those temples, many brands today aspire to appear as luxury brands, persuaded by the fact that the word "luxury" has a special selling power. Even if it is only when goods or services incorporate a series of specific features that they can be considered materializations of luxury, in this overpopulated scenario, the concept is stretched in a way that diminishes its strength and seems to lose any efficiency or appeal:

> To expand the definition to these claimants to luxury, new terms even have been invented, such as accessible luxury, popular luxury, and casual luxury,

with the goal of leveraging the benefits of the "luxury" tag for non-luxury brands. But these developments also have disrupted the positioning of luxury, pushing it to the extreme spheres with terms such as "überluxury," "high luxury," or "ultra luxury." As a result of the proliferation of luxuries, the word also has lost some substance. (Kapferer 2015, p. 27)

In this cascading movement, the world of luxury goods production has deeply changed. Material artefacts, services and other cultural products—along with being democratized, have actually undergone diverse moments of crisis, located between the 1970s and the 2014 and affecting different groups at different times. In particular, the period between 2009 and 2013 has seen the industry witnessing a deep transformation both on the side of consumption, and of production, with the rise of luxury multibrand conglomerates such as LVMH, Kering, and Richemont as new pivotal players in the system. The scenario has thus been reframed and constituted of the acquisitions of traditional family-run brands and other luxury brands (usually family-owned) that resisted being taken over by the above-mentioned conglomerates and that nonetheless grew alongside those conglomerates (Som and Blanckaert 2015). With those changes, the idea of luxury is also modified, and the family brands have started to use specific strategies as presenting luxury as part of their brand heritage and DNA; and recurring to vertical integration and the purchase of suppliers to face the challenge of the conglomerates. The strategy of the luxury firm has thus shifted and now focuses on brand equity, investments in international expansion while repurchasing franchises and licenses to gain more control over their retail operations (ibidem). Nonetheless, just like the life in the metropolis, the market of luxury has increasingly turned into a paradoxical reality, in which:

> Luxury operates, among other things, as social distinction. It is the sign of a practice reserved for the happy few and thus circumvents the masses. At the same time, contemporary luxury is promoted by many brands that remain linked to the logic of volume of production and product distribution. How, therefore, can distinction and selectivity be acquired? Such is the dilemma for luxury brands. They will try to solve it by adjusting their

positioning through innovative strategies of creation, communication, and distribution. (Mazzalovo and Chevalier 2012, p. 33)

Therefore, in order to provide an appropriate identity for a luxury brand it seems also useful to identify elements that will actually operate to build a suggestive but memorable idea of luxury in the minds of people and at the same protect consumers' need for exclusivity and distinction, but: are they all looking for luxury as an undisputable fact, or is everyone searching for a specific individual interpretation of luxury for temporary identifications and self-expression?

## Luxuriousness, Between Luxury and Necessary Gains

The issues related to the interpretation and identification of luxury are the first and most obvious problems encountered by the scholars who have been trying to understand the concept. This is partly due to the fact that the term has often been—and still is—used and abused in innumerable manners both in the discourse of commercial communication and in everyday life, to the extent that, as said above, it not only has lost explicative power but it continually needs to be reinvented in order to guarantee the exclusivity that consumers wish to conquer.

In contemporary and ancient societies luxury has frequently been defined through its opposite, the idea of "need" or "necessity". In this perspective, basic needs are considered the minimum for living; while, luxury, in a sense, represents the maximum. The apparent separation between need or necessity and luxury is thus represented by a combination of elements in which one term makes sense only if compounded with the other. This dialectical opposition is what makes 'luxury' a relational term (Berry 1994).

In this framework, in which luxury and necessities are coupled together, we might wonder what can actually help us discriminating luxury artefacts and experiences from other more necessary or merely different products of our everyday life, or, in other words, where the borders stand between the two realities, and more importantly, how this separation might shift in relation to time and space.

This is no easy job given the constant complexification of the scene, where brands appear as the main factor in the recent transformations of the concept of luxury (Mazzalovo and Chevalier 2012). The academic reflection on this topic has been growing in the recent years, and acknowledging an increasing difficulty to find a unique answer or agreement about the definition, which seems to be the most apparent result of the debate (Miller and Mills 2012). In a sociohistorical perspective, indeed, the phenomenon of luxury seems impossible to be reduced to a few elements or unique dimension and to require as a consequence that the observers take into account many variables ranging from the social and cultural context to the issue of time liability, from factors related to consumers' individual perceptions to specific product features, etc. (see Berthon et al. 2009). Given this complexity of factors and being the major discrepancy between luxury and non-luxury revealed by the relativity of the concept, it is clear that any definition can only be temporary and transformable depending on the idea of each individual or group, and their social position. Both terms can be conceived according to specific social norms, respected and accepted by a community, but for that same reason they can differ according to the changes of time and costume. The classifications of what is to be located beyond mere necessity in contemporary societies or within a specific cultural communities seems not suitable to be set once and for all, more importantly the same luxurious object that today are regarded with desire and envy for those who can buy them might become an unquestionable need in the eyes of the following generations or within the closest community (Berry 1994; Kapferer and Bastien 2009, p. 38).

There is another perspective about the complex pattern of the luxury world, which is represented by the reflection of brand management and marketing and that seems instead to insists on a relative group of features that connects specific products, brands and services, and position them at the end of a scale marking superior quality (Vigneron and Johnson 2004; Kapferer and Bastien 2009). This definition appears indeed as an efficient way of making sense of the specific goals and factors related to the management of the company and the production of goods, but it seems to undermine the dimension of social and cultural influence, when it is not struggling against it. It is indeed the very way in which brands operate to create a cultural frame of interpretation of their goods that modifies and blurs the concept of luxury, so even if boundaries exist set by traditional processes they are continually trespassed by ways in which the newcomers move inside the market, as experts suggest: "mass brands have learned to manage their operations by adopting the rules of traditional luxury. Therefore, what may differentiate a true luxury brand, in the sense that was intended fifty years ago, from a new entrant with a proper strategic understanding of the luxury industry and the talent to run an intermediate luxury positioning?" (Mazzalovo and Chevalier 2012, p. 15).

An extremely important aspect of the relation between luxury and need is also provided in the interplay between the notions of 'need' and 'desire', which have been held as vital preconditions for the presence of luxury in a society. The concept of desire is difficult to be defined, or rather, it's difficult to identify what characterizes the nature and the dimension of desire and if it is enough to influence our perception of luxury. Even if the idea of luxury often entails a desiring dimension (for exclusiveness, expensiveness, rarity) the very sensation of it is variable in quantity and quality due to its general incidence, the very extent of its diffusion or merely the intensity with which it is held (Berry 1994, p. 5). Luxury goods are expected to be widely desired and even to produce a certain sensation of envy among those who can't afford them, nonetheless desirability alone is not sufficient quality to guarantee that we are dealing with luxury products. This condition can be better expressed by the case of the products of (mass) fashion which are widely desired even though they are far from being legitimated as high gamut products pertaining the luxury sector of production, since they are generally not the result of sophisticated techniques of production or long periods of manual work, but that are nonetheless associated with an idea, an experience, a value, a possibility to make a statement about one's ownership to anyone (Bovone 2014).

Moreover it is the very way in which desire is managed in the communication of luxury products that transforms the concept into another ambivalent variable. The narration about luxury seems to be oriented to arouse desire in two ways: on the one hand, it tells the story of the event staged when the brand launched its latest product or new collection, and who was invited (or not), and it let people know which luxury brands are the most profitable. Such information aims to attach feelings of exclusivity to the brand and disseminate a sense of prestige (Kapferer 2015, p. 27), but it is reinforced by another typology of narration online. Through social media, in particular, any exclusive luxury event "can be immediately shared with the masses, building their desire" but what has to appear extremely clear to them is the fact that they are longing "for something they can dream of but not access", this kind of information is fundamental because it is "the measure of greater interest to a luxury brand: luxurious margins" (ibidem). It is difficult to tell if desire operates for the definition of luxury or to articulate it and make the boundaries between goods less clear since that pattern seems ultimately to be rooted in the rise of the bourgeoisie—as a typically aspirational kind of social group—and sustained through the centuries by the culture of consumption:

> The boundless capacity of manufacturers to produce goods ever more rapidly and in ever greater quantities meant that it was no longer sufficient to rely on the secular 'democratisation of luxury' that accompanied the rise of the bourgeoisie. The presence of cultural obstacles to continuous acquisition meant that strategies of enticement were required to manipulate wants and needs, to attract interest, to promote aspirations and create rituals that made consumption satisfying. Consequently, techniques of persuasion were necessary as the previous emphasis on production gave way to a new preoccupation with consumption. (Gundle and Castelli 2006, p. 33)

A similarity can be also identified between desire and want, as Berry (1994, pp. 10–11) suggests: 'want' is different from 'need', while wants are intentional and refer to privileged constitutions of our minds and thoughts, needs are more related to physical, objective, or even universal conditions of life. Having a shelter represent a more or less universal need, and we can easily assume that it addresses everybody, but we cannot know how actually they expect this need to be satisfied—weather having a mansion in the countryside or a small flat in the city centre—, here the issue of want appears as a particularization of a basic need. Another difference between needs and wants includes the aspect of refinement which, again, has little to do with the level of needs: we need to eat and drink for our sustenance, but if we choose to make a dinner having gourmet food and champagne we are not merely guaranteeing our survival, we are choosing goods that are deemed as more refined and positively pleasing for ourselves and our social group.

The issue of luxury thus seems conceptually fleeting and deeply entangled in the sociocultural context of both products and consumers, more importantly, being related to refinement, desires (that cannot be satisfied), subjective perceptions of wants, and positive reinforcements it also acquires a symbolic dimension widely exploited by marketing and management experts in a way that blurs the boundaries between luxury and ordinary (mass) goods. We might indeed continue to enrich the list of differences between luxury and other subtle typologies of concepts, but at the same time we need to point out how many of those conceptualizations cannot avoid the influence of socio-cultural conditions. Nonetheless, the specific facet of luxury that appears as more qualitative and consumer-driven seems to have not been investigated in-depth nor it has been clarified what such a consumer-centred interpretation of luxury stands for (Turunen 2018, p. 86).

## Consumer Culture and the Taste for Luxuriousness

The role of the consumer has been presented as crucial to justify the identity of luxury goods: luxury needs to be widely desired by those who cannot afford it and visibly manifested by those who can, therefore luxury goods seem in return capable—and need to be able—to guarantee the status of contemporary social actors, to set boundaries, as well as to provide the experience of membership in a community of privileged people. If we pay attention to the side of consumers' interpretation indeed the issue of perception appears crucial in order to clarify the connecting feature of luxury as relative positioning. What is regarded as luxury—products, brands and services—is located at the far end of a continuum, and those goods need to be acknowledged as high-class, being endowed with superior qualities (see Vigneron and Johnson 2004; Kapferer and Bastien 2009). But the superiority of those qualities, as said above, is the result of a careful planning and strategic communication through competent management of so-called "artificial rarity" (Kapferer 2015, p. 31).

> What quality difference could possibly justify a price multiplier of 163 between core luxury and mass market watches? There is not one; the difference is due to intangibles, the signaling dimension of the brand, and the resulting ego benefits that purchases have for buyers. Luxury is a business of self- and social elevation; luxury brands are visas of class and good taste, as well as the access fee required to enter a restricted club of owners. Price is not the measure of value; price creates value. (ibidem, 32)

Luxury therefore becomes strictly intertwined with issues of perception, or better of self-centred experiences. But if luxury lies in the eye of the beholders, still, what are they looking at?

In order to fill the gap in the landscape mentioned above, Turunen (2018, p. 86) suggests to introduce another term: "luxuriousness", that emphasizes the 'symbolic to self' facet of luxury. The concept of luxuriousness is thus referred to a consumer-centred interpretation of luxury that is different from the definitions presented in the realm of brand management and that locates the subjective interpretations of individual consumers at the core of the concept. In this perspective the meanings associated to luxurious object and services are rooted in the individual experiences of the consumers as subjects, their own life situations and sociocultural contexts.

This is a particularly tantalizing issue because it is related to the way in which consumers approach goods and experiences in their everyday life as well as they develop their taste, as Turunen puts it (2018, p. 93) "*Luxuriousness* evolves from the interpreter—the consumer. It gets its value in relation to the perceiver or interpreter, and thus cannot be separated from the person who is making sense of the world". Luxuriousness is to be understood as a combination of four different elements, that interact to produce an ambiguous and complex consumer emotion, more in particular they are: *extended product* (value in use and consumption), *perceived authenticity, perceived uniqueness* and *context specificity*. Among those, the concept of extended product (i.e. the product and its characteristics) plays a central role and is regarded as an element of the conceptual model of perceived luxuriousness, because it emphasizes consumers' active role in value creation thus expanding the discussion of the characteristics attached to luxury branded products. In this perspective, interpretations of the luxuriousness of a brand need to include all those forms derived from the actual uses and practices of consumption of those goods, thus combining concrete attributes and intangible components of individual experience (Turunen 2018, p. 94). Perceived uniqueness and perceived authenticity add on that nuances derived from consumers' own involvement and activity in (co)creating the characteristics of the products with the brands or the companies producing the goods.

Perceived luxuriousness appears as embedded in the aesthetic dimension of objects and services and is indeed evaluated in terms of the level of affective features and product design attributes (Bahn et al. 2009; Turunen 2018). Although, in this aesthetic dimension lies the reason of all everyday experiences with objects and the possibility of assessing one's subjectivity:

> nothing is more distinctive, more distinguished, than the capacity to confer aesthetic status on objects that are banal or even 'common' (because the 'common' people make them their own, especially for aesthetic purposes), or the ability to apply the principles of a 'pure' aesthetic to the most everyday choices of everyday life, e.g., in cooking, clothing or decoration, completely reversing the popular disposition which annexes aesthetics to ethics. (Bourdieu 1984, p. 7)

As Bourdieu point out, the aestheticization of things and services is relevant and even take on ethical connotations. In late modern societies the experience of consumption is characterized by an emphasis on *aestheticization* that can be referred to three different aspects of the phenomenon:

the fact that the boundaries between art and life have been blurred, starting with the of Surrealist and Dada movement during the 1920s; the project of turning one's life into a work of art, which was initially developed by the Bloomsbury group and then continued by the followers of dandyism; and, the fact that the reality is increasingly transformed in aesthetic terms, due to the proliferation and increasing saturation of pictures and signs which, through commercial manipulation, aim at releasing dream-images which mirror our desires, and at the same time de-realize reality (Featherstone 1991). All those aspects contribute to renew the idea that individuals should desire and look for a perfect body or being sensitive and refined as their *raison d'être*, everyone has to aspire, or is unconsciously becoming, *homo aestheticus* (Lipovetsky and Serroy 2013).

Another important aspect to take into account is the fact that the ways in which people are socialized to consumption rules and practices is also related to their taste, and more importantly as Bourdieu (1984) suggests, that taste represents at the same time an element of identification and a structure, which let consumers emphasize or avoid the aesthetic dimension of the goods they choose. Taste and consumption are both part of a process of comprehension in which the boundaries between legitimated culture and ordinary practices are erased in order to make sense of the system of dispositions (habitus) that characterizes each different class and class fraction:

> Taste classifies, and it classifies the classifier. Social subjects, classified by their classifications, distinguish themselves by the distinctions they make, between the beautiful and the ugly, the distinguished and the vulgar, in which their position in the objective classifications is expressed or betrayed. […] The antithesis between quantity and quality, substance and form, corresponds to the opposition—linked to different distances from necessity—between the taste of necessity, which favours the most 'filling' and most economical foods, and the taste of liberty or luxury—which shifts the emphasis to the manner (of presenting, serving, eating etc.) and tends to use stylized forms to deny function. (Bourdieu 1984, pp. 6–7)

Even in the category of taste we see a combination of factors at work and more notably we can detect another differentiation between perception of luxury associated to liberty, form, and having a qualitative stance, as opposed to quantitative aspects regulated via necessity and economical motives.

These elements are part of an ambivalent attitude that seems to characterize the behavior of late modern social actors, deeply engaged in a plurality of enticing images, produced by many sources (e.g. magazines, the fashion industry, film and television industries, advertisement and public relations companies), thus fostering an idea of glamour as "an accessible ideal, a touch of sparkle that can add something to every life" (Gundle 2008, p. 387). It is this idea that continues to work in the niche forums of new media, socializing consumers at appropriating products as a reproduction of a glamorous taste and lifestyle:

> Advertising, celebrity linkages, and visible logos made prestige goods desirable for all and brought the glamour of luxury within the purview of groups which had no previous contact with it. Such strategies turned them into aspects of popular culture. The appropriation of signature products by fast-money and downmarket celebrities, and even working-class subcultures, soon followed. This could not readily be prevented even though the potential damage for labels could be considerable. (Gundle 2008, p. 377)

Owing to the subjectivity of interpretations and context specificity the industry of luxury aims to create dream-images of intangible value that let luxury brands appear unique in a way that they cannot be paralleled with any other brand, and escape the process of commodification. In this respect, luxury brands try to point out differences between luxury and premium products, but if they undermine reasonability or the role of e-commerce sites, they might miss the point: "The latter [premium products] mostly rely on tangible characteristics to build their attractiveness. Premium brands compete by looking for comparisons (compare-by-reason), but as soon as any reason is more important than emotion, consumers would quit buying luxury offerings. E-commerce sites that sell luxuries at discounted prices contribute to commoditization and dangerously assimilate luxuries with premium products" (Kapferer 2015, p. 32). If the experience of luxury comes into existence through consumption, it seems that consumers resist the process of education that brands would like to impart them, besides, as the majority of research settings reveals, consumers' active role is a uniting factor in determining, negotiating, perceiving and interpreting the luxuriousness of a brand (Turunen 2018, p. 85).

We can thus try to approach the phenomenon from a different perspective, which insists on the idea that almost any goods can enter the realm of luxury, but that also acknowledges the fact that some specific features need to be found in the products deemed as element of the luxury world by right (Appadurai 1986, p. 38). In this view, both the variability of luxury and the specific relation between luxury goods and experience of the individual consumers are taken into account as well as their aesthetic dimension.

Luxury goods can be interpreted as "incarnated signs" having a predominantly social and rhetorical function (Appadurai 1986, p. 38). From the point of view of their social life, they are similar to any kind of product or service because there appears to be no luxury in essence, while all goods are suitable to change their conditions in a particular moment or period of time and thus enter and exit what Appadurai has labelled as the "luxury register".

Even though this conception shares with other perspectives the idea of the variability of the concept, along with its socio-relational structure, it seems to offer useful insights into the topic in order to move away from the relational dimension (i.e. need vs. luxury) and to tackle issues that appear as a part of a common ground for the conditions presented above and that are related to specific experiences about: restriction to elites by law or price; complexity of acquisition—which may or may not reflect real scarcity; semiotic virtuosity; codes for appropriate consumption (demanding a form of specialized knowledge); high degree of linkage between their consumption and body, person or personality.

Aspects related to restriction to elites by law or prices seem to encompass features of luxury such as extra value, high quality to the extent that extra quality translates into extra-prices (Csaba 2008, p. 7). In terms of experience and luxuriousness it addresses what is perceived in products and brands that are not regarded as luxury brands in the social context (Turunen 2018, p. 179), or better the affective experience consumers undergo in not having or gaining access to goods that are regarded as luxurious by someone.

Complexity of acquisition is not equivalent to real scarcity but focuses instead on the way in which that idea becomes part of the experience for the consumer and how it is managed in everyday life. It seems to go hand in hand with perceived uniqueness as a component of luxuriousness and part of the consumers' participation in (co)creating the characteristics of the products as pointed out by Turunen (2018).

Semiotic virtuosity regards the capability of certain goods to send complex messages and is often assimilated to luxury goods, which have a communicative nature and can even be conceived as *message-goods* (Amatulli 2009). But this also addresses the experience of the consumer, who is the main source of meaning and interpretation, and can rearticulate in terms of luxuriousness the whole story with the goods.

As to the codes for appropriate consumption, again we see the intertwining of issues of appreciation of quality and value but also the point of view of the consumers who are active participant in the experience and can partly bend the appropriateness or educated themselves by choosing the sources of their knowledge form the media, the web, etc.

The last aspect, sensory stimulation, which might occur on many levels but strongly influences the emotional experience and the sensation of luxuriousness as affective features and product design attributes, as pointed out above.

Following this conception we will try to shed light on the topic considering two typologies of experience of consumption related to the Italian and the Chinese production.

# Italian Experience: Luxury Products for Luxurious Experiences

In the global scenario of luxury Italy is considered one of the examples of most established and developed markets along with France. Moreover, luxury goods have traditionally been associated with those countries, and with Italy in particular that is still producing one third of all of the world's luxury goods, making it "the largest luxury-goods-producing nation" (Som and Blanckaert 2015, p. 47). It is therefore crucial to observe this country in order to understand part of the different possible nuances attributed to the experiences with luxury and the perception of luxuriousness.

The manifestation of Italian luxury in the international market seems to be rooted the development of the manufacturing sector producing clothing and accessories, which starts to transform itself into a fashion industry since the 1950s and then refocus on the production of luxury goods especially since the 1970s onwards (Merlo 2018). In this perspective, we not only need to go back in time, but we also have to focus more specifically on the moment when a small group of emerging Italian designers joined the project of a man, Giovanni Battista Giorgini, who was actually an experienced buyer of Italian artisan products for some US department stores. His aim was to show in his villa in Florence the work of acknowledged Italian designers to an international audience of fashion journalists and American buyers. The project, which presented the collections of nine maisons and two boutiques, succeeded and is generally regarded as the birth of Italian style. Italian creativity in clothing production was thus launched to the international markets and was prone to become an important player in the scene, only after the acquisition of a new know-how (Vergani 1992).

According to some observers (Merlo 2018; Mora 2009; Colaiacomo 2006; White 2000), the newly born Italian fashion was still lacking any industrial consistency: it was mainly made up of small manufacturing units, and conserved an extremely fragmented structure, which resembled the one applied to craftsmanship production of accessories with only few exceptions in the sector of shoe production (e.g. Ferragamo) and bags production (e.g. Gucci) that could count on a well-established reputation and had been present for a long time in the foreign markets.

At the beginning of its history Italy was therefore much less experienced in clothing manufacturing than other countries in the international market (e.g. Germany, the United States, Great Britain), it not only needed to acquire and develop an organizational model but also to improve the system of machinery and managerial skills. The point of reference in this case seem to have been given the

American exemplar—along with its economic support (Mora 2009)—carefully examined and then readapted to meet the needs of the local context (White 2000). Retail chains have represented a pivotal factor in this development and in the constitution of a system of large investments in physical capital and technological knowledge, as well as in the import of human capital and the expansion of marketing and distribution (Merlo 2011). Italian style started to gain importance and achieve success in the atmosphere of active transformation typical of the period after the war, Italian production was articulated in order to provide experiences with different typologies of goods: haute couture (evening and daywear); boutique; ready-to-wear (high quality) (White 2000).

The processes of reorganization that reshaped the biggest Italian clothing firms subsequently reached its peak by the 1970s, and it was characterized by specific conditions that have been assumed as "distinctive, country-specific assets within the international arena for a long time" as Merlo (2018, p. 40) puts it, namely a close collaboration between industry and fashion designers along with an extensive presence of industrial districts.[1] The developing Italian industry could take an advantage of the high level of productive specialization displayed by the companies collected around industrial districts as realities deeply rooted in long-established manufacturing traditions: "Specialization prompts the search for both vertical and horizontal linkages between firms. As a result, this kind of industrial agglomeration usually spans the entire pipeline, from the selection of raw materials to product labelling" (ibidem).

What characterizes the Italian way of production is a SMEs reality, which, according to Merlo (2018, p. 40), can be found both in the Italian industry as a whole and in the local industries broadly related to fashion and luxury, and which is due to the fact that Italian districts consist on average of 8173 local units and employ 34,663 workers. This structure was crucial in the phase of transformation from mere clothing industry to fashion industry.

Starting from the 1970s onwards the Italian clothing industry undergoes important transformations (Pent Fornengo 1992; Colaiacomo 2006) that turns it into a fashion system similar to the one we experience nowadays. As a reaction to the oil crisis in 1973, Italy operates a form of delocalization on a domestic scale, and carries out the process of decentralization within the country. This is due to the fact that different from other countries who could count on satellite economic areas (e.g. US, France, and Germany) Italy had to count on the widespread presence of domestic SMEs, many of which were agglomerated in industrial districts. This change could prepare the way to a new phase of reorientation to luxury goods production, because "these conditions made it possible to exploit the advantages of large-scale production without giving up the flexibility peculiar to small firms, which was essential to promptly adapt to the changing trends of fashion" (Merlo 2018, p. 44) in order to create a subsequent system.

It is exactly after this new constitution that the Italian luxury industry starts to acquire a specific connotation in terms of production as well as it operates to maintain a specific place in the global market and imagery (Colaiacomo 2006), to the extent that a specific Italian way of approaching luxury can be detected and outlined in the sector (Som and Blanckaert 2015, p. 220).

In this reconstruction of the Italian industry, luxury appears as experience with specific typologies of goods that are conveyed as exclusive products, and that are meant to invite high net worth individuals, therefore they are high priced and mostly sold through selective channels. Luxury nonetheless is presented as the attribute of a wide spectrum of items located in different market segments, that range from traditional ultra-luxury to affordable luxury, and can include super-premium and aspirational luxury (Merlo 2018, p. 41). Therefore we can assume that the experience related to the purchase and use of Italian luxury products does entail a dimension of luxuriousness, especially if we focus on novelty, diversity, and reach. As Som and Blanckaert (2015, p. 239) suggest: "a point to be noted about the Italian brands is that they mostly started out with accessories: the beginning of great designers was in Gucci handbags, Fendi fur, and Prada shoes. However, they slowly increased their reach to include ready-to-wear collections, which became an instant hit with the ladies. Despite never having promoted haute couture (which is a very French concept), these Italian brands were never afraid to hit Paris fashion week with their latest collections".

In this variety the category of luxury goods for personal use (i.e. designer apparel and footwear, bags and accessories, jewellery, watches, cosmetics, and fragrances) seem to stand out and to allow interpretations in which the perspectives of management scholars and historians conflate. As said above, luxury goods can be observed in an eminently cultural perspective as objects that are characterized by a capability to accomplish specific social tasks and to endorse specific narrations about the users and their (social) experience (semiotic virtuosity). The experience offered and acknowledged with Italian products seems based on their semiotic virtuosity as well as on the perceived uniqueness they grant the consumer, since they appear prone to be readapted to their lifestyle based on perception and (social) uses. We can see this epitomized by Armani's production who is regarded as a champion in terms of making luxury affordable "a long time before the concept of 'masstige' came up in the marketing arena" (ibidem). Different typologies of consumers are offered a gamut of options including *privé* collections and in this experience the factor of extended product is embedded in the strong brand identity, highly constructed through heritage, and placing paramount emphasis on product and service quality, as well as on creativity and innovation. These elements in particular can provide an experience of perceived uniqueness as well as rebuild an idea of complexity of acquisition and appropriate consumption in the mind of the consumer. But are global consumers looking for those features?

# Chinese Consumers: In Search for Luxuriousness?

"China emerged as the luxury market in which to have a presence, a market that didn't exist 10 years before in 2003. China saved many brands from sliding into the red. [...] China's economic growth in 2013, China represented around a quarter of global luxury purchases" (Som and Blanckaert 2015, p. 15). In this perspective, we might assume that if Italians can be regarded as the main creators of meanings for luxury goods and luxurious experience in late modern societies, Chinese appear as the crucial component in the interpretation of those meanings and in their use for individual purposes. In particular, they seem to pay particular attention to specific issues related to the changes of the Chinese luxury landscape, namely, a meaning and perception of luxury that is embedded in the past, but is responding to the changing public sentiment; the influence of new regions in China that represent an increasingly significant market opportunity for long-term luxury brand sustainability; and, the increasing significance of heritage and country of origin, which enable international luxury brands to connect with current, but also prospective Chinese luxury consumers (Rovai 2015, 130). These factors are to be taken into account in understanding the changing nature of the different typologies of luxury(ous) experience contemporary consumers are looking for.

In this perspective, it is also important to point out that Chinese culture and way of thinking insist on concepts of rites and harmony as inspired by Confucian thought. As a consequence of this, the experience with luxury goods is generally lived and interpreted as an affirmation of individualism and distinction, reflecting at the same time the structure of social dynamics. Such a traditional interpretation of the relationship with goods and services is also related to the concept of inequality between individuals and the spiritual forces existing between them. In this framework, luxury goods participate in a ritual hierarchical pattern in which status and social obligations are reflected. Besides, they represent the character and spirit of each individual (who can afford them), since traditional Confucian culture does not consider luxury as something superfluous or frivolous (Rovai 2015).

This attitude seems to reverse the typical perspective traditionally attached to old luxury by Western observers, scholars, and marketing managers: luxury is not exclusively reserved for the rich, or considered as a waste of money, instead many aspire to a luxurious lifestyle, or a lifestyle that distinguishes them from other people through a display of wealth and social status. As Chen (2013, p. 114) suggests: "in an attempt to reach the same level as those rich people, the middle class in China may consume luxury beyond their income in order to feel that they belong to a certain elite group", indeed, "due to urbanization and the ever-rising number of middle classes, the demand for luxury in China has grown rapidly in recent years".

Consumer behavior nonetheless appears as significantly differentiated and is regarded as an effect of the rapid expansion of luxury consumption. In more economically advanced regions, Chinese customers still adopt a highly knowledgeable and refined approach towards the purchase of luxury brands (Rovai 2015) and they are able to spend long time looking for the best solution in terms of money invested and expression of their own personality and individuality: this process of information research and evaluation can last up to 2–3 months before the actual purchase (Panchout 2013).

Engaging with luxury consumers in China also means recognizing their attention for the symbolic dimension of things and experiences. China appears to the observers as a country that places great importance on its cultural heritage and traditions, to the extent that the social organization allows luxury brands to be used as "amulets, instantly recognizable and acknowledged as a sign of personal success and social status". Consumer behaviour is supported by this symbolism and those values, producing a striking resonance between individual and the symbolic values of brands (and in particular luxury brands) in the mind of the consumer (Panchout 2013, p. 92):

The role of symbolism as a leverage for brand associations can be seen in the ownership of luxury brands. Their symbolic values of quality, exclusivity, craftsmanship, heritage, authenticity and product excellence are just as important as the functional benefits of the brand itself. Ownership of these brands and the appropriation of brand meaning by association allow the Chinese consumer to differentiate himself, build self-concept and create individual self-expression. The link between brand user and self-image associations defines the notion of self-concept and serves as a uniform, denoting membership of certain reference groups and by definition, selected brand communities.

Since the landscape of the possible experiences with luxury goods is increasingly taking on the features of creation of a 'lifestyle', the relationship Chinese consumers aim to establish with luxury brands and products has undergone a series of steps in which the role of individual perception has increased in terms of importance. In the first phase, logos have represented the main source of attraction, providing a demonstration of status for the aspiring segment, an attitude that is still particularly present in the newer Chinese luxury territories (i.e. the third tier cities). In another phase, detectable in other environments (e.g. ter one cities) consumers have revealed great maturity and experience, and refer to heritage as an increasingly important attribute of the (brand) story, in this perspective the 'Made in …' approach is deemed not only a key success factor and an effective entry mode strategy (Rovai 2015, p. 133).

Another interesting aspect of those consumers is the fact that they have a specific profile. They have been labelled as "solitary Little Emperors" (Panchout 2013, p. 93) and mainly tend to an online mediated experience with luxury, they are often only children of less then 45 years of age (more often less than 35). They are also digitally native and have developed an understanding and awareness of brand heritage and codes due to a socialization to look for a high standard and expect the best that money can buy. In this sense they have acquire a good knowledge about brand and brand recognition and their subjective perception of luxury is moving from an interpretation of cultural display of self-expression: "Yi jin huan xiang" (return home in golden robes), into a mainstream cultural phenomenon in which complex emotional and psychosocial considerations are intertwined (ibidem).

Eastern cultures are considered particularly focused on interdependent self-construal, in a way that the line between collective self and brand communities can be easily trespassed.

In this perspective, the emotional experience individuals try to have with luxury(ous) goods is partly influence by the affection for the brands and partly dependent on the lifestyle enhancement motivations suggested by their narrations. Issues like core values of luxury brands; superior craftsmanship, exclusivity, quality, heritage, innovation and international standing seem consistent within the changing frame of reference, as well as high prices are seen as a guarantee of quality and peer-group evaluation via e-communities is crucial (Panchout 2013).

The interest of Chinese consumers on heritage, "made in…", and craftsmanship seem particularly aligned with the symbolic dimension entailed in the experience with Italian luxury production, at the same time it reveals similarities with the main source of perceived luxuriousness, insisting on elements of product extension, perceived uniqueness and authenticity. But are those two countries speaking the same globalized language of luxuriousness?

## Concluding Remarks

The concept of luxury has been radically transformed since its birth on the international cultural scene and it has been increasingly stretched to include a variety of interpretations that can find now a place in the articulated continuum which includes options reflecting the originally opposed mentalities: the elitist aristocratic view and the democratized and exhibitionist understanding of the bourgeoisie. What has become crucial for the perception of luxury and can impinge on the process of globalization of taste, is the fact that products are carefully aestheticized regardless their actual material or functional qualities and in this process a reflection is required about issues related to values, heritage, standardization of procedures.

In the transformation of consumer culture the role of glamour and the glamourization of society as well as the search for an enchanting and dreamlike experience with goods and services have played an important role: the democratization of elite products as well as transformation of luxury into something that is intrinsically embedded in the art of seduction and make believe.

This auratic dimension attached to places and things has entered the everyday experience and permeated consumer culture to the extent that anyone can have access to the dream of exclusivity and uniqueness in the form that best suits their needs. This elements are nowadays better understood in terms of luxuriousness, radically located in the mind of the consumers and in their work of interpretation of the symbolic world attached to the wide range of luxury products available.

Glamour, [...] starting as magic, developed into a very specific form of individualism via the dandies of the Regency period, and Byron. With the dandies it took the form of personal charisma. The individual imposes himself upon society by means not of power but of beauty and personality, unanchored and divorced from traditional social relations. The dandy, in other words, is a performance and, individual that he is, paradoxically anticipates the rise of spectacular mass culture—for eventually, "stars" replace aristocrats and princes as figures of glamour. (Wilson 2007, p. 97)

The luxury industry has strategically exploited those processes in order to arouse the desire of consumer and remark the distinctions between groups. The Italian industry seems to epitomize this conception of production (of luxuriousness) and to have undergone the same process of glamourization and democratization of its products—always allowing consumers to find the most appropriate personal experience with the goods produced.

The way in which Chinese consumer are now approaching the experience with luxury reveals many similarities with the concept of luxuriousness as it is strongly centred on the idea of perceived uniqueness as well as it aims to construct an individuality useful to impose oneself on society, or better to easily move along the borders between groups and hierarchies.

All those elements seem to draw a picture of Chinese experience with luxury that, on the one hand, fits in the strategy and way of managing meanings that Italian brands (like other similar firms in the sector) have been carrying out for a long time (and that now are recalling in order to escape the absorption by the conglomerates). On the other hand it seems to slowly erode the boundaries meant to create an elite of selected consumers.

If it seems that a strong interest in luxury products is established in Chinese society, a certain taste for luxuriousness is emerging among Chinese consumers, as part of the transformation of the globalized culture: in their experience with goods elements can be detected that differentiate them from the idealized character of modernity—the aristocrat—who was not interested in suitable investments nor in pleasurable enchantments but was searching for aesthetics and refinement as goals in themselves.

If luxuriousness is becoming the new idiomatic expression of luxury, it will be useful to collect the stories of the new consumers in terms of their experience with the semiotic virtuosity of the goods, their capability to shift them in the luxury register, and to reinvent or avoid rules for restriction and complicated acquisition, because its in their right to classify and being classified by those stories.

# Note

1. District is here meant as "socioterritorial entities that are characterized by the active presence of both a community of people and a population of firms in one naturally and historically bounded area" cfr. Merlo (2018, p. 40).

# References

Amatulli, Cesare. 2009. *Il lusso esteriorizzato e il lusso interiorizzato*. Bari: Cacucci.

Appadurai, Arjun. 1986. *The Social Life of Things: Commodities in Cultural Perspective*. Cambridge: Cambridge University Press.

Bahn, Sangwoo, Cheol Lee, Chang S. Nam, and Myung H. Yun. 2009. "Incorporating Affective Customer Needs for Luxuriousness into Product Design Attributes." *Human Factors and Ergonomics in Manufacturing and Service Industries* 19 (2): 105–127.

Berthon, P.R., L. Pitt, M. Parent, and J.-P. Berthon. 2009. "Aesthetics and Ephemerality: Observing and Preserving the Luxury Brand." *California Management Review* 52 (1): 45–66.

Berry, Christopher. 1994. *The Idea of Luxury: A Conceptual and Historical Investigation*. Cambridge: Cambridge University Press.

Bovone, Laura. 2014. *Rappresentarsi nel mondo. Comunicazione, identità, moda*. Milano: FrancoAngeli.

Bourdieu, Pierre. 1984. *Distinction: A Social Critique of the Judgement of Taste*. Cambridge: Harvard University press.

Campbell, Colin. 1987. *The Romantic Ethic and the Spirit of Modern Consumerism*. Oxford: Blackwell.

Campbell, Colin. 1994. "Consuming Goods and the Good of Consuming." *Critical Review* 8: 503–520.

Chen, Joanna. 2013. "Luxury Shopping Places in China." In *Global Luxury Trends: Innovative Strategies for Emerging Markets*, Chap. 8. Basingstoke: Palgrave Macmillan.

Colaiacomo, Paola. 2006. *Fatto in Italia. La cultura del made in Italy (1960–2000)*. Roma: Meltemi.

Csaba, F.F. 2008. "Redefining Luxury: A Review Essay." Creative Encounters Working Paper No. 15. Copenhagen: Copenhagen Business School.

Dewald, J. 1996. *The European Nobility 1400–1800*. Cambridge: Cambridge Unversity Press.

Dubois, Bernard, and Gilles Laurent. 1995. "Luxury Possessions and Practices: An Empirical Scale." *European Advances in Consumer Research* 2: 69–77.

Fabris, Giampaolo. 2010. *La società post-crescita*. Egea: Milano.

Featherstone, M. 1991. *Consumer Culture and Postmodernism*. London: Sage Publications.

Gundle, Stephen. 2008. *Glamour: A History*. Oxford: Oxford University Press.

Gundle, Stephen, and Clino T. Castelli. 2006. *The Glamour System*. Basingstoke: Palgrave Macmillan.

Kapferer, Jean-Noël. 2015. *Kapferer On Luxury: How Luxury Brands Can Grow Yet Remain The Same*. London: Kogan Page.

Kapferer, Jean-Noël, and Victor Bastien. 2009. *The Luxury Strategy: Break The Rules of Marketing to Build Strong Brands*. London and Philadelphia: Kogan Page.

Lipovetsky, Gilles, and Jean Serroy. 2013. *L'esthétisation du monde. Vivre à l'age du capitalisme artistique*. Paris: Gallimard.

Mazzalovo, Gerald, and Michel Chevalier. 2012. *Luxury Brand Management: A World of Privilege*. Singapore: Wiley.

Merlo, Elisabetta. 2011. "Italian Fashion Business: Achievements and Challenges (1970s–2000s)." *Business History* 53 (3): 344–362.

Merlo, Elisabetta. 2018. "Italian Luxury Goods Industry on the Move: SMEs and Global Value Chain." In *Global Luxury: Organizational Change and Emerging Markets Since the 1970s*, edited by Pierre-Yves Donzé and Rika Fujioka, 39–64. Basingstoke: Palgrave Macmillan.

Miller, Karen W., and Michael K. Mills. 2012. "Contributing Clarity by Examining Brand Luxury in the Fashion Market." *Journal of Business Research* 65 (10): 1471–1479.

Mora, Emanuela. 2009. *Fare moda. Esperienze di produzione e consumo.* Milano: Bruno Mondadori.

Panchout, Katrina. 2013. "Engaging with the Luxury Consumer in China." In *Global Luxury Trends: Innovative Strategies for Emerging Markets*, edited by Jonas Hoffman and Ivan Coste-Maniére, Chap. 6. Basingstoke: Palgrave Macmillan.

Pent Fornengo, Graziella. 1992. "Product Differentiation and Process Innovation in the Italian Clothing Industry." In *Industry on the Move: Causes and Consequences of International Relocation in the Manufacturing Industry*, edited by Gijsbert van Liemt, Chap. 8. Geneva: International Labour Office.

Rovai, Serena. 2015. "The Evolution of Luxury Consumption in China." In *Luxury Brands in Emerging Markets*, edited by Glyn Atwal and Douglas Bryson, Chap. 11. Basingstoke: Palgrave Macmillan.

Som, Ashok, and Christian Blanckaert. 2015. *The Road to Luxury.* Singapore: Wiley.

Turunen, Linda L.M. 2018. *Interpretations of Luxury: Exploring the Consumer Perspective.* Basingstoke: Palgrave Macmillan.

Veblen, Thorstein. 1912. *The Theory of the Leisure Class.* New York: Penguin (Original work published 1899).

Vergani, Guido. 1992. *Sala Bianca: Nascita della Moda Italiana.* Milano: Electa.

Vigneron, Frank, and Lester W. Johnson. 2004. "Measuring Perceptions of Brand Luxury." *Journal of Brand Management* 11 (6): 484–506.

Warde, Alan. 2005. "Consumption and the Theories of Practice." *Journal of Consumer Culture* 5 (2): 131–153.

White, Nicola. 2000. *Reconstructing Italian Fashion: America and the Development of the Italian Fashion Industry.* London: Bloomsbury.

Wilson, Elizabeth. 2007. "A Note on Glamour." *Fashion Theory* 11 (1): 95–108.

# 4

# The Dark Side of Luxury: When Negative Emotions Are Felt by Very Wealthy Consumers

Virginie De Barnier and Elyette Roux

## Introduction

In the current financial crisis, the global luxury market is also facing a recession. However, the high unemployment has not affected the affluent class in the U.S., and rich Chinese consumers continue to burn money during their luxury travels. Luxury democratization is a new market trend (Silverstein and Fiske 2003) that may have been overestimated by previous studies' focus on student populations to investigate consumer attitudes towards luxury (Dubois et al. 2001; Vigneron and Johnson 2004). As a matter of fact, luxury brands target both populations; the wealthy are the core target, and the middle class is targeted for more democratized product categories. However, do the people at the top of the social and financial pyramid feel the same way about luxury as mass consumers do?

V. De Barnier (✉) · E. Roux
IAE Aix Center for Studies and Research in Management (CERGAM),
Aix Marseille University, Aix en Provence, France
e-mail: virginie.de-barnier@iae-aix.com

© The Author(s) 2020
I. Cantista and T. Sádaba (eds.), *Understanding Luxury Fashion*,
Palgrave Advances in Luxury, https://doi.org/10.1007/978-3-030-25654-8_4

Luxury objects serve to signal the differences in economical capital (Veblen 1899) and cultural capital (Bourdieu 1984). Luxury brands also create a dream effect (Dubois and Paternault 1995) and sensory pleasure (Roux and Floch 1996) for consumers. Researchers have widely discussed the benefits that consumers can gain from the consumption of luxury goods. However, the negative side of luxury consumption, such as the negative emotions it might evoke, has rarely been studied. This research therefore aims to explore the emotions, particularly of a negative variety, that affluent consumers experience in the consumption of luxury goods and services. Therefore, we conducted an interpretative, qualitative research in China and Brazil, which are two of the most important emerging markets for luxury goods in the world (Lu 2008; Galhanone 2009). Brazil scores higher than China on the Hofstede cultural index (i.e., index of individualism-collectivism: Brazil 38, China 20). With a score of 20 China is a highly collectivist culture where people prefer to act in the interests of the group rather than for themselves. Brazil has a score of 38 which means that it is a more individualistic country than China. However, individualism is not regarded as positively in Brazil as it is in the United States. On the contrary, individualism is perceived as a negative concept and *"against the laws that define and emanate from union"* (DaMatta 1985, p. 64). Comparing individualistic and collectivistic culture, Wong and Ahuvia (1998) argue that a reinterpretation of the consumer theories grounded in the Western rationality is necessary to understand luxury consumption in Eastern countries: *"because the Asian interdependent self focuses more on the public, outer self than the Western, independent self, Asian group norms and goals frequently emphasize public and visible possessions"* (Wong and Ahuvia 1998, p. 437).

In both countries, Brazil and China, luxury consumption is concentrated among the few people who can afford it. However, specific characteristics of each country may interfere or impact luxury consumption, i.e., religious, economic or cultural factors. For example, would people in a country like China, influenced by Buddhist doctrine, consider it a shame to purchase things like a Louis Vuitton bag while others are starving or earning only a fraction of the price of that bag? In Brazil, where the richest 10% of the population holds almost 50% of the national wealth, do very rich people feel guilty while driving their luxury cars close to the "favelas[1]"? Finally, what should luxury brands attend to when consumers link brands to negative emotions?

The first part of this chapter focuses on literature review about luxury and emotions, the second part presents research methods and results. Finally, we stress the limits of our study and propose avenues for future research.

## Luxury and Culture

Luxury is hard to define and lacks a universal conception (Berry 1994). In marketing, analysts have developed this concept from the perspective of consumers in a long process from simple models up to multi-dimensional frameworks. Roux and Floch (1996) suggested that luxury has two inseparable dimensions: one ethical and one aesthetic. The ethical dimension represents the anti-economic character of luxury, and the aesthetic refers to the poly-sensuality that luxury brands provide. Vigneron and Johnson (2004) proposed a model of luxury comprising two components, "personal vs. non-personal", and five dimensions, "hedonic, extended self, conspicuousness, uniqueness, and quality". Consumer understand well the luxury market and perceive the three luxury levels: accessible, intermediate and inaccessible (De Barnier et al. 2012).

The concept of luxury is also closely linked to culture. Dubois et al. (2001) studied over twenty geographic areas and identified three basic attitudes to luxury: "elitism, democratization, and distance". To some extent, these attitudes reflect the specific cultures, values, and even religions of an area. For example, different aspects of luxury attract French, British and Russian consumers (De Barnier and Valette-Florence 2013). Recently, due to the cultural complexity of luxury, researchers proposed a framework based on consumers' perceptions of luxury values. With individual, social, financial and functional dimensions, this value-based

---

[1]Favelas is a shantytown or slum, especially in Brazil.

model identifies the drivers of luxury value more broadly than previous studies. It is also considered an adequate conceptual structure for cross-cultural studies (Wiedmann et al. 2009).

## Luxury and Emotions

Psychologists and marketers have studied emotions for decades. In marketing, Olshavsky and Granbois (1979) first recognized that consumers are not always rational in the sense that their purchases are not always the result of a decision process. Instead, they showed that purchases can be driven by culturally mandated lifestyles, conformity to group norms or the imitation of others. Holbrook and Hirschman (1982) pioneered the study of consumer emotions and opened the way for further exploration of this subject.

In the luxury field, there is no doubt that consumers experience emotions when they buy expensive objects. Those emotions are multiple and not always positive (Kessous et al. 2017). However, a cross-cultural study raises the question of how universal emotions are across cultures.

Although emotions and their expression and interpretation vary among cultures, there is a general consensus that happiness, fear, anger, and sadness are universal to human beings (Kemper 1987). Those universal emotions, or primary emotions, combine to create secondary emotions. However, combinations of happiness, fear, anger, and sadness may result in many different secondary emotions. Bierbrauer (1992) studied people's reactions to the violation of norms in a cross-cultural environment and showed that different emotions are dominant according to culture, especially according to the culture's collectivist or individualistic dimension. Specifically, Bierbrauer pointed out that individualistic cultures react with greater guilt, and collectivistic cultures tend to react with more shame. He defined shame as the reaction to others' criticism and a fear of rejection and the withdrawal of love. In contrast, guilt results from the violation of personal standards; it is a form of self-criticism that results from comparing one's actions with internalized standards. His research showed that shame results from social influence or from anger with the self for not being able to conform to social norms, but guilt results from the internalization of norms or from fear of the consequences of breaking them.

Turner and Stets (2005) argued that guilt and shame are secondary emotions produced by a combination of sadness, anger and fear and that the relative intensity of the primary emotions is what differentiates them. Guilt is a combination of intense sadness, relatively intense fear (of the consequences for the self) and less intense anger. Shame results from intense sadness, relatively intense anger (with the self), and less intense fear.

The objective of this study is to identify emotions felt during luxury consumption, especially negative emotions such as guilt and shame, and therefore the discrete approach for emotions was chosen. Consequently, this study focuses on identifying five negative emotions. Three are the primary universal emotions of fear, anger, and sadness, and the remaining two are the secondary emotions of guilt and shame.

# Research Method

Since the focus is on negative emotions such as guilt and shame, a qualitative approach to probe more in-depth information (Brennan and Binney 2010) was chosen. Data were collected through phenomenological interviews (Thompson et al. 1989). Interviews took place in two main phases. The first was an introduction or warm-up, which was designed to inform participants about the main rules of the interview, make them feel comfortable and give them a sense that they had a lot to contribute. The second phase targeted luxury to understand how the participants defined luxury in their lives; we focused on their personal feelings toward luxury, including both the positive and negative feelings that they experienced while consuming luxury products and/or brands.

Interviews were carried out in the mother languages of the consumers (Portuguese in Brazil and Chinese in China) by Brazilian natives in Brazil and Chinese natives in China. The interviews lasted from 30 minutes to one hour. They were tape-recorded, transcribed in the domestic language, and translated into English. After translation, they were back-translated into Portuguese and Chinese by independent researchers to verify the accuracy of the translations. Any divergences were eventually discussed by the research team and adjusted to guarantee the transcript's original meaning.

Due to the high financial status of the participants, they were chosen based on the researchers' personal acquaintances or by snowball sampling (Cooper and Schindler 2010). It was critical for the participants to be frequent customers of luxury products, and thus the selection criterion was a participant's standard of living and income. Therefore, the sample can be classified as purposive (Cooper and Schindler 2010). The informants' monthly income ranged from 13,600 to 68,000 USD for Brazil and from 13,600 to 136,000 USD for China. A total of 14 Brazilian and 15 Chinese were interviewed (see Table 4.7 in Appendix for sample specification). In both countries, our sampling and interview processes followed the rules of equivalence that are recommended for cross-cultural qualitative research (Polsa 2007).

# Findings

## Negative Emotions—Fear, Anger, Sadness

The feelings of fear that are associated with luxury consumption are listed in Table 4.1. Both Brazilian and Chinese consumers feared violence and being envied during the consumption and display of their luxury possessions.

However, in a typical Confucian society, the Chinese consumers' fears seemed to be shaped by social pressure and cultural values. Wong and Ahuvia (1998) suggested that Confucian, Asian consumers would prefer publicly visible luxury goods to symbolize and communicate their positions in the social hierarchy. However, this proposition neglects another facet of Confucianism: the doctrine of the Mean, or, "being without inclination to either side" (Legge 1960). The internal harmony that Confucianism emphasizes refers to the regulation of one's passions and impulses. This aspect of Confucianism also led several studies to characterize traditional Chinese people as humble

**Table 4.1** Negative emotions evoked during luxury consumption—fear

| Type of fear | Verbatim |
| --- | --- |
| Fear of violence | 1.1 "I think security is the most luxurious thing someone can have, and, because of this, I only ride in an armored car with dark glasses and a driver trained in defensive driving…" (Marcos-Brazil) |
| | 1.2 "To avoid catching the attention of thieves, I cut the logo off my LV bag. We should choose things with a high price, but with a poor appearance…" (Zhang-China) |
| Anxiety of being envied | 1.3 "But luxury is very good when it draws good energy to you and to those you love, or because it's a synonym of comfort and beauty… but when it becomes a reason for others to envy you and send harsh thoughts your way, then I think it isn't worth it… I swear that I prefer people to think I'm an insignificant person than for them to think that I'm someone to be envied or imitated…" (Ana-Brazil) |
| | 1.4 "Because I work in government, it's not good to be too flaunty and extravagant. Sometimes my colleagues ask me about my Gucci bag, and I tell them it's a counterfeit…" (Bailu-China) |

(Zhang and Jolibert 2003) and moderate (Xiao and Kim 2009). In our study, several informants seemed to live under the pressure to be humble because they exhibited anxiety and caution to avoid being envied or noticed for their wealth (Comments 1.2, 1.5). Some negative emotions appeared to be specific to China (see Table 4.2).

The Chinese consumers feared being distant from others because they believed that something bad would befall them if they tried to be different or to show off (Comment 2.1). They also feared losing face by selecting an unrecognized brand (Comment 2.2) and were concerned about the devaluation of their luxury possessions (Comment 2.3). Some Chinese participants reported their fears of retribution (Comment 2.4). This fear originates in Buddhism, which emphasizes that a person's fate and fortune are predetermined and suggests that "life and death are fated; wealth and honors hinge on the will of providence" (Legge 1960). Luxury consumption is incompatible with Buddhist doctrine because the Buddhist concept of "Jie" requires people to control their desires for

**Table 4.2** Fear evoked during luxury consumption specific to China

| Type of fear | Verbatim |
| --- | --- |
| Anxiety of being different | 2.1 "…I have a rule for myself, which is not to be too different. I should let others know that I am similar to them. My clothes and the way I speak should match others'. Actually, to be different and individual is very easy, but you cost yourself a lot by doing so, especially in Chinese society…" (Pan-China) |
| Fear of losing face | 2.2 "…I choose some good brands to wear for sportswear, at least Nike or Adidas. If I wear Lining (a local sportswear brand), I will feel I'm losing face, especially now that I represent the image of my company, which I shouldn't degrade…" (Xiaofeng-China) |
| Concern of devaluation | 2.3 "…. For me, I always purchase the jewelry of 100% rare materials, like 999 platinum, because the jewelry that emphasizes the design but not the material, like Swarovski, will lose value when it is not in vogue…" (Yunxi-China) |
| Fear of retribution | 2.4 "…One's wealth is given by heaven. If you don't use your wealth properly, you will be punished, and heaven will take away your wealth…" (Yuse-China) |

material wealth, emotions and mood swings and encourages a simple life. This healthy Buddhist lifestyle enables to keep inner peace.

When the interviewer probed the participants' opinions on luxury consumption, some of them described the doctrines of predetermination and theological control over human fate (Comments 2.4). These participants seemed to fear losing their fortunes. To avoid this possibility, they believed that it is necessary to behave well, by avoiding extravagance, and to obey Chinese philosophy.

Like the Brazilian sample, some of the Chinese participants criticized the improper behavior of the new rich. Influenced by the Mean value, traditional Chinese people tend to be more cautious in verbalizing their responses (Yang 1981) and to use indirect forms of communication (such as metaphors) to express criticism (Gries 2004). Therefore, the Chinese participants expressed a kind of sadness for the new rich (Comment 3.4), but the Brazilian participants expressed indignation or disdain for the new rich's uncultivated behavior (Comment 3.1). The Chinese participants' feelings were limited to sadness and calm, and anger was unnecessary. However, when the participants were mentioning the possibility of new rich behavior damaging the image of the wealthy class, they responded very differently. Ms. Fanyi expressed irritation and tried to find more precious goods to defend her status in the hierarchy when the mass consumption of luxury goods threatened to neutralize the distinction between social classes (Comment 3.2) (Table 4.3).

## Shame and Guilt

Researchers have suggested that shame and guilt differ in terms of the focus on others or the self (Glenn and Glenn 1982; Lebra 1973; Abe 2004). Shame results from the failure to meet others' expectations and is therefore assumed to be more relevant for collectivistic cultures. Guilt is defined as having a negative view of the self and is more relevant for individualistic cultures (Triandis et al. 1985). Although Brazil is not classified as an individualistic culture, it scores higher than China on the Hofstede cultural index (2019) (index of individualism-collectivism: Brazil 38, China 20). According to DaMatta (1985), for instance, individualism is not regarded as positively in Brazil as it is in the United States. On the contrary, it is perceived as a negative concept and "against the laws that define and emanate from union" (DaMatta 1985, p. 64). These cultural differences might explain why more of the Chinese informants reported no guilt but reported more shame than their Brazilian counterparts (Table 4.5).

Although most of Brazilian participants reported that they did not feel guilt, some others did admit to experiencing this feeling. For instance, Mr. Celso (Brazil) reported feeling guilty when he realized that he enjoys a very different lifestyle compared to the majority of the Brazilian population (Comment 4.4). He also mentioned religion as the source of his guilt (Comment 4.5). However, it should be emphasized that this sensation did not last long (Comment 5.1). Those participants who admitted feeling guilty immediately justified themselves by arguing

**Table 4.3** Negative emotions evoked during luxury consumption—anger and sadness

| Types of emotion | | Verbatim |
|---|---|---|
| Anger specific to Brazil | Irritation, disdain and disgust for the improper behavior of new rich or luxury buyers | 3.1 "I see people buying deliriously in this crisis time in the country...People buy more than they need and rush to places to show off... It's a ridiculous excess... the kind of thing done by people who don't realize what's going on... When everything is ok it's already like this, imagine now, isn't it?" (Maria-Brazil) |
| Anger specific to China | Irritation with the mass consumption of luxury brands | 3.2 "...I purchased LV and Prada bags, but after a while, I found that everyone has LV and Prada; even my employees have the same bags that I have. I can even imagine the scene in which they are whispering that the president has the same bag as her employees. So, I prefer to purchase products of limited edition now. At least they are not something that a regular white collar can afford..." (Fanyi-China) |
| Sadness specific to Brazil | Sorrow, anguish and pain for not being able to identify the right products or services to be accepted in a specific group | 3.3 "...sometimes I realize that even if I really try hard to follow those rules, even if I really value the tradition, the usual practices and all, I feel lost... I often feel like a fish out of water. Nobody is hostile... on the contrary ... but I always have the sensation that I've arrived just after a secret has been told... as if I'm permanently late... or for some reason I wasn't invited to take part in the group..." (Penelope-Brazil) |

(continued)

**Table 4.3** (continued)

| Types of emotion | | Verbatim |
|---|---|---|
| Sadness specific to China | Sadness for the improper behavior of the new rich | 3.4 "...I respect LV, but it doesn't suit me...I have seen many men carrying a LV bag, but the bag is just like an unsuitable decoration. The bag and its user can't match each other. I feel a little bit sad for this type of people because they don't look nicer with the bag..." (Laoye-China) |

that social differences are not their fault, that they earned their fortunes through hard work, or that they contribute to society in some way (i.e., generating jobs, paying taxes, or using their money to buy gifts for family and friends). Brazil has a long history of social inequality and, although it is slowly decreasing (Soares 2006), this inequality remains among the worst in the world (CIA World Factbook 2019). Not all participants were blind to Brazil's social inequality, and some of them expressed grief about the situation (Table 4.4).

Religious practices in Brazil are unique. Although most of the population defined themselves as Catholics (74%) in the last national census (IBGE 2010), religious practices involve a mix of several different religions (DaMatta 1984). Catholicism was the official colonial religion and compulsory even for foreigners who wished to buy land or marry a local woman (Freyre 2006). As Gracino (2008) and Siqueira (2006) pointed out, religious practices in Brazil are very dynamic and continually evolving. Thus, even though Catholicism may evoke a sense of guilt for social inequality, it nevertheless has a minor effect on the population's attitudes and behaviors concerning luxury, as our results show.

We found that, for the Chinese consumers, Buddhism was the first norm to provoke their guilt during luxury consumption. Buddhism suggests that luxury goods are unnecessary (Zhang and Jolibert 2003). Buddhist participants felt rather guilty for the contradiction between luxury consumption and frugality and for the fear of retribution. Influenced by the Buddhist tradition of frugality, Mr. Chen was parsimonious in his personal consumption, but generous with business

**Table 4.4**  Guilt for luxury consumption

| Themes | | Verbatim |
|---|---|---|
| Selfish | | 4.1 "It weighs on my conscience that I have something that is so much better than what the majority has, and still I don't have any intention of sharing that with others... It sounds kind of selfish..." (Celso-Brazil) 4.2 "...I don't dare to tell my husband and children about my purchases of luxury clothes because I am afraid that I will be seen as too selfish..." (Xiaotu-China) |
| Specific to Brazil | Realizing social inequality | 4.3 "Actually, if you think rationally, as I am now, most things I consume are luxury products...some things, of course, we are aware of even if we use them on a day-to-day basis... others not... It's the most natural thing in the world that Bic pens to other people are Montblanc... After all, such a pen costs at least a minimum salary... but at the same time it's very normal that everybody has it in my environment... God, I never thought of it like that... yes..." (Celso-Brazil) |
| | Because of religion education (Catholic) | 4.4 "But on the other hand, this contrast between wealth and poverty is very shocking and very strong... That's when guilt appears... nothing more Catholic, isn't that so? For the Catholics, success and money are sins..." (Celso-Brazil) |
| Specific to China | Contradictory to the frugal tradition | 4.5 "...I was born in the countryside. We followed the frugal tradition when we were young, so I seldom spent a big amount of money on personal purchases. Once my wife bought some jewelry, and I was very unhappy because she doesn't need those at her age..." (Chen-China) |
| | Fear of retribution | See Table 4.2. |

expenses (Comment 5.7). He also donates to charity. We inferred that he might do so to relieve his guilt by giving back to society (Comment 5.4); and on the other hand, he seemed more interested in investing money in beneficial projects. According to Zhang and Jolibert (2003), Buddhist doctrine leads to a consumption preference for utilitarian products. Luxury goods differ from utilitarian products, but they have several useful attributes. Therefore, it seems that consumers adopt "spending rationally and practically" as an extended principle to respond to the Buddhist doctrine of frugality. They tend to emphasize the useful functions of luxury goods or spend for practical reasons to minimize the incompatibility of luxury consumption with Buddhist norms. The fear of retribution is also an outcome of Buddhism's influence. For Buddhism, causality naturally exists in life and Chinese people often refer to it as karma. This implies that there is a reason for all actions taken by individuals, and these actions may come back, no matter good or bad. Therefore, fear for retribution is high in China and creates tensions. Ms. Yuse alleviated her fear of retribution by giving to charity (Comment 5.10). Two other participants who were willing to give charity explained they wanted to do good deed based on their respect for tradition (Comment 5.3). However, they also seemed to believe in the rules of retribution. Ms. Mei followed her family's tradition, but she also believed that donating to charity protects her family from harm (Comment 5.3).

Some participants regarded the personal consumption of luxury goods as selfish behavior (Comments 4.1, 4.2), and thus they felt guilty for purchasing luxury goods for themselves. They reported that, to justify this consumption, they often spend more on their family and children than on themselves (Comments 5.5, 5.6).

Today, increasing numbers of consumers choose to buy environmentally friendly products (Laroche et al. 2001; Montoro et al. 2006). However, these environmental concerns seem to conflict with the desire for precious materials in luxury goods. In our study, Ms. Yuse confronted this conflict because she owned a Shahtoosh, which is shawl woven with the down hair of Tibetan antelope. As the numbers of Tibetan antelope continue to drop yearly, the hunting of antelope and the consumption of Shahtoosh in China are illegal. Ms. Yuse intended to show off her precious shawl, but, at the same time, she tried to hide the dark side of her consumption. She first specified that the wool came from domesticated antelope but then realized that this approach was not a good explanation; thus, she ended the conversation by pointing out that her consumption might help the development of local industry (Comment 6.10). Recently, there has been an increasing tendency towards "consumer nationalism" in China, which refers to buying domestic products or brands instead of foreign brands (Wang and Wang 2007). Ms. Yuse tried to justify her guilt for consuming non-environmentally friendly products by appealing to another accepted ethical principle in China (Table 4.5).

None of the Brazilian participants reported feeling shame. On the contrary, when the interviewer directly asked about shame, the participants did not seem to understand why they should feel this emotion. Chinese consumers fear losing face because it is a source of social shame (King and Myers 1977). Several participants reported that they choose luxury brand clothes because they feel safer in these clothes and there is less risk of losing face (Comment 2.2). These Chinese consumers need luxury goods to save face, but, on the other hand, excessive extravagance also causes negative feelings like shame or sadness. Mr. Laoye reported feeling sad for the "new rich" people showing off and having improper behaviors (Comment 3.4). Mr. Xiaofeng reported feeling uncomfortable with showing off his accessories (Comment 6.1) because this type of display is the typical image for uncultured, new rich consumers. "Following the middle way", an interpretation of the Mean value in China, seems to be the best rule for Chinese consumers to avoid shame and embarrassment in their consumption of luxury goods.

Turner (2000) suggested that shame results from a person's disappointment and sadness at behaving inadequately, both in his own eyes and the eyes of others. Mr. Pan reported being disappointed in himself for pursuing luxury goods as his goal in life (Comment 6.2). Thus, he started donating to charity, which he found to be a more fulfilling and encouraging goal. This finding is congruent with Guy and Patton's (1989) suggestion that, among other reasons, individuals donate to charity to enhance their self-esteem. Hirschman (1985) observed that not all the new rich consumers engage in conspicuous consumption

**Table 4.5**   The way to alleviate feelings of guilt

| Themes | | Verbatim |
|---|---|---|
| I gave or I will give charity | Justify guilt feeling | 5.1 *"Generally speaking, this guilt doesn't last and ends fast… first because I help some charity institutions…" (Ana-Brazil)* <br> 5.2 *"I want to set up a foundation of jade because I have seen a lot of people who starve and live in poor conditions. I really want to help them…" (Yuse-China)* |
| | Following tradition— specific to China | 5.3 *"I am Buddhist, and Buddhism asks us to do good deeds, to do charity. In my family, from my grandmother, we started to give money to the temples and to help the constructions of road. I think it's also why we always had a good life until now. Buddha blessed us…" (Mei-China)* |
| | For image enhancement | 5.4 *"As lawyers we don't have much money, but we should still give back to society. We have already set up scholarships in 6 universities for 10 years. With these public welfare gifts, we also built up a very good image for our company…" (Chen-China)* |
| I spend for others | Spend for family | 5.5 *"When I shop for gifts, I'm always a bit nervous, hoping that I choose the right gift… I usually feel happy because I can buy things for my children… to supply them with everything that they need or desire, obviously within certain limits" (Ingrid-Brazil)* <br> 5.6 *"I spend more on my children. If I travel alone, I often choose a business hotel, but if I travel with my family, I will choose a much better hotel, usually a 5 star hotel…" (Yixiang-China)* |
| | Spend for business development | 5.7 *"We treated many friends in luxury restaurants last year. About ten generals attended as well. The cost of each table is about 30000 yuan (about 4400 USD), and we organized more than 30 tables…" (Chen-China)* |

(continued)

**Table 4.5**  (continued)

| Themes | Verbatim |
|---|---|
| I pay taxes to the government | 5.8 "I pay a lot of money on taxes… over employees' salaries, office's revenues… so you can have an idea, we paid in 2008 almost twenty-five … let me say it again… twenty-five million reais in taxes…" (Marcos-Brazil) |
| Social and economic problems are not my fault | 5.9 "I don't think like this, not… and there is more, I didn't cause what is on the streets. I didn't take part in this, and I took no benefit from this… on the contrary…" (Marcos-Brazil) |
| My consumption supports the development of local industry—specific to China | 5.10 "It looks like a normal shawl. It is woven with the down hair of Tibetan antelope. They raise the antelopes, but the survival rate is very low. That's why it's so precious. I think my consumption somewhat supports the development of our local industry…" (Yuse-China) |

and that some of them attribute more importance to the meaning of life than to material possessions. In this case, it seems that, after acquiring his wealth, Mr. Pan needed to find a new goal because material possessions could no longer satisfy him (Comment 6.3) (Table 4.6).

# Discussion and Conclusion

Results show that wealthy Brazilian and Chinese consumers experience negative emotions that are similar in many respects but differ in others. "Gaining face" is a very important issue in Chinese culture and, therefore, stands out for Chinese wealthy people. In contrast, "having a cradle", or a noble origin, is a source of pride for Brazilian consumers and distinguishes between "luxury buyers", the people who merely buy luxury products, and "luxury customers". This latter group of consumers understands the meaning of luxury and, consequently, knows how to behave and how to use luxury products and brands. "Gaining face" is a social value, that allows a person to be included in a specific group; in

**Table 4.6**  Shame for luxury consumption and the way to justify it (specific to China)

| Sources and the way to justify | | Verbatim |
|---|---|---|
| Losing face | | *See Table 4.2* |
| Social and cultural pressure—anti-luxury | | *6.1 "…I think it's also related to my personality. I don't like to show off. I would feel so uncomfortable if I wore a big gold necklace around my neck…" (Xiaofeng-China)* |
| Frustration | Having set a luxury good as the goal of life | *6.2 "…After I purchased my first BMW, I felt I am so worthless. I set this car as my goal, but once this goal was achieved, I felt that this luxury car humiliated me. Am I worth just a car? It represents all my value? I should be worth much more than this. I was totally lost. I don't know the meaning of being rich…" (Pan-China)* |
| | Justify: I will give charity | *6.3 "…Right now, I am no longer lost and confused. I have a new goal. I will start to do charity work when I am 40. I can start right now. I have a plan to run an animal shelter…" (Pan-China)* |

contrast, "having a cradle" is a personal value because it depends exclusively on the person's origin.

Wealthy consumers in both cultures fear violence and being envied. However, the Chinese participants more specifically expressed a fear of being different in a collective culture and a fear of losing face. We only observed a concern for the devaluation of luxury products among the Chinese participants. This observation might be explained by the fact that China's market was opened relatively recently, and thus Chinese consumers are relatively new to the luxury market. As a result, they are not completely confident about which brands are the most valuable. Another aspect reported exclusively by the Chinese participants is the fear of retribution, which originates from the Buddhist concept of "Jie". This doctrine requires people to control their desires for material possessions, their emotions and mood swings. This lifestyle advocated by Buddhism helps individuals keep their inner peace and encourages a simple life.

Results show that not all the interviewees admit experiencing guilt and shame. Participants from both countries cite hard work as the main justification for consumption, which is a "reward" for their efforts. This rationalization is individualistic and, therefore, contradicts the collectivism in both cultures. Brazilian interviewees tend to express slightly more guilt but do not express shame, while Chinese interviewees express more shame. In China, shame is linked to social values, such as the fear of losing face, social pressure and the failure to achieve a specific status.

Cultural differences may explain why Chinese participants do not report guilt but report more shame than their Brazilian counterparts. Chinese consumers adopt the extended principle of "spending rationally and practically", following the Buddhist doctrine of frugality. Chinese consumers tend to emphasize the functionality of luxury goods, explaining that they spend for practical reasons to minimize the cognitive dissonance resulting from the incompatibility of luxury consumption with Buddhist norms.

The phenomenon of new rich consumers' improper behavior and consumption provoked two different reactions between the samples; the Brazilians reported anger, and the Chinese reported sadness. Although the Brazilian interviewees occasionally expressed sadness, their dominant emotions were disgust, disdain and even clear irritation for "new rich" behavior. The Chinese participants only expressed irritation when they noticed the mass consumption of luxury brands.

Not all the interviewees admitted to experiencing guilt and shame. Participants from both countries cited hard work as the main justification for their consumption, which is a "reward" for their efforts. This rationalization is individualistic and, therefore, contradicts the collectivism in both cultures. Although the Brazilian interviewees tended to express slightly more guilt and no shame, the Chinese expressed more shame. This emotion is linked to social values such as the fear of losing face, social pressure and the failure to achieve a specific status. None of the Brazilian interviewees expressed any kind of shame, and they could not understand why someone could experience this emotion while buying luxury products.

Like any research, this study has limitations. The most important concerns the sampling procedure. It was essential to have very rich people in the sample, and, because this target is difficult to reach, we used purposive sampling. Thus, personal acquaintance was the main criterion for sample selection. Therefore, we should be cautious in our generalizations. Furthermore, interpretative research is always subject to different points of view. However, our continuous interaction as a multicultural team that questioned and reviewed each member's interpretations reasonably reduced this limitation.

This study has several conceptual and managerial implications. On a conceptual level, it is interesting to make clear that secondary emotions, such as guilt and shame, associate less with brands than do primary emotions. Secondary emotions link more frequently to general luxury consumption rather than to specific brands. However, this study cannot examine the underlying mechanism of these cognitive or affective linkages. Future research should explore these questions.

On a managerial level, this research shows that luxury brand managers should pay particular attention to the Chinese market to limit the negative emotions linked to their brands. Obviously, some brands, such as Louis Vuitton, are associated with negative emotions among very rich customers, probably due to the extended strategy of the brand, simultaneously targeting different customer groups. The elite of society consume Louis Vuitton products, but so do newly rich and less rich people. Those different targets are incompatible, and the elite class feels that other Louis Vuitton consumers often display improper behavior, which generates negative feelings toward the brand. Although democratization strategies may generate more profits, the negative emotions linked to the brand can badly harm brand image and reputation, which could injure the company in the long run. These results can also forewarn brand managers working in other emerging markets, such as Brazil. When sales volume of luxury goods in these markets increases to a level comparable to the Chinese market, the masses will consume more luxury goods and brands, possibly linking luxury brands to either good or bad emotions for consumers. Therefore, market research is essential to assess customer emotions toward brand democratization.

Companies that produce or sell luxury brands should carefully manage both the brands and, more importantly, the different marketing strategies that target consumers. Rich customers are extremely demanding, and they feel pride and joy when they know how to use luxury brands unlike others who don't. They cherish the uniqueness of what they use, which emphasizes their own uniqueness, and they feel the self-confidence of being members of a privileged class because they do not only own things, they also know the "codes" of how to use them, and how to behave as owners. Moreover, they seem displeased with the "mass consumption" strategy of some luxury brands. Thus, managers should consider whether wealthy consumers will stop buying "masstige" brands and thereby establish a brand hierarchy, in which the wealthy will only consider consuming the top brands. This study observed such a phenomenon, but further research might contribute to a better understanding of such very rich consumers.

# Appendix

See Table 4.7

**Table 4.7** Sample characteristics for Brazil and China

| Country | Fictitious name | Profession | Age | Gender | Family status | Monthly revenue, $ |
|---|---|---|---|---|---|---|
| Brazil | Penelope | Lawyer | 37 | Female | Married | 40,800 |
| $n = 14$ | Maria | Economist | 40 | Female | Married | 68,000 |
| | Celso | Physician | 42 | Male | Married | 20,400 |
| | Débora | Entrepreneur | 47 | Female | Married | 47,600 |
| | Ingrid | Entrepreneur | 35 | Female | Married | 34,000 |
| | Marcos | Lawyer | 45 | Male | Divorced | 40,000 |
| | Ana | Entrepreneur | 41 | Female | Married | 40,000 |
| | Claudia | Fashion consultant | 34 | Female | Married | 13,600 |
| | Luiz | Private banker | 36 | Male | Single | 34,000 |
| | Angela | Housewife | 41 | Female | Married | 27,000 |
| | Bob | Entrepreneur | 55 | Male | Separated | 27,000 |
| | Cristina | Entrepreneur | 50 | Female | Divorced | 20,400 |
| | Davi | Entrepreneur | 31 | Male | Single | 20,400 |
| | Clarissa | Administrator | 28 | Female | Single | 20,400 |

(continued)

**Table 4.7**   (continued)

| Country | Fictitious name | Profession | Age | Gender | Family status | Monthly revenue, $ |
|---|---|---|---|---|---|---|
| China n = 15 | Song | Company owner | 28 | Female | Married | 13,600 |
| | Chen | Lawyer, company owner | 65 | Male | Married | 81,000 |
| | Fanyi | Entrepreneur | 50 | Female | Separated | 68,000 |
| | Bailu | Company owner | 50 | Female | Married | 13,600 |
| | Zhang | Mine owner | 44 | Male | Married | 40,800 |
| | Xiaotu | Entrepreneur | 39 | Female | Married | 13,600 |
| | Laoye | Company owner | 42 | Male | Married | 109,000 |
| | Pan | PR Company CEO | 27 | Male | Single | 13,600 |
| | Xiaofeng | Company owner | 40 | Male | Married | 34,000 |
| | Duanyu | Trade company owner | 38 | Male | Married | 13,600 |
| | Yunxi | Trade company owner | 41 | Female | Married | 109,000 |
| | Yinxiang | Company owner | 45 | Female | Married | 20,400 |
| | Yuse | Mine owner | 47 | Female | Divorced | 109,000 |
| | Tupi | Mine owner | 46 | Male | Separated | 136,000 |
| | Mei | Entrepreneur | 46 | Female | Married | 13,600 |

# References

Abe, Jo Ann. 2004. "Shame, Guilt and Personality Judgment." *Journal of Research in Personality* 38: 85–104. http://dx.doi.org/10.1016/S0092-6566(03)00055-2. Accessed on 27 April 2019.

Berry, Christopher J. 1994. *The Idea of Luxury: A Conceptual and Historical Investigation.* Cambridge: Cambridge University Press.

Bierbrauer, Günter. 1992. "Reactions to Violation of Normative Standards: A Cross-Cultural Analysis of Shame and Guilt." *International Journal of Psychology* 27: 181–193. https://doi.org/10.1080/00207599208246874. Accessed on 28 April 2019.

Bourdieu, Pierre. 1984. *Distinction: A Social Critique of the Judgment of Taste.* London: Routledge.

Brennan, Linda, and Wayne Binney. 2010. "Fear, Guilt, and Shame Appeals in Social Marketing." *Journal of Business Research* 63: 140–146. https://doi.org/10.1016/j.jbusres.2009.02.006. Accessed on 28 April 2019.

Cooper, Donald R., and Pamela S. Schindler. 2010. *Business Research Methods.* 10th ed. New York, NY: McGraw-Hill.

DaMatta, Roberto. 1984. *O que faz o brasil, Brasil?* Rio de Janeiro: Rocco.

DaMatta, Roberto. 1985. *A Casa e a Rua.* São Paulo: Brasiliense.

De Barnier, Virginie, and Pierre Valette-Florence. 2013. "Culture and Luxury: An Analysis of Luxury Perceptions Across Frontiers." In *Handbook of Luxury Marketing*, edited by K.P. Wiedmann and N. Hennigs. Wiesbaden: Springer Gabler. https://halshs.archives-ouvertes.fr/halshs-00786051. Accessed on 28 April 2019.

De Barnier, Virginie, Sandrine Falcy, and Pierre Valette-Florence. 2012. "Do Consumers Perceive Three Levels of Luxury? A Comparison of Accessible, Intermediate and Inaccessible Luxury Brands." *Journal of Brand Management* 19: 623–636. https://halshs.archives-ouvertes.fr/halshs-00786023. Accessed on 28 April 2019.

Dubois, Bernard, and Claire Paternault. 1995. "Observations: Understanding the World of International Luxury Brands: The 'Dream Formula'." *Journal of Advertising Research* 35: 69–76.

Dubois, Bernard, Gilles Laurent, and Sandor Czellar. 2001. "Consumer Rapport to Luxury: Analyzing Complex and Ambivalent Attitudes." Research Paper HEC Jouy-en-Josas, 736.

Freyre, Gilberto. 2006. *Casa-Grande E Senzala.* São Paulo: Global Editora e Distribuidora.

Galhanone, Renata F. 2009. "O Mercado do luxo: Aspectos de marketing." In *IX SEMEAD - Seminários em Administração*, São Paulo.

Glenn, Edmund S. 1982. *Man and Mankind: Conflict and Communication Between Cultures.* Norwood, NJ: Ablex.

Gracino, Paulo Júnior. 2008. "Dos interesses weberianos dos sociólogos da religião: um olhar perspectivo sobre as interpretações do pentecostalismo no Brasil." *Horizonte* 6: 69–92.

Greis, Peter Hays. 2004. *China's New Nationalism: Pride, Politics, and Diplomacy.* Berkeley: University of California Press.

Guy, Bonnie S., and Wesley F. Patton. 1989. "The Marketing of Altruistic Causes: Understanding Why People Help." *Journal of Consumer Marketing* 6: 19–30. https://doi.org/10.1108/eb024711. Accessed on 28 April 2019.

Hirschman, Elizabeth C. 1985. "Primitive Aspects of Consumption in Modern American Society." *Journal of Consumer Research* 12: 142–154. https://www.jstor.org/stable/254347. Accessed on 29 April 2019.

Hofstede, Geert. 1991. *Cultures and Organizations: Software for the Mind.* London: McGraw-Hill.

Holbrook, Morris B., and Elizabeth C. Hirschman. 1982. "The Experiential Aspects of Consumption: Consumer Fantasies, Feelings, and Fun." *Journal of Consumer Research* 9: 132–140. https://doi.org/10.1086/208906. Accessed on 29 April 2019.

IBGE. 2010. "Census 2000." Available at www.ibge.gov.br. Accessed on 29 April 2019.

Kemper, Theodore D. 1987. "How Many Emotions Are There? Wedding the Social and Autonomic Components." *American Journal of Sociology* 93: 263–289. https://www.jstor.org/stable/2779585. Accessed on 29 April 2019.

Kessous, Aurélie, Pierre Valette-Florence, and Virginie De Barnier. 2017. "Luxury Watch Possession and Dispossession from Father to Son: A Poisoned Gift?" *Journal of Business Research* 77: 212–222. https://doi.org/10.1016/j.jbusres.2016.12.006. Accessed on 29 April 2019.

King, Ambrose Y., and John T. Myers. 1977. "Shame as an Incomplete Conception of Chinese Culture: A Study of Face." In *Research Monograph*, H.K. Social Research Institute, Chinese University of Hong Kong.

Laroche, Michel, Jasmin Bergeron, and Guido Barbaro-Forleo. 2001. "Targeting Consumers Who Are Willing to Pay More for Environmentally Friendly Products." *Journal of Consumer Marketing* 18: 503–521. https://scinapse.io/papers/2055949247. Accessed on 29 April 2019.

Lebra, Takie Sugiyama. 1973. "The Social Mechanism of Guilt and Shame: The Japanese Case." *Anthropological Quarterly* 44: 241–255. https://www.jstor.org/stable/3316971. Accessed on 29 April 2019.

Legge, James. 1960. *The Chinese Classics.* Hong Kong: Hong Kong University Press.

Lu, Pierre Xiao. 2008. *Elite China, Luxury Consumer Behavior in China.* Singapore: Wiley.

Montoro Rios, Francisco J., Teodoro Luque Martinez, Francisca Fuentes Moreno, and Paloma Cañadas Soriano. 2006. "Improving Attitudes Towards Brands with Environmental Associations: An Experimental Approach." *Journal of Consumer Marketing* 23: 26–33. https://doi.org/10.1108/07363760610641136. Accessed on 29 April 2019.

Olshavsky, Richard W., and Donald H. Granbois. 1979. "Consumer Decision Making—Fact or Fiction?" *Journal of Consumer Research* 6: 93–100. https://www.jstor.org/stable/2488867. Accessed on 29 April 2019.

Polsa, Pia. 2007. "Comparability in Cross-Cultural Qualitative Marketing Research Equivalence in Personal Interviews." *Academy of Marketing Science Review* 8: 1–18.

Roux, Elyette, and Jean-Marie Floch. 1996. "Gérer l'ingérable: La contradiction interne de toute maison de luxe." *Décisions Marketing* 9: 15–25. https://www.jstor.org/stable/40592555. Accessed on 29 April 2019.

Siqueira, Deis. 2006. "Religiosidade contemporânea brasileira: estilo de vida e reflexividade." *Sociedade e Cultura* 9: 13–26. https://doi.org/10.5216/sec.v9i1.209. Accessed on 29 April 2019.

Silverstein, Michael J., and Neil Fiske. 2003. "Luxury for the Masses." *Harvard Business Review* 81: 48–57.

Soares, Sergei Suarez Dillon. 2006. "*Distribuição de renda no Brasil 1976 – 2004 com* ênfase no Período Entre 2001 e 2004." Discussion Text 1166. Brasília: IPEA—Instituto de Pesquisa Econômica Aplicada. Ministério do Planejamento. http://www.ipea.gov.br/portal/images/stories/PDFs/TDs/td_1166.pdf. Accessed on 29 April 2019.

Thompson, Craig J., William B. Locander, and Howard R. Pollio. 1989. "Putting Consumer Experience Back into Consumer Research: The Philosophy and Method of Existential-Phenomenology." *Journal of Consumer Research* 16: 133–146. https://www.jstor.org/stable/2489313. Accessed on 29 April 2019.

Triandis, Harry C., Kwok Leung, Marcelo J. Villareal, and Felicia I. Clark. 1985. "Allocentric Versus Idiocentric Tendencies: Convergent and Discrimination Validation." *Journal of Research in Personality* 19: 395–415. https://doi.org/10.1016/0092-6566(85)90008-X. Accessed on 29 April 2019.

Turner, Jonathan H. 2000. *On the Origins of Human Emotions.* Stanford, CA: Stanford University Press.

Turner, Jonathan H., and Jan E. Stets. 2005. *The Sociology of Emotions.* New York: Cambridge University Press.

Veblen, Thorstein. 1899. *The Theory of the Leisure Class.* New York: Macmillan.

Vigneron, Franck, and Lester W. Johnson. 2004. "Measuring Perceptions of Brand Luxury." *Journal of Brand Management* 11: 484–506. https://doi.org/10.1007/978-3-319-51127-6_10. Accessed on 30 April 2019.

Wang, Jian, and Zhiying Wang. 2007. "The Political Symbolism of Business: Exploring Consumer Nationalism and Its Implications for Corporate Reputation Management in China." *Journal of Communication Management* 11: 134–149. https://doi.org/10.1108/13632540710747361. Accessed on 30 April 2019.

Wong, Nancy Y., and Aaron C. Ahuvia. 1998. "Personal Taste and Family Face: Luxury Consumption in Confucian and Western Societies." *Psychology & Marketing* 15: 423–432. https://doi.org/10.1002/(SICI)1520-6793(199808)15:5<423::AID-MAR2>3.0.CO;2-9. Accessed on 30 April 2019.

Wiedmann, Klaus-Peter, Nadine Hennigs, and Astrid Siebels. 2009. "Value-Based Segmentation of Luxury Consumption Behavior." *Psychology et Marketing* 26: 625–651. https://doi.org/10.1002/mar.20292. Accessed on 30 April 2019.

Xiao, Ge, and Jai-Ok Kim. 2009. "The Investigation of Chinese Consumer Values, Consumption Values, Life Satisfaction, and Consumption Behaviors." *Psychology & Marketing* 26: 610–624. https://doi.org/10.1002/mar.20291. Accessed on 30 April 2019.

Yang, Kuo-Shu. 1981. "Social Orientation and Individual Modernity Among Chinese Students in Taiwan." *Journal of Social Psychology* 113: 159–70. https://doi.org/10.1080/00224545.1981.9924368. Accessed on 30 April 2019.

Zhang, Meng Xia, and Alain Jolibert. 2003. "Les valeurs traditionnelles des acheteurs chinois: raffinement conceptuel, mesure et application." *Recherche et Applications en Marketing* 18: 25–42. https://www.jstor.org/stable/40589354. Accessed on 30 April 2019.

# 5

# Future Luxury: Fashioning Wellbeing Through Holistic Design

Kirsten Scott

## Luxury in the Anthropocene: *Introduction*

Luxury is a construct that reflects the material tastes and aspirations of a society or an individual; it is therefore relative in nature, may evolve over time and space, and be geographically, socio-culturally or demographically located. Of course, the paradigm of luxury that has most widely been accepted—in relation to luxury brands—identifies quality, craftsmanship, heritage, durability, rarity, art, superfluousness and style as characteristics of the luxury product (Kapferer and Bastien 2012, p. 85). True luxury has always celebrated the slow values of artisanal production and the tacit knowledge embodied in artefacts created in this way. The commercial desirability for luxury brands to demonstrate social and environmental responsibility has led to calls for ethics and sustainability to be mandated as essential components of the luxury paradigm (Kapferer and Bastien 2012, pp. 21, 47; Hennigs et al. 2013,

K. Scott (✉)
Istituto Marangoni, London, UK
e-mail: k.scott@istitutomarangoni.com

© The Author(s) 2020
I. Cantista and T. Sádaba (eds.), *Understanding Luxury Fashion*,
Palgrave Advances in Luxury, https://doi.org/10.1007/978-3-030-25654-8_5

p. 27; Maisonrouge 2013, pp. 119–120). Arguably, these additional facets are harmonious with the true luxury product, in which quality is valued over quantity, as well as timelessness and durability (Kapferer 2010, p. 40); but are there additional ways in which luxury might evolve in response to new emerging imperatives?

## The Contemporary Luxury Landscape

The massification strategies of many luxury brands, with globalised supply chains and products that reflect seasonal trends and relative ubiquity rather than traditional luxury values, have contributed to the problematics of the global fashion industry. Issues such as environmental pollution, over-production and mass-consumption, waste, exploitation and human rights abuses in the supply chain are ongoing subjects of scrutiny and remain critical to any discourse about the future of luxury fashion. As these begin to be fully comprehended—if yet to be fully addressed—and luxury's involvement measured, many luxury brands continue to develop more socially and environmentally responsible business models. Luxury conglomerates have forged partnerships with academic institutions in order to find solutions to the challenges they face in these areas, for example LVMH with Central Saint Martins and Kering with London College of Fashion. These relationships enable international, luxury fashion brands to benefit from the new knowledge and innovations generated by research communities, which feed into both parties' product, marketing, communications, CSR policy and strategic vision. Kering's support for the Centre for Sustainable Fashion at LCF has enabled significant progress to be made in devising greener production strategies, even if its business model is still based on the orthodoxy of growth. There is an intensifying movement in western societies and in the academic community, that advocates against growth as the accepted objective of business—arguing instead for an ecology of diverse, small businesses: for niche, independent brands which reflect authentic, ethical values in every aspect of their organisation and which have a positive impact on society. Business models focused on growth seem outmoded, as the imminently finite nature of the earth's resources and the impacts of climate change become clear in this anthropocene era. 'Degrowth' was the mantra of at least two international fashion conferences in 2018: Fashion Colloquium: 'Searching for the New Luxury' hosted by ArtEz University and the Global Fashion Conference: 'What's Going On?' hosted by London College of Fashion. There is seismic change in the wind and Schumacher's (1974) "small is beautiful" is resonating once more: McRobbie et al.'s (2016) study for CREATe looked at micro-enterprises in the creative industries in Berlin, London and Milan, some of which may be categorised as luxury fashion. These small, varied businesses were able to operate sustainably and to define themselves on their own terms:

> My brand is about emotion, and I don't want to waste that by playing marketing games. (Anon, in McRobbie et al. 2016, p. 40)

Many of the brands interviewed in this study expressed unhappiness with how the fashion industry works and were looking for new ways of doing things at a slower pace that challenges the status quo. Some incorporated aspects of social entrepreneurship in their business models to bring about positive social change (McRobbie et al. 2016, pp. 18, 21, 40, 41). Small, agile, luxury brands continue to emerge that not only offer diversity, but are governed by strong, values-based approaches (Gardetti 2014, pp. 28–29; Gardetti and Giron 2016; Gutsatz and Heine 2018, p. 409). For example, Eden Diodati works with women survivors of the Rwandan genocide, who produce beads for her jewellery brand; Elvis and Kresse works with recycled materials to create beautifully crafted accessories, from which 50% of their profits are donated to charities; Beulah creates employment for marginalised women in India for their luxury clothing line and campaigns against modern day slavery.

Of course, there are more established luxury brands that have a positive impact on others, embedding strong values in all or part of their business models, such as social concerns, community development and environmental sustainability; for example, the well-documented work of Brunello Cucinelli or Loro Piana. However, large luxury brands remain subject to criticism: recent revelations, such as Burberry burning £28 million worth of excess stock in 2018; Richemont destroying around £430 million of watches (Ferrier 2018; Pinnock 2018) have raised concern amongst consumers and generated bad publicity, even if understood within the industry as a normative of luxury strategy (Kapferer and Bastien 2012, p. 228; Pinnock 2018): if the image of luxury is to be protected, its products should never be devalued by marking down prices to move unsold stock. The dream of luxury must be preserved, but that dream is changing:

> Things like health, enlightenment, freedom, social and environmental responsibility - these are the new luxuries, and they all come from within, not without. That's the challenge that traditional luxury brands will have to contend with in the mid-to-long-term future. (Bina 2018 in Pinnock 2018)

In busy lives, with physical and mental space at a premium and with mounting levels of stress, anxiety and depression in western societies, consumers are searching for more opportunities to foster wellbeing in their lives and in the lives of others (Global Wellness Economy Monitor 2018, p. 7). If 'the credibility of luxury products and services will be derived from their ability to generate wellbeing, not only to consumers, but also for those involved in (or affected by) their production, use, reuse and disposal' it therefore raises the question: how might luxury fashion respond to this new imperative? (Bendell and Kleanthous 2007, p. 2).

# Wellbeing as the New Luxury

## Wellbeing Today

In 2018, 74% of people in the UK reported feeling "overwhelmed or unable to cope". Amongst 18–24 year olds that were suffering from stress in 2018, comparison to others, unhappiness with their own appearance and body image issues were cited as reasons and 60% said that pressure to succeed (however that may be perceived) was a factor

(Mental Health Foundation 2018). Stress, anxiety and depression are frequent causes of employee ill health and absenteeism, accounting for 57% of working days lost in 2017/2018 in the UK (Health and Safety Executive 2018). The World Health Organization (2019) calls for preventative strategies to be devised that improve physical and mental wellbeing and resilience (WHO 2019).

There are many measures of wellbeing, but most include "feeling good and functioning well", and embrace psychological as well a physical health (Department of Health and Social Care 2014, p. 6; Centers for Disease Control and Prevention 2019). A state of wellbeing may add years to life expectancy, improve emotional resilience, resistance to and recovery from illness, and may positively affect the wellbeing of those around us (DHSC 2014, pp. 9–10, 13). With an increasing recognition of the benefits of wellbeing, the global wellness industry is growing exponentially—at a rate that exceeds economic growth (Global Wellness Institute 2018, p. 3). A report by the Global Wellness Institute indicates the potential to add deeper value to products in ways that contribute to health and wellbeing:

> With consumers beginning to feel as though they've got a handle on the traditional dimensions of wellness, such as physical activity, nutrition and sleep, their attention is beginning to move elsewhere. (Global Wellness Institute 2018, p. 3)

## Some Dynamics of Luxury and Wellbeing

The relationship between luxury, fashion and wellbeing is complex. As the statistics above suggest, fashion may be complicit—with other socio-cultural factors—in encouraging dissatisfaction with one's appearance and lifestyle. People who focus most on their appearance, wealth, status and possessions tend to be less happy than those that don't (New Economics Forum 2006, p. 31), as this tends to reflect a need for the validation of others. Links between social media usage and feelings of inadequacy have been well established, as well as those between feelings of inadequacy and of stress (Abel et al. 2016, p. 34). As social media is an important communication channel for luxury fashion brands, which present a dream lifestyle that indelibly associates luxury with beauty, status and perfection, it may feed the insecurities of consumers who purchase items they may not be able to afford in a cycle of desperate aspiration and self-gratification (Wu et al. 2015, p. 19; Abel et al. 2016, p. 34; Kapferer 2010, p. 42). In a study by Kennedy and Bolat (2017), subjects reported feelings of anxiety if they did not get enough likes on social media and looked for products that would bring them the most likes: those were usually luxury items. Luxury consumption may therefore be understood to be part of the problem.

On the other hand, there are 'feel good' factors associated with purchasing and wearing luxury items that include a heightened sense of status; greater feelings of self-worth; a sense of belonging to a social elite; a sense of security in the quality and longevity of the product (while paradoxically being 'on trend'); impressing other people; and simply pampering oneself—which may have a beneficial effect on symptoms of stress (Wu et al. 2015, pp. 5, 20, 23; Kennedy and Bolat 2017, p. 6; Kapferer and Bastien 2012, p. 36). Is seems that the construction of an idealised self, enacted through the acquisition of luxury goods and broadcast on social media, actually improves the self-esteem of some consumers (Kennedy and Bolat 2017, p. 6).

However as consumer values shift, with increasing emphasis placed on personal health and growth, and more concern for ethical, political and environmental issues, there is an urgent need for "luxury with good intentions" (Gutsatz and Heine 2018, p. 409). As Gutsatz and Heine (2018) imply in the following quotation, this should not be just another marketing strategy but rather a sincere acknowledgement by luxury brands that they should have a positive impact on society:

> There is a growing desire for authentic products that are good for the environment and especially for personal health, while at the same time also being good for the people involved. (Gutsatz and Heine 2018, p. 409)

A new methodology is needed for future luxury fashion that is more ambitious than simply doing less harm to people and planet, but rather one that is pro-actively positive in every possible way in how it conceives and creates luxury goods. Luxury is the perfect arena in which to explore and resolve new, holistic approaches to sustainable fashion design—where the costs of research, development, prototyping and production are unlikely to be a prohibiting factor to consumers and where a high premium is placed on beauty and uniqueness (Kapferer 2010, pp. 41, 45; Maisonrouge 2013, p. 119). And where luxury leads, others will follow.

# Luxury with Good Intentions: Formulating a Holistic Design Methodology for Luxury Fashion

## Lessons from Other Disciplines

In order to develop a more holistic design methodology for luxury fashion that supports individual, social and environmental wellbeing and resilience, it is necessary to explore approaches from outside the normatives of fashion and to journey into foreign disciplinary territories where potential solutions might lie. Science and engineering have generated a variety of design methods to inform the development of new materials and products that are inspired by nature—including bioengineering, biomimetics, biodesign, biomimicry and biomechanics—and which increasingly are influencing the creative disciplines. Contact with nature has been shown to be beneficial to human health and wellbeing. For thousands of years, our affiliation with nature has led us to build gardens, bring plants into our homes and more recently into our workspaces (Grinde and Patil 2009, pp. 2333–2335). Spending time amongst nature is a luxury that most urban dwellers find difficult to include in their busy lives, but research shows that its potential benefits to health and wellbeing are significant, having a restorative effect on people suffering from a range of mental health disorders including stress and anxiety (Kellert et al. 2008, p. 4; Bell and Ward Thompson 2014, p. 82). Walking in forests enables *phytoncides*—chemicals released into the air by trees—to stimulate the immune system in ways that may prevent certain diseases, such as cancer, from forming as well as to improve our ability to manage stress (Hansen et al. 2017, pp. 3, 38, 41; Bell and Ward Thompson 2014, p. 11; Grinde and Patel 2009, pp. 2334–2335). Calm is improved and blood pressure decreased merely by touching the leaves and the bark of trees (Putra et al. 2018, p. 6654). Even indoors, the aesthetic values of nature, such as certain colours, materials and textures, reduce stress and anxiety levels, improve attention, and confer a sense of wellbeing (Grinde and Patil 2009, pp. 2334–2335; Kellert et al. 2008, p. 6).

Designers for the built environment use biophilic design strategies that are endorsed by mental and physical health research (Kellert et al. 2008, p. 4; Bell and Ward Thompson 2014, pp. 10–11), and which acknowledge human affiliation with nature through the use of certain materials and forms (Kellert et al. 2008, pp. 6, 15; Coutts and Hahn 2015, p. 9779). For example, in interior design, the proven links between time spent in forests and human wellbeing are frequently addressed through specific materials: timber products have important visual, haptic, and scent qualities and continue to store carbon even after wood has been cut and treated (Bell and Ward Thompson 2014, pp. 7, 9; Grinde and Patel 2009, p. 2333). There are

> ..... opportunities for luxury brands to develop methodologies for well-being, develop products made from species of plants that can be used for healing while protecting biodiversity, and contribute to healthier working conditions in their supply chains through health programs. (Hashmi 2017, p. 8)

Therefore ways must be found to engage further with nature through design, to formulate new strategies that may successfully be applied to luxury fashion in order meet the complex needs of the twenty-first century, luxury consumer. For example, what if we were to wrap ourselves in the skins of trees rather than the skins of animals? What if the bark of trees could become a new luxury fabric? What might the benefits of wearing a tree-based textile be to health and wellbeing in a strategically designed luxury garment? Elements of biophilia have been integrated into a design strategy for propositional luxury garments created by the Barkcloth Research Network, described later in this chapter, in order to develop individually and socially beneficial—as well as environmentally sustainable, luxury fashion.

## A Holistic Methodology for Future Luxury Clothing

A holistic methodology for creating luxury fashion must encompass social and environmental sustainability, but it should go further to actively promote human and environmental wellbeing. As such, there are additional factors to be considered and addressed beyond reducing the harm done by conventional modes of production and consumption. The framework below (Table 5.1) has been born from the reflective practice of the Barkcloth Research Network and will continue to evolve as new opportunities to add value emerge.

## Case Study: The Barkcloth Research Network— A Holistic Research Project for Luxury Fashion

### Background

The Barkcloth Research Network (Kirsten Scott, Mevin Murden and Karen Spurgin from Istituto Marangoni London and Praburaj Venkatraman from Manchester Metropolitan University) was established in 2016. Our initial aim was to examine Ugandan barkcloth—a non-woven, fibrous textile that has been produced from the wild fig tree (*ficus natalensis*) since at least the thirteenth century (Rwawiire and Tomkova 2013, p. 649)—from multiple perspectives to discover its full potential as a sustainable, luxury, fashion textile. Through technical sampling, through aesthetic experimentation, through design and through laboratory testing, we continue to develop a series of speculative, luxury, fashion garments and artefacts. We aim to generate a report to disseminate our research along with other, more experiential forms of dissemination such as an exhibition of our work, including film and

**Table 5.1** Holistic Design Methodology

| Holistic design methodology explained | |
| --- | --- |
| Design approach | Future luxury clothing should be designed to produce tangible and intangible benefits to the wearers, to the makers and to the plant: the styles, shapes, details, materials and textures used should contribute human wellbeing, informed by research from psychology, health and other disciplines. Design must consider waste minimization, waste repurposing and ensure that all components are reusable, recyclable or compostable. Luxury fashion should be innovative, but timeless—not tied to seasonal trends—and be produced in small collections, in limited runs or as bespoke. Great care should be taken to promote lasting value through design, technique and process |
| Materials | Natural, sustainably sourced materials should be used for future luxury clothing that help to connect the wearer to the environment and to global, artisan communities. It should be sourced from small producers, from artisan groups, and handcrafted in a way that helps to ensure the preservation of heritage or endangered textile traditions. The materials used should promote lasting value through the craft of their making, their beauty and the stories behind them. They should, as much as possible, provide therapeutic benefits to health and wellbeing and be reusable, recyclable or compostable |
| Dyes | Natural, sustainably sourced dyestuffs should be used that add distinctive aesthetic qualities to materials. As much as possible, any dyes used should impart additional properties to the clothes and their wearers, such as benefits to health and wellbeing or strengthening properties. Colours should be used that age well, to promote lasting value, and the materials should remain fully recyclable or compostable after dyeing |
| Treatments | Any treatments applied to the materials to improve properties such as strength, body, wear, and their aesthetic values, must be natural and biodegradable. These might include surface treatments that add colour, lustre, decoration or water resistance, or natural stiffening or softening agents. Any interfacings used must be natural and recyclable or fully compostable |

(continued)

**Table 5.1**  (continued)

| Holistic design methodology explained | |
| --- | --- |
| Making | Making processes must follow a circular approach that considers the values of longevity through lasting attachment, as well as end of life/next life of the garment in all decision-making. The making techniques used for new luxury clothing must show a high level of neocraft that promotes the value of the handmade in contemporary luxury—thus establishing a connection between consumers and makers. Technology will be incorporated as appropriate. Embellishments should provide additional benefits such as strengthening the cloth or adding properties to support wellbeing. Fabric waste must be reused, perhaps in decorative finishes, or repurposed; it should be fully compostable; any beading used should be reusable |
| Sourcing | Materials should be sourced transparently, direct from makers, and in ways that provide benefits to those makers beyond the short term. Opportunities for further investment in community and environmental projects should be sought. The story behind the sourcing should be considered crucial to the future of luxury |
| Branding | The branding should reflect the ethical position of the brand as well as its other distinctive characteristics. It should acknowledge the supply chain, so emphasis should be given to the makers, their stories and their craft. The use of ingredient branding is recommended for specific materials to highlight their authenticity and to help protect the intellectual or cultural property of the makers |
| Promotion | The storytelling about the product, its qualities, and the makers involved in its creation should be central, with strong educational content to promote social and environmental sustainability and awareness of the lives of others. Promotion should be honest and inclusive, and models used should be diverse and representative of contemporary western societies. It is envisaged that small installations will provide the best way to showcase and promote new luxury clothing, where contact with the product and its story will forge a bond with consumers, and allowing detailed information to be communicated about the processes of their creation. This approach will link the product with art and thus reinforce its status. Technologies such as Virtual and Augmented Reality and 360 degree film will be harnessed for installations and pop-ups. A website will provide information about the brand, its values, the clothing, its makers and events, with a strong presence on social media |

(continued)

Table 5.1  (continued)

| Holistic design methodology explained | |
| --- | --- |
| Selling | Small collections of limited edition, luxury clothing should be sold through the installations described above, by invitation, and orders taken for bespoke items. In addition, pop up shops should be used in proximity to selected stores that share similar values. Selling will therefore be face-to-face, reinforcing connection between the brand and the consumer; there will be no online retailing—the website should be used to steer potential consumers towards events |
| Wear | The clothing should be innovative and designed to wear well, working with the specific qualities of the materials used to promote lasting value and emotional attachment. All materials used should be of good quality. The wearer should feel uplifted when wearing the clothing, as elements have been integrated in its design and creation to foster wellbeing. The clothing should fit its function, adopting aspects of biomechanics to improve comfort |
| End of life | Everything used in the creation of these luxury garments should be reusable, recyclable or fully compostable, to provide biological nutrients to the soil |

photography of the barkcloth makers, their craft and the wild fig tree. Our objectives include raising awareness of the beneficial properties of barkcloth; of the plight of this rare material; to develop strategies for improving its strength and versatility; to sustainably improve the market for Ugandan barkcloth; and to determine practical branding strategies for its makers. This iterative research builds upon fieldwork conducted in Uganda in 2013 and 2014, where I was able to meet with barkcloth makers and local environmentalists in order to assess their needs and to purchase barkcloth.

## The 'Borrowed Cloth' Model

Our methodology employs the metaphor of *borrowing* in an attempt to navigate and frame the ethical complexities of working with the cultural heritage of others. Using the metaphor of *borrowing*, the barkcloth will be returned to its community with *interest*, in the form of the new

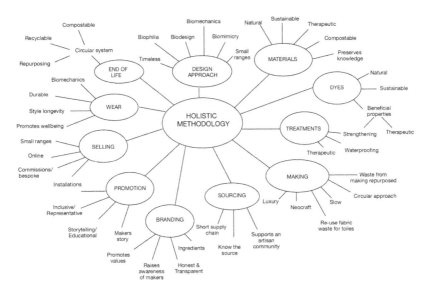

**Fig. 5.1**  Holistic Design Methodology Map

knowledge generated, enhanced market awareness and recommenda-
tions that we hope will be beneficial to them; then we will plan together
the next steps. We suggest that our 'borrowed cloth' model represents
an ethical, non-exploitative approach to interventions of this nature—
when working with the cultural property of others—and may be transferrable to other contexts for the luxury market. As the research has
progressed, we have increasingly drawn on cross-disciplinary perspectives to envision a new, holistic methodology for small-scale design initiatives for the luxury fashion market. The Holistic Design Methodology
Map (Fig. 5.1) details the main features of this approach.

## Holistic Design for a New Luxury

Our holistic design strategy aims to be pro-actively beneficial, generating value for people and planet at every stage we encounter. Whilst
our methodology bears some similarity to Hashmi's (2017) excellent,
holistic, value creation model for the luxury sector (Hashmi 2017,
p. 10), our approach largely is born from design and making activities,

emphasises product, and offers additional factors. In tandem with a review of the literature, we use our engagement with materials, techniques and processes as a medium for reflection and idea generation, from which to envision new potentialities for luxury fashion that incorporates attributes designed to benefit the health and wellbeing of its consumers, its makers and the environment. Our design process is therefore informed by our practice as well as disciplines such as the natural sciences, architecture, health and wellbeing—specifically by strategies associated with biophilia, biodesign and biomechanics (Kellert et al. 2008, p. 15; Gupta 2011, p. 328; Benyus 2008, p. 30) where significant understanding of how our affiliation with nature may be addressed through design already exists.

As the project has progressed we have looked for ways to impart benefits to health and wellbeing through design and making processes. In order to illustrate how this approach may be operationalized for a new conception of luxury fashion, I will present some of the most significant ways in which our holistic design methodology has been implemented through the Barkcloth Research Network to date.

## Material for a New Luxury

Barkcloth is a rich red-brown, relatively unmediated, non-woven, endangered textile that is designated a Masterpiece of the Intangible Cultural Heritage of Humanity by UNESCO (2005) and is deeply tied to the identity of the Baganda of south-western Uganda as a signifier of status, culture and beliefs (Nakazibwe 2005, p. 86, Figs. 5.2 and 5.3). Barkcloth has historic associations with royalty and for centuries was an item of local and regional economic importance. However the introduction of woven textiles, by Swahili-Arab traders in the mid 1800s and later by the British, undermined barkcloth's importance and ultimately production (Nakazibwe 2005, pp. 114–115). In recent decades, barkcloth has become more associated with tourist crafts and funeral shrouds, although still worn for ceremonial occasions by Bagandans— including the Kabaka of Buganda. Therefore barkcloth has heritage and

**Fig. 5.2**   Ugandan barkcloth

rarity, a powerful narrative, is handcrafted, and has historic links to royalty, thus meeting some important requirements of luxury.

Handcrafted objects or textiles that employ traditional techniques and natural materials have always been essential to luxury and represent a powerful articulation of the value of highly skilled, unalienated labour. The challenges of using such materials, though, can be their inconsistency. As a handmade, naturally derived textile, each piece of barkcloth is different from another. However the small irregularities that characterize the natural and the handmade, and which may be considered a flaw in mechanically produced commodities, are appreciated by discerning, eco-conscious, luxury connoisseurs as markers of uniqueness and

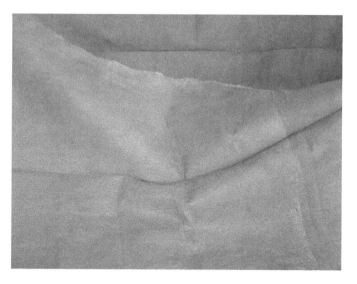

**Fig. 5.3** Finished piece of Ugandan barkcloth

authenticity (Kapferer and Bastien 2012, pp. 66–67). These qualities foreground human activity, promoting awareness of the maker, their skills and their circumstances, and may promote lasting value and emotional attachment. As such, they offer an antidote to the uniformity of mass-produced goods while adding to the beauty of the product itself (Scott 2011, p. 61).

Interviews in Uganda revealed that the bark of the wild fig tree is known locally to have anti-bacterial, mosquito repellent and medicinal properties that are used in traditional medicines. Our initial tests have indicated that barkcloth is anti-bacterial, but future research will measure the extent of this, define other attributes that may contribute to wellbeing, and discover the potential of these to add value to luxury garments as well as transferrable benefits for other sectors. In addition, this knowledge has prompted our use of plant fibres and natural dyes that are beneficial to human health and wellbeing.

## Therapeutic Dyes for a New Luxury

Nature continues to point to more positive ways of living: our research into natural dyes has led us to re-conceptualise future luxury clothing. The ancient Indian wisdom of Ayurveda, a holistic system of treatment for the mind, body and soul, includes the use of medicinal herbs to dye fabrics used for clothing, known as Ayurvastra (Jyothirmi and Panda 2016, p. 1166). The skin is an excellent conduit through which the body may absorb medicines and clothing made from organic, natural fibres dyed with medicinal plants has been understood to impart thera-peutic benefits to its wearers for over 5000 years. This cloth is believed to protect the body from infection and to heal a wide range of condi-tions, including skin diseases, rheumatism, arthritis, diabetes, respira-tory problems, heart conditions, hypertension, high blood pressure and depression, as well as to improve calm, sleep quality and general wellbe-ing (Jyothirmi and Panda 2016, pp. 1166–1167). Clinical trials at the Government Ayurveda College in Kerala indicated that certain natu-ral dye treatments improved the conditions of patients and some also improved the strength, abrasion resistance and general wear of cotton fabric (Jyothirmi and Panda 2016, p. 1170; Mader 2011, pp. 16–18).

It therefore seems likely that any beneficial properties that are intrin-sic to barkcloth may be delivered to wearers through clothing; we have attempted to further enhance these by using natural dye pigments that have been shown to improve the strength and wear of other materials, as well as for their aesthetic or therapeutic characteristics. Tests dipping barkcloth in indigo solution have attempted to confer on it medic-inal and strengthening properties (Chiao et al. 2016, pp. 238–239; Wells 2013, pp. 2, 7–8) and team member Karen Spurgin has inves-tigated alternative ways of applying indigo and other natural pigments (Figs. 5.4 and 5.5). Karen's experiments include using logwood as a sur-face application to create a glossy black, inspired by techniques used by the Miao people of south-western China/Vietnam. She has also adapted historic painting mediums such a glair and medieval tempera to create dye finishes that are beautiful, luminous and compostable, but which also improve the strength and water resistance of barkcloth.

**Fig. 5.4**   Karen Spurgin dye experiments

**Fig. 5.5**   Karen Spurgin black dye sample

## Sourcing for a New Luxury

We believe passionately in sourcing directly from small, artisan producers of rare textiles in order to assist in preserving their cultural heritage. If luxury brands are to address the need for more socially and environmentally sustainable production, the traditional practices of global artisans—many of which are endangered and in need of new markets—might offer solutions. Traditional craft embodies precious, tacit knowledge and offers uniqueness, authenticity, quality, heritage and environmental stewardship. Luxury brands have the opportunity to source exquisite, ethically produced products while participating in the promotion and conservation of cultural heritage, with additional opportunities to develop positive social entrepreneurship activities such as sponsorship of local education or healthcare.

However, sourcing from artisan producers is not without challenges for luxury brands: it may be difficult for artisan groups in developing countries to understand the requirements of distant markets without training or close collaboration. Artisanal textile crafts face enormous—although not insurmountable—difficulties in the face of globalisation: local markets have been undermined by cheap, imported, mass-produced fabric; in some communities, handicrafts have become more associated with tradition rather than modernity; there may be a lack of access to new markets; insufficient capacity to adapt to new requirements or to innovate new designs; inconsistency in product quality—to name but a few (USAID 2006, p. vii; Scott 2012, p. 87). Therefore, support is likely to be needed to enable artisans to partner effectively with luxury designers in product creation. These designers can play a crucial role in actively problem solving aesthetic, technical and quality issues when adapting traditional skills to new contexts (Scott 2012, p. 86; Brown 2015, p. 3).

There are numerous ethical debates about how external agents' input might shape crafts away from their indigenous norms and their cultural relevance (Craft Revival Trust et al. 2005, p. v), but unless these traditions find a market they may be lost forever (Scott 2012, pp. 86–87). Significant investment of time and resources is needed to insure high quality and sustainable outcomes for all parties, but luxury brands are well positioned to make that investment.

Our barkcloth is sourced directly from its makers in Bukomansimbi, south-western Uganda, where an apprenticeship programme is enabling a new generation to learn the specialist skills required before this knowledge vanishes. The Bukomanbsimbi Organic Tree Farmers Association (BOTFA) (Fig. 5.7) has implemented a tree-planting project to insure the future availability of wild fig trees and other plants used in local crafts. The bark of each tree may sustainably be harvested annually by splitting its outer layer down the length of the tree before gently peeling it off (Fig. 5.6). The naked trunk is then wrapped in banana leaves for a few days to protect the tree as it recovers. The bark is then steamed or soaked in water to soften it, before being beaten by wooden mallets; in this way, the bark fibre felts, becomes finer, softer and more pliant, and grows in size significantly (Nakazibwe 2005, pp. 73, 78, Fig. 5.7). The techniques and processes used to harvest and create barkcloth show

**Fig. 5.6**  Wild fig tree, bark harvested

strong, environmental stewardship and help to preserve both the wild fig tree and the cultural heritage of Baganda, but the makers need to find a sustainable market. As the project progresses, a Fair Trade framework will be used to agree pricing, however opportunities will be sought to create additional value through support for local community and environmental enterprises.

## Designing a New Luxury

Aspects of biophilic design have been adopted to inform our design process. A biophilic design strategy includes two main dimensions: the first is an organic dimension, which may be expressed through materials, shapes and forms that are reflective of those found in nature; the second relates to forms that may foster connection to culture and locality and to the emotions and meanings that these hold (Kellert et al.

**Fig. 5.7**  BOTFA barkcloth makers

2008, p. 6). Looking at luxury fashion design through the lens of bio-philia has enabled us to conceive silhouettes, garments and details that include curved or pod-like forms and seam lines that carry subtle con-notations of nature, while being sympathetic to the unique qualities and limitations of the cloth itself. In addition, biomechanical considerations (Gupta 2011, p. 328) have been seamlessly integrated in our design process to enable the barkcloth effectively to respond to how the body moves and interacts with each garment created. For example, we have emphasized particular stress points—such as across the upper back and the elbows—by expanding them to enable unhindered movement that minimizes issues of wear. Speculative garments have been completed that demonstrate these approaches to shape making and how to maxim-ise the versatility of the barkcloth (Figs. 5.8 and 5.9).

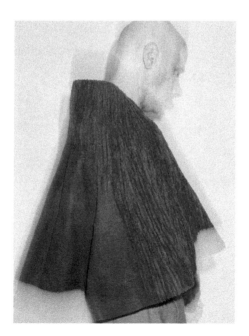

**Fig. 5.8**  Proposition 1

## Crafting a New Luxury

Neocraft involves the modernisation of the handmade for contemporary contexts (Alfoldy and Nova Scotia College of Art and Design 2007, pp. xiv, xix) and is vital to the creation of luxury. Traditionally, craft places an emphasis on the relationship between maker, materials, techniques, skill, environment and end user; it therefore embodies concern for people and planet. Future luxury clothing must be sustainably crafted and hold a timeless beauty that promotes lasting emotional attachment—qualities which are compatible with the values of true luxury: where the beauty and uniqueness of the materials, the skill of the maker and the excellence and innovation of design promote care being taken to cherish, retain and repair handcrafted items. Therefore, we strongly assert the contemporary relevance of the handmade in luxury clothing, embracing technology where desirable as one of many tools in the hand of the maker. Our aesthetic experimentation has used a range of techniques to explore and embellish barkcloth's surface, such as embroidery, appliqué, printing, beading, gilding, laser etching and laser cutting (Figs. 5.10 and 5.11). We have tested a variety of seams, surface treatments and fusing. Working with barkcloth in this way has enabled us to discover its material qualities and to develop techniques that add to its strength and durability. By working sympathetically with barkcloth using slow, neocrafting techniques, coaxing it towards a pre-defined goal but responsive to how its dynamic qualities might lead to unforeseen outcomes, we have made some important breakthroughs in shaping our design methodology and have advanced a series of decorative techniques that add actively benign features to our work, for example appliqué and embroidery that strengthen as well as embellish (Figs. 5.10 and 5.11), biomechanical cutting to synergise the specific qualities of the cloth with body movement requirements which improve style and wear, and dyes that strengthen and enhance therapeutic qualities (Gupta 2011, p. 328; Scott 2018).

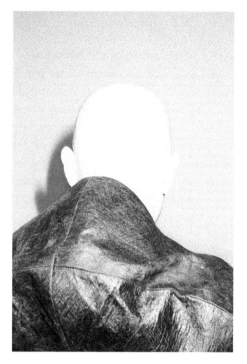

**Fig. 5.9** Proposition 2

## Goodness as Luxury

Some cultures seem to believe that the very act of decorating an object might imbue it with an essential *goodness*, beyond a superficial beauty. In many African languages beautiful and good are denoted by the same word. For example, in Lusoga, the language of the Ugandan Basoga people, *obúlúngi* means beauty and also goodness (Cultural Research Centre 2000, p. 14). In ancient Greek, both virtue and good-looking came from the same language root of *agathos* (Appiah 1985, p. 18). Through decorative processes, makers have communicated the cosmological ideas and other values of a community: goodness—a quality that all cultures acknowledge—may be represented through technical accomplishment in craft and through ornamentation (Appiah 1985, pp. 18–19). Therefore making something well, to be both functionally

**Fig. 5.10**  Indigo-dyed appliqué

and aesthetically pleasing, is making it the best it can be on a deeper level, implying an almost spiritual dimension that provides a counter-narrative to a world dominated by—and polluted by—mass-produced disposable goods. However, our conception of making *fashion* well has been limited in western societies until now, with couture and bespoke tailoring representing the finest approaches to the craft of luxury garment creation.

## Imparting Wellbeing Through Luxury Fashion

As we begin to envisage a transition to post-sustainability, other urgent imperatives arise—such as the increased levels of stress and anxiety in city populations—as well as other health conditions—perhaps related to a disconnect from nature. The concept of what constitutes true luxury is changing and requires an alternative design approach to develop fewer and better products that meet the deeper needs of both consumers and makers. Luxury fashion is well placed to pioneer new, values-based

**Fig. 5.11**  Crafting the cape

initiatives in product creation, but an alternative design methodology is needed for creating luxury clothing that is pro-actively positive in addressing the deeper needs of individuals, of society and of the planet. Obviously consideration of sustainability must be embedded in all product creation from the design stage, by adopting circular systems; but in addition ethically produced, natural materials should sustainably be sourced from global artisans, to preserve their knowledge and skills and to promote their wellbeing and that of their communities; supply chains must be short and wholly transparent, with the makers of materials and products acknowledged so as to forge connection between consumers and makers and appreciation of how the materials are made to encourage lasting value; these materials should—as much as possible—hold additional beneficial properties beyond the aesthetic, such as anti-bacterial and medicinal qualities to promote the health and wellbeing of wearers; materials, techniques and processes should connect consumers with the natural world, through surface, shape, detail and colour; designs should show a high degree of individuality and innovation, unrelated to seasonal trends, but having unique qualities which render them exclusive and timeless; neocrafting techniques should be used to add exquisite detail and finish, imparting goodness through lasting quality and emotional attachment. Future luxury fashion must therefore evolve in order to address the changing needs of its consumers by adopting a benign and truly holistic way of envisioning luxury fashion that promotes the wellbeing of its wearers, of its makers and of the planet.

# References

Abel, Jessica P., Cheryl L. Buff, and Sarah A. Burr. 2016. "Social Media and the Fear of Missing Out: Scale Development and Assessment." *Journal of Business and Economics Research* 14 (1): 33–41. https://doi.org/10.19030/jber.v14i1.9554. Accessed on 17 February 2019.

Alfoldy, Sandra, and Nova Scotia College of Art and Design. 2007. *NeoCraft: Modernity and the Crafts*. Halifax, NS: Press of the Nova Scotia College of Art and Design.

Appiah, Kwame A. 1985. "An Aesthetics for the Art of Adornment." In *Beauty by Design: The Aesthetics of African Adornment*, edited by Marie-Therese Brincard, 15–19. New York: The African American Institute.

Armstrong, Cosette M., Kirsi Niinimäki, and Chunmin Lang. 2016. "Towards Design Recipes to Curb the Clothing Carbohydrate Binge." *The Design Journal* 19 (1): 159–181. https://doi.org/10.1080/14606925.2016.110920 7. Accessed on 22 February 2019.

Bell, Simon, and Catherine Ward Thompson. 2014. "Human Engagement with Forest Environments: Implications for Physical and Mental Health and Wellbeing." In *Challenges and Opportunities for the World's Forests in the 21st Century: Forestry Sciences*, edited by Trevor Fenning, Vol. 81, 71–92. Dordrecht: Springer Netherlands. https://doi.org/10.1007/978-94-007-7076-8_5. Accessed on 4 May 2019.

Bendell, Jem, and Anthony Kleanthous. 2007. *Deeper Luxury*. http://assets.wwf.org.uk/downloads/luxury_report.pdf.

Benyus, Janine. 2008. "A Good Place to Settle: Biomimicry, Biophilia, and the Return of Nature's Inspiration to Architecture." In *Biophilic Design: The Theory, Science and Practice of Bringing Buildings to Life*, edited by Stephen R. Kellert, Judith Heerwagen, and Martin Mador, 27–42. Hoboken, NJ: Wiley.

Bina, Jasmine. 2018. Cited in Pinnock, Olivia. 2018. "No One in Fashion Is Surprised Burberry Burnt £28 Million of Stock." *Forbes*, July 20. https://www.forbes.com/sites/oliviapinnock/2018/07/20/no-one-in-fashion-is-surprised-burberry-burnt-28-million-of-stock/#3cf18bde4793. Accessed on 16 February 2019.

Brown, Sass. 2015. "Can Global Craft and Artisanship Be the Future of Luxury Fashion." Paper presented at Product Lifetimes and the Environment Conference (PLATE), Nottingham Trent University, June 17–19. https://www.plateconference.org/category/conference-2015-proceedings-papers/. Accessed on 17 February 2019.

Centers for Disease Control and Prevention. 2019. *Well Being Concepts*. https://www.cdc.gov/hrqol/wellbeing.htm#three. Accessed on 4 May 2019.

Chiao, Ying H., Jennifer Y. Chang, Gerald L. Riskowski, Wai K. Chan, Jinn T. Lai, and Audrey C. Chang. 2016. "Antimicrobial Activity of Indigowoad (Isatis indigotica Fort) and Plains Wild Indigo (Baptisia bracteata) Roots." *Research Journal of Medicinal Plants* 10 (3): 237–245. https://scialert.net/abstract/?doi=rjmp.2016.237.245. Accessed on 4 May 2019.

Coutts, Christopher, and Micah Hahn. 2015. "Green Infrastructure, Ecosystem Services, and Human Health." *International Journal of Environmental Research and Public Health* 12: 9768–9798. Basel: MDPI AG. http://www.mdpi.com/1660-4601/12/8/9768/htm. Accessed on 4 May 2019.

Craft Revival Trust, UNESCO, and Artesanias de Colombia. 2005. *Designers Meet Artisans: A Practical Guide*. http://unesdoc.unesco.org/images/0014/001471/147132eo.pdf. Accessed on 9 September 2017.

Cultural Research Centre. 2000. *Dictionary: Lusoga-English, English-Lusoga*. Jinja, Uganda: Cultural Research Centre.

Department of Health and Social Care. 2014. *Wellbeing and Why It Matters to Health*. https://assets.publishing.service.gov.uk/government/uploads/system/uploads/attachment_data/file/277566/Narrative__January_2014_.pdf.

Ferrier, Morwenna. 2018. "Why Does Burberry Destroy Its Products and How Is It Justified?" *The Guardian*, July 20. https://www.theguardian.com/fashion/2018/jul/20/why-does-burberry-destroy-its-products-q-and-a.

Gardetti, Miguel A., and Maria E. Giron, eds. 2016. *Sustainable Luxury and Social Entrepreneurship: Volume II, More Stories from the Pioneers*. Sheffield: Greenleaf Publishing.

Gardetti, Miguel A. 2014. "Stories from the Social Pioneers in the Sustainable Luxury Sector: A Conceptual Vision." In *Sustainable Luxury and Social Entrepreneurship: Stories from the Pioneers*, edited by Miguel A. Gardetti and Maria E. Giron, 23–34. Sheffield: Greenleaf Publishing.

Global Wellness Institute. 2018. *Global Wellness Economy Monitor.* https://globalwellnessinstitute.org/industry-research/2018-global-wellness-economy-monitor/. Accessed on 16 February 2019.

Global Wellness Summit. 2018. *2019 Wellness Industry Trend Report.* https://www.globalwellnesssummit.com/2019-global-wellness-trends/.

Grinde, Bjorn, and Greta Grindal Patil. 2009. "Biophilia: Does Visual Contact with Nature Impact on Health and Well-Being?" *International Journal of Environmental Research and Public Health* 6 (9): 2332–2343. https://doi.org/10.3390/ijerph6092332.

Gupta, Deepti. 2011. "Design and Engineering of Functional Clothing." *Indian Journal of Fibre & Textile Research* 36 (4): 321–326. http://nopr.niscair.res.in/handle/123456789/13226. Accessed on 4 May 2019.

Gutsatz, Michel, and Klaus Heine. 2018. "Luxury Brand-Building and Development: New Global Challenges, New Business Models." *Journal of Brand Management* 25 (5): 409–410. https://doi.org/10.1057/s41262-018-0093-5. Accessed on 22 February 2019.

Hansen, Margaret M., Reo Jones, and Kirsten Tocchini. 2017. "Shinrin-Yoku (Forest Bathing) and Nature Therapy: A State-of-the-Art Review." *International Journal of Environmental Research and Public Health* 14 (8): 851. https://doi.org/10.3390/ijerph14080851. Accessed on 17 February 2019.

Hashmi, Zeynep G. 2017. "Redefining the Essence of Sustainable Luxury Management: The Slow Value Creation Model." In *Sustainable Management of Luxury: Environmental Footprints and Eco-design of Products and Processes*, edited by Miguel A. Gardetti and Maria E. Giron, 3–27. Sheffield: Greenleaf Publishing.

Health and Safety Executive. 2018. *Work Related Stress, Depression or Anxiety Statistics in Great Britain, 2018.* http://www.hse.gov.uk/statistics/causdis/stress.pdf. Accessed on 16 February 2019.

Hennigs, Nadine, Klaus-Peter Wiedmann, Christiane Klarmann, and Stefan Behrens. 2013. "Sustainability as Part of the Luxury Essence." *The Journal of Corporate Citizenship* 58: 25–35. https://doi.org/10.9774/GLEAF.4700.2013.de.00005. Accessed on 9 February 2019.

Jyothirmi, Singothu, and Sasmita Panda. 2016. "Ayurvastra Herbal Clothing (A New Technology to Heal Naturally)." *International Journal of Advanced Research and Innovative Ideas in Education* 2 (4): 1166–1171. https://www.researchgate.net/publication/307580444_AYURVASTRA_-_HERBAL_CLOTHING_A_new_technology_to_heal_naturally. ISSN(O)-2395-4396.

Kapferer, Jean-Noel. 2010. "All That Glitters Is Not Green: The Challenge of Sustainable Luxury." 40–45. www.europeanbusinessreview.com/. Accessed on 17 February 2019.

Kapferer, Jean-Noel, and Vincent Bastien. 2012. *The Luxury Strategy: Break the Rules of Marketing to Build Luxury Brands.* 2nd ed. Philadelphia, PA: Kogan Page.

Kellert, Stephen, R., Judith Heerwagen, and Martin Mador, eds. 2008. *Biophilic Design: The Theory, Science, and Practice of Bringing Buildings to Life.* London: Wiley.

Kennedy, G., and E. Bolat. 2017. "Meet the HENRYs: A Hybrid Focus Group Study of Conspicuous Luxury Consumption in the Social Media Context." Paper presented at the Academy of Marketing Conference 2017, Hull, United Kingdom, June 3–7. https://core.ac.uk/download/pdf/84144510.pdf.

Mader, Lindsay Stafford. 2011. "Ayurvastra: Dyeing Fabric with Medicinal Ayurvedic Plants." *HerbalGram: The Journal of the American Botanical Society* 92: 16–18. http://cms.herbalgram.org/herbalgram/issue92/ORGNEWS-ayurvastra.html?ts=1551512695&signature=fbb8e8addee584a7c4369ebc9beec3aa. Accessed on 19 February 2019.

Maisonrouge, Ketty Pucci-Sisti. 2013. *The Luxury Alchemist.* New York, NY: Assouline.

McRobbie, Angela, Dan Strutt, Carolina Bandinelli, and Bettina Springer. 2016. "Fashion Micro-enterprises in London, Berlin, Milan." CREATE Working Paper 2016/13, November 2016. https://doi.org/10.5281/zenodo.162668.

Mental Health Foundation. 2018. *Stressed Nation: 74% of UK 'Overwhelmed or Unable to Cope' at Some Point in the Past Year*, May 14. https://www.mentalhealth.org.uk/news/stressed-nation-74-uk-overwhelmed-or-unable-cope-some-point-past-year. Accessed on 19 February 2019.

Nakazibwe, V. 2005. "Barkcloth of the Baganda People of Southern Uganda: A Record of Continuity and Change from the Late 20th Century to the Early 21st Century." PhD Thesis, Middlesex University. http://ethos.bl.uk/SearchResults.do.

New Economics Foundation (NEF). 2006. *The (Un)Happy Planet Index: An Index of Human Well-Being and Environmental Impact.* https://www.researchgate.net/publication/312602893_The_unHappy_Planet_Index_An_index_of_human_well-being_and_environmental_impact. Accessed on 17 February 2019.

Pinnock, Olivia. 2018. "No One in Fashion Is Surprised Burberry Burnt £28 Million of Stock." *Forbes*, July 20. https://www.forbes.com/sites/oliviapinnock/2018/07/20/no-one-in-fashion-is-surprised-burberry-burnt-28-million-of-stock/#3cf18bde4793. Accessed on 16 February 2019.

Putra, R.R.F.A., D.D. Veridianti, N. Evelyn, D. Brilliant, G. Rosellinny, C. Suraz, and A. Sumarpo. 2018. "Immunostimulant Effect from Phytoncide of Forest Bathing to Prevent the Development of Cancer." *Advanced Science Letters* 24 (9): 6653–6659(7). https://doi.org/10.1166/asl.2018.12804. Accessed on 17 February 2019.

Rwawiire, Samson, and Blanka Tomkova. 2013. "Thermo-physiological and Comfort Properties of Ugandan Barkcloth from Ficus Natalensis." *The Journal of the Textile Institute* 105 (6, 2014): 648–653. https://doi.org/10.10 80/00405000.2013.843849.

Schumacher, Ernst F. 1974. *Small Is Beautiful: A Study of Economics as if People Mattered.* London: Blond & Briggs.

Scott, Kirsten. 2011. "Meeting the Maker: Warm Irregularity in Traditional African Craft Practice." *Craft Research Journal* 2 (1, June): 61–82. https://doi.org/10.1386/crre.2.61_1.

Scott, Kirsten. 2012. "Pidgin Plait: Fashioning Cross-Cultural Communication Through Craft." PhD Thesis. http://researchonline.rca.ac.uk/view/creators/Scott=3AKirsten=3A=3A.html.

Scott, Kirsten. 2018. "Borrowed Cloth: A Holistic Design Intervention for Sustainable Fashion and Wellbeing." Paper presented at Global Fashion Conference October 2018, London College of Fashion, October 31–November 1. http://gfc-conference.eu/proceedings/.

UNESCO. 2005. *Bark Cloth Making in Uganda.* http://www.unesco.org/archives/multimedia/?pg=33&s=films_details&id=641. Accessed on 16 February 2019.

USAID. 2006. *Global Market Assessment for Handicrafts.* https://pdf.usaid.gov/pdf_docs/PNADN210.pdf. Accessed on 9 February 2019.

Wells, Kate. 2013. "Colour, Health and Wellbeing: The Hidden Qualities and Properties of Natural Dyes." *Journal of the International Colour Association* 11: 28–36. http://hdl.handle.net/10545/297603. Accessed on 15 February 2019.

World Health Organization. 2019. *Promotion of Mental Well-Being.* http://www.searo.who.int/entity/mental_health/promotion-of-mental-well-being/en/#. Accessed on 18 February 2019.

Wu, Meng-Shan S., Isabella Chaney, Cheng-Hao Steve Chen, Bang Nguyen, and T.C. Melewar. 2015. "Luxury Fashion Brands: Factors Influencing Young Female Consumers' Luxury Fashion Purchasing in Taiwan." *Qualitative Market Research: An International Journal* 18 (3): 298–319. https://doi.org/10.1108/QMR-02-2014-0016.

# Part III
## Understanding Luxury and Society

# 6

# Sustainable Luxury: The Effect of Corporate Social Responsibility Strategy on Luxury Consumption Motivations

Carmela Donato, Matteo De Angelis and Cesare Amatulli

## Introduction

Sustainable development, introduced in 1987 by the World Commission on Environment and Development, encompasses three dimensions of human well-being (Langenwalter 2009)—social justice, environmental preservation, and economic prosperity—for both present and future generations (Fletcher 2013). The social dimension

C. Donato (✉) · M. De Angelis
Department of Business and Management,
LUISS University, Rome, Italy
e-mail: donatoc@luiss.it

M. De Angelis
e-mail: mdeangelis@luiss.it

C. Amatulli
Ionian Department of Law, Economics and Environment,
University of Bari, Bari, Italy
e-mail: cesare.amatulli@uniba.it

© The Author(s) 2020
I. Cantista and T. Sádaba (eds.), *Understanding Luxury Fashion*,
Palgrave Advances in Luxury, https://doi.org/10.1007/978-3-030-25654-8_6

assumes that sustainable development leads to a general improvement of life quality in terms of environmental protection and trust in social relationships. The environmental dimension depends on the idea that sustainable development reduces natural resource usage, thus preserving the natural resources that are fundamental for the fulfillment of material needs. Finally, the economic dimension captures the paramount importance of regulating the usage of resources to minimize excessive levels of consumption that decrease the presence of non-renewable resources and shorten the rotation times of renewable ones. Environmental preservation is considered the cornerstone of the sustainability concept, as it provides the foundation for establishing prosperity and justice.

Given its multidimensional relevance, sustainability has been risen at the forefront of public discourse (Bansal and Roth 2000). Consumers are in fact showing increased interest in products that use fewer natural resources, cause less pollution, and are less harmful to the environment (Luchs et al. 2010), as well as in companies that do good for employees, contribute to surrounding communities, and benefit the society at large (Amatulli et al. 2017). Perhaps as a consequence, today, many companies from different sectors are highly committed to the different facets of sustainable development (e.g., Gershoff and Frels 2015; Luo and Du 2015). Due in part to this mounting interest, there has been a proliferation of products that include components made with materials that reduce the environmental impact (Delmas and Burbano 2011). For example, IKEA invested in sustainability throughout its entire business operations, starting with their supply chain, where the Swedish furniture-maker has sourced close to 50% of its wood from sustainable foresters and 100% of its cotton from farms that meet the Better Cotton standards, which mandate reduced usage of water, energy and chemical fertilizers and pesticides. Firms such as Unilever and Panasonic have made similar strides: The former created a Sustainable Living Plan that set targets for sourcing, supply chain, and production on everything from energy and water use to treatment of suppliers and communities where it operates. The latter moved its North American headquarters to a LEED-certified building in downtown Newark in order to reduce employees' drive to work, thus reducing their carbon footprint.

A similar trend can be seen among fashion brands. *Recover Brands* produces and sells clothing that is made entirely out of recycled material, such as discarded water bottles and cotton. The company also uses environmentally sustainable manufacturing methods, such as restricting the use of dyes as well as minimizing chemical, water, and energy use. Similarly, the firm Mango has launched two fashion collections produced with materials such as organic and recycled cotton, recycled wool, modal, and lyocell. The shoe company, *Allbirds*, created an innovative wool fabric made specifically for footwear: a fine merino wool upper and base made from castor bean oil, a natural substitute for plastic and rubber. By wearing a pair of these shoes consumers can wear a pair of sneakers from a company that found a new use for naturally existing materials, rather than relying on cheaper and unsustainable synthetics. In the fast fashion industry, Swedish retailer H&M has implemented several practices, including a sustainability report website and a recycling initiative that provides vouchers to customers who return old used clothing.

The impulse toward sustainability has even spread to luxury fashion—paradoxical as that might seem. Many recent initiatives by luxury companies fall into the domain of Corporate Social Responsibility (hereafter CSR; Janssen et al. 2014; Maignan and Ferrell 2001), which can be defined as a company's ongoing commitment to behaving ethically and contributing to the improvement of the quality of life of all stakeholders, as well as the society in which they operate. Through CSR-oriented initiatives, luxury brands are increasingly trying to cater to consumers that, even in the luxury industry, have become more sensitive to environmental and social issues. In this way, such brands seek to make a positive worldly contribution that aligns with the prestige and excellence expected of luxury goods. There have been several notable examples so far: Tiffany started to certify its diamonds as "conflict free"; Chanel incorporated "earthy materials" in its 2016 collection, and Bulgari recently funded the restoration of the famous Spanish Steps in Rome.

Despite the recent proliferation of such activities, little is known about whether they are successful for luxury brands—in particular, whether and how they might positively influence consumers' attitudes and behavior. Some studies suggest that luxury consumers consider sustainability elements as irrelevant, if not deleterious factors to their purchase decisions (e.g., Achabou and Dekhili 2013; Davies and Ahonkhai 2012; Griskevicius et al. 2010). However, others argue that a potentially positive effect of sustainability and CSR-oriented activities on luxury consumption might indeed exist (e.g., Amatulli et al. 2017; De Angelis et al. 2017; Kapferer 2010; Janssen et al. 2014).

The present chapter aims to shed new light on the role of CSR in luxury consumption. Specifically, we propose that different types of CSR activities might have different effects on luxury consumers' perceptions and behaviors. Such a differential effect, we propose, might be attributable to the variance in consumers' approaches to luxury purchasing and consumption. Whereas some consumers buy luxury goods mainly to display their social status, others buy them mainly to satisfy their personal tastes, preferences, and style codes (Amatulli and Guido 2012). From a methodological standpoint, we combine qualitative and quantitative methods: We first describe the cases of four luxury companies deeply engaged in CSR initiatives. Afterward, we present the results of an experimental study aimed at testing our hypothesis that consumer' reactions to luxury brands' CSR initiatives vary depending both on the type of CSR initiative and consumers' motivations for luxury consumption. This research is, to the best of our knowledge, the first to empirically investigate the conditions under which luxury brands' CSR initiatives might be perceived favorably by consumers. Through this endeavor, we hope to offer important suggestions to luxury managers about currying favor with consumers through CSR activities.

## Conceptual Framework

The public's increasing attention to issues concerning the environment, workers, customers, and society is pushing companies to behave ethically (e.g., Gershoff and Frels 2015). Luxury is one industry in which such pressure has steadily mounted in the last decade (Davies et al. 2012; Janssen et al. 2014), which has prompted many luxury firms to embed CSR in their marketing strategies. However, the literature is ambiguous about the role of CSR activities in the luxury industry. According to some streams of research (e.g., Achabou and Dekhili 2013; Griskevicius et al. 2010), the majority of consumers see luxury and CSR as incompatible concepts. These scholars reason that luxury is generally associated with hedonism, excess, and ostentation (Cristini et al. 2017; De Barnier et al. 2012), while CSR is associated with sobriety, moderation, and ethics (Lochard and Murat 2011).

While quite pervasive, this idea has been challenged by recent studies suggesting that luxury and sustainability might be more compatible than initially thought (e.g., Amatulli et al. 2017; De Angelis et al. 2017; Janssen et al. 2014). The central belief is that both luxury and sustainability "focus on rarity and beauty" (Kapferer 2010, p. 41). A recent book by Amatulli et al. (2017) strengthened this concept by advancing the idea that luxury is *inherently* sustainable, as some of luxury goods' most distinctive characteristics—such as limited production, reliable quality, craftsmanship, and the associated preservation of valuable artisanal jobs—render them naturally more sustainable (i.e., beneficial to the environment and the surrounding community) than mass market goods. Building on this idea, we propose and empirically test the notion that CSR initiatives may play a positive role in luxury consumption. Our goal is to show whether and under what conditions consumers might react positively to luxury companies' CSR initiatives.

Underlying our proposition is the idea that CSR is a multidimensional construct, as originally conceptualized by Archie B. Carroll (1979, 1991). According to Carroll, CSR can be split into four dimensions that correspond to four categories of responsibilities. Carroll portrayed these dimensions (summarized in Table 6.1) as a pyramid following this hierarchy: The economic dimension, at the bottom of the pyramid, reflects the belief that businesses have an obligation to be productive and profitable in striving to meet consumer needs. The next level, the legal dimension, refers to the laws and regulations that serve as boundaries to the firm's economic responsibilities. The third level, the ethical dimension, reflects unwritten codes, norms, and values that are implicit in a society and transcend mere legal requirements. The philanthropic dimension, at the top of the pyramid, refers to firms' volitional

Table 6.1  A multidimensional model of CSR

| CSR dimensions | Responsibilities | Main potential goals |
|---|---|---|
| Philanthropic | Behaving as good corporate citizens | Contributing to the community |
| | | Improving quality of life |
| Ethical | Being ethical | Doing what is fair and moral |
| | | Avoiding harm |
| Legal | Following the law | Providing goods and services that meet legal requirements |
| Economic | Making acceptable profits | Creating the basis for all the other responsibilities |

*Source* Adapted from Carroll, A. B. (1991)

discretionary responsibilities that qualify them as "good corporate citizens."

In this chapter, we look at the four dimensions in greater detail by identifying an aspect that importantly differentiates such dimensions: their visibility to consumers. In line with recent work about food consumption behavior by some of this chapter's authors (Pino et al. 2016), we argue that initiatives in the legal and philanthropic dimensions are readily visible to consumers, while those in the economic and legal dimensions are less so. Based on this distinction, we identify two categories of CSR dimensions: the "internal" category (which encompasses the economic and ethical dimensions) and the "external" category (which encompasses the legal and philanthropic dimensions). We empirically investigate whether internal or external CSR initiatives are more or less likely to increase consumers' willingness to buy (hereafter, WTB) from luxury companies.

Importantly, we hypothesize that the effect on WTB might depend on luxury consumers' intrinsic motivations toward luxury purchasing. Indeed, we believe that the particular nature of luxury goods (e.g., high prices, largely inaccessible to the masses, an emphasis on creative and self-fulfilling content, etc.; e.g., Atwal and Williams 2009; Fionda and Moore 2009) merits a distinction between *externalized* and *internalized* consumption (e.g., Amatulli and Guido 2012). Consumers who embody the externalized motivation typically buy luxury products to fulfill their dispositional need to be admired and validated by other people. In other words, such consumers mainly buy luxury goods that are highly visible and noticeable by others (i.e., products that carry a visible logo) (e.g., Han et al. 2010; Nueno and Quelch 1998) in order to showcase their social status. On the other hand, consumers who abide by the internalized motivation typically buy luxury products to experience pleasing feelings and emotions. In other words, these consumers generally avoid buying highly visible and noticeable luxury items (e.g., Amatulli et al. 2015) because their main interest is satisfying their individual taste, preferences, and style. In short, externalized luxury consumption places greater importance on the "visibility" component, whereas the internalized approach places greater importance to the luxury product itself.

In conjunction with this dichotomy, we hypothesize that externally motivated customers could be particularly interested in CSR initiatives that are highly visible to others, such as those in the legal and philanthropic spheres. Likewise, internally motivated customers could be particularly interested in CSR initiatives that are more "quiet" and "discreet," such as those in the economic and ethical dimensions. In short, we expect that the effectiveness of internal versus external CSR initiatives in driving consumers' WTB luxury products will depend on the personal benefits that the consumer derives from those initiatives (Bhattacharya and Sen 2004). Formally,

$H_1$: Internal (vs. external) CSR initiatives undertaken by a luxury brand are more likely to increase consumers' WTB products from that brand, but only for consumers characterized by internalized (vs. externalized) luxury consumption motivation.

We first present a case study analysis that provides detailed anecdotal evidence about luxury companies engaged in CSR initiatives. We specifically align those initiatives with the CSR dimensions described above. Afterward, we present the procedure and results of an experimental study aimed at offering an empirical test of our hypothesis.

# Case Studies' Analysis

In this section we present four cases of well-known luxury fashion brands that have made CSR a core pillar of their strategy, undertaking specific initiatives that have strengthened, rather than diluted, the brand's prestige and perceived quality. We also align the four cases with Carroll's (1979, 1991) CSR pyramid: Specifically, the first two cases—Brunello Cucinelli and Armani—portray activities that belong to the internal CSR dimensions (i.e., economic and ethical dimensions, respectively), while the other two cases—Prada and Fendi—portray activities that belong to the external CSR dimensions (i.e., legal and philanthropic dimensions, respectively).

## The Case of Brunello Cucinelli

Brunello Cucinelli S.p.A. was established in 1978 in the central Italian region of Umbria. Today, the company is globally recognized as a leading producer of cashmere. Its revenues (about 500 million euros) grew by 10% in 2017, with particularly positive performances in Europe, the US, and China. Mr. Brunello Cucinelli, the company's founder, has been deeply inspired by the idea of making a positive contribution to the society in which the company operated. In 1985, the company bought a fourteenth-century castle in Perugia (Italy), which has become the company's headquarters. In 2000, the company bought a working production plant located at the foot of the Solomeo hill and molded it into a symbol of culture and progress, with a built-in Forum of the Arts, library, theatre, and amphitheater. In 2015, the brand launched an initiative called "Project for Beauty," which involved the creation of three big parks in the Solomeo area. These initiatives reflect the founder's interest in preserving and improving the local community.

Mr. Cucinelli's deep commitment to sustainable development has been formally recognized at both the national and international level through several awards and honors. Acclaimed for his "Neohumanistic Capitalism," he has received an honorary degree in Philosophy and Ethics of Human Relations from the University of Perugia; the

Sustainability Award from the Green Carpet Fashion Awards in Milan; and the Global Economy Prize from the Kiel Institute for the World Economy, which noted that Mr. Cucinelli "personifies perfectly the figure of the Honorable Merchant".

Brunello Cucinelli S.p.A is worth being mentioned also for its economic sustainability. To illustrate, in 2012, Brunello Cucinelli S.p.A., following its listing on the Italian Stock Exchange, distributed a relevant portion of the year's net profit (5 million Euro) to its 783 employees, each of whom received a Christmas bonus of 6385 Euro. Mr. Cucinelli intended this bonus as a proper recognition of his employees' good work in helping the company's profits grow by 25%. Such a profoundly sustainable action can be regarded as an instance of initiative belonging to the economic CSR dimension.

## The Case of Armani

Giorgio Armani S.p.A., founded in 1975 by the famous Italian designer Giorgio Armani, is one of the world's leading luxury fashion houses. Mr. Armani remains the firm's main shareholder, as well as its managing director and chairman of the board. Over the years, Giorgio Armani has made control over manufacturing and distribution activities tighter and tighter, thus remaining aloof from the waves of consolidation which often characterize the luxury industry. The group has about 250 outlets in 34 countries and markets its wares through exclusive and selective distribution strategies.

The Armani Company has been successful since its beginning, as indicated by the establishment of Giorgio Armani Corporation in United States in 1979. Part of the success was due to Armani's bold design gambles, including the famed "destructured" men's suit jacket.

In 2000, the Armani Company earned operating profits of $374 billion (EUR 193 million) on consolidated net revenues of $2 trillion (EUR 1.03 billion), which were up 20% for the year. Global retail sales exceeded $7 trillion (EUR 3.6 billion). During 2000, the company launched a joint venture with the Zegna Group, called Trimil, to produce and distribute the Armani Collezioni line of men's clothing.

Giorgio Armani Cosmetics debuted. Armani Casa, a home fashion store, opened after years of planning. A series of Armani-related web sites were launched and plans for a new headquarters office were underway. Armani, though, was unable to acquire the armani.com name, which was held by a Canadian artist named Anand Ramnath Mani. During the years, Armani was honored with an exhibit at New York's Guggenheim Museum for having changed the way people dressed in the previous quarter century. At this stage in his career, Armani was finding inspiration in the marriage of Eastern minimalism and Western luxury.

The Armani Group is aware that the responsible use of natural resources, environmental protection, and respect for the communities and territories in which it operates are essential requirements for a company that operates at a global level. For this reason, the Group has for some time been engaged in a worthwhile initiative for the development of projects that are aligned with the leading international principles concerning the combination of economic, environmental, and social sustainability. For example, in 2016 they announced they would no longer use animal fur in any of their fashion collections. Through such a decision the Italian luxury brand gave a clear answer to a growing consumer demand for ethical and sustainable fashion.

Armani's fur-free collections decision can be identified as an ethical CSR activity according to Carroll's model, as it demonstrates a respect for animal life. Thus, it aligns with societal expectations, ethical norms, and ethical behaviors that are independent from legal regulations.

## The Case of Prada

Prada S.p.A. is an Italian fashion brand specializing in luxury goods for men and women. It was founded in 1913 by Mario Prada and his brother Martino in Milan, as a leather goods shop called Fratelli Prada. Mario Prada started designing and selling handbags, shoes, trunks, and suitcases through two boutiques in Milan. His granddaughter, Miuccia Prada, took over leadership of the company in 1978. Under her leadership, Prada became a premium status symbol for women, particularly business women. To appeal to a larger customer base, Miuccia developed the more affordable Miu Miu line in 1992, followed by Prada Sport and a line of menswear and lingerie. By 1995, Prada was operating in 40 locations worldwide. Prada continued to expand its global footprint, first through a series of acquisitions and then by opening and running its own stores around the world.

Nowadays the company is highly committed to reducing the environmental impact of its production activities. To illustrate, the company devotes considerable amounts of money on a multiannual basis to the reduction of land consumption, energy usage, and waste, including the responsible use of paper and packaging when developing plans for its branches. Moreover, in 2016 the Prada Group achieved LEED (Leadership in Energy and Environmental Design) Gold certification on 7 stores: 6 Prada stores between China, Australia and Switzerland, and 1 Miu Miu store in China. This certification is one of the most popular green building certification programs used worldwide. Developed by the non-profit U.S. Green Building Council (USGBC), it includes a rating system for the design, construction, operation, and maintenance of green buildings, homes, and neighborhoods that aims to help building owners and operators be environmentally responsible and use resources efficiently.

Prada's effort and success in obtaining LEED certification represents an activity in the legal CSR dimension. Compared to Brunello Cucinelli's and Giorgio Armani's initiatives, belonging to economic and ethical CSR dimensions, respectively, LEED certification for Prada represents an achievement that is more visible and noticeable by customers and other stakeholders.

## The Case of Fendi

Fendi is an Italian luxury fashion brand founded in 1925 by Adele and Eduardo Fendi in Rome. Nowadays, the brand is recognized for producing refined clothes, accessories, shoes, fragrances and eyewear. In 1946, the couple's five daughters—Paola, Anna, Franca, Carla and Alda—joined the family business, bringing with them research and innovation. In 1965, the Fendi sisters hit the fashion house with a wave of innovation after bringing on the talented fashion designer Karl Lagerfeld. A year later, the designer presented the first successful haute couture collection in Rome.

Like the previous luxury brands, Fendi is also highly committed to CSR activities. It is particularly recognized for its philanthropic initiatives in its home-town of Rome. For instance, in 2015, the company initiated the *Fendi for Fountains* project, donating 2.18 million euros to the renovation of Rome's Trevi Fountain, and another 320,000 euros to the restoration of the Four Fountains located in Rome's city center. Pietro Beccari, Fendi's president and chief executive officer, said about the project: "The works won't only bring back the Trevi Fountain to its former splendor but will also give the chance to tourists to visit the fountain from a completely new perspective and from an incredible short distance. Rome and its fountains gave a lot to Fendi over the years and we are honored to give back one of Rome's symbols to people."

Fendi's significant contribution to the restoration of Rome's historical fountains clearly constitutes an initiative in the philanthropic dimension of CSR. The high visibility of this initiative to the public aligns it with the external CSR category.

# Experimental Study

The goal of the following experiment is to test $H_1$. To recap, we expected that a luxury brand's internal (vs. external) CSR initiatives might lead to an increase in consumers' WTB products marketed by that brand, but only if said consumers abide by an internalized (vs. externalized) motivation to buy luxury goods. We chose an experimental design so that we could make causal inferences (Cook et al. 2002) about the relationship between our independent and dependent variables—in our case, the type of CSR initiative and consumers' responses, respectively.

## Methodology

One hundred and sixty-two respondents (97 females; $M_{age} = 40.76$, $SD_{age} = 13.01$) took part in one online experimental study. We first asked participants to indicate their luxury consumption dispositional motivation using one item rated on a seven-point scale (i.e., "*Please indicate why you would buy a luxury product …*" 1 = "Mainly for an internal motivation, related to my individual style and my taste"; 7 = "Mainly for an external motivation, related to my economic and social status").

Then, using a between-subjects design, we manipulated the type of CSR initiative (internal vs. external) undertaken by a fictitious luxury fashion brand (which we named "Shine") and observed its effect on consumers' WTB a product (i.e., a jacket) from that same brand. In particular, participants were randomly assigned to one of two experimental conditions corresponding to our manipulation of CSR (internal vs. external). Specifically, in the internal CSR condition, participants read a scenario reporting that Shine brand had recently developed ethical initiatives (i.e., it had bequeathed extra benefits to its employees) alongside economic sustainability initiatives (i.e., it had bought software intended to reduce internal production costs). In the external CSR condition, the scenario reported that Shine brand had recently engaged in philanthropic initiatives (i.e., it had donated money to a pediatric hospital) as well as attained an important legal certification (i.e., a certification confirming the traceability of its raw materials). Table 6.2 provides the text we used in our scenarios.

Following CSR manipulation, we measured the WTB from Shine using a three-item, seven-point scale (i.e., "*I would purchase the jacket from this brand,*" "*I would consider buying a jacket from this brand,*" and "*The probability that I would consider buying a jacket from this brand is high*", 1 = strongly disagree, 7 = strongly agree; see Dodds et al. 1991). We averaged the three items to form an overall WTB score ($\alpha = .92$). Next, as a check of our manipulation, we asked participants to indicate to what extent they perceived the aforementioned initiatives as visible and observable from outside the company ("*To what extent do you*

**Table 6.2**  Scenarios employed to manipulate type of CSR initiative

| Internal CSR condition | External CSR condition |
|---|---|
| SHINE is a luxury brand that has recently developed the following initiatives, an ethical and an economic one | SHINE is a luxury brand that has recently developed the following initiatives, a philanthropic and a legal one |
| • Concerning the ethical initiative, the company offers to its employees a series of working benefits for them and their children | • Concerning the philanthropic initiative, the company has donated money to help the building of a new pediatric hospital |
| • Concerning the economic initiative, the company has bought a software able to optimize the manufacturing process thus reducing internal production costs | • Concerning the legal initiative, the company has acquired a certification attesting the traceability of its raw materials, thus having now the opportunity to put this certification on the label of its products |

*perceive as visible and observable from outside the company (that is from people who are not part of the firm, such as consumers) the initiatives developed by the brand and previously described?"* 1 = not at all, 7 = a lot). Finally, we collected demographic information (age and gender) before debriefing and thanking the respondents for their participation (see Appendix A for further details).

# Results

We firstly checked our manipulation, and results indicated that on average participants recognized the initiatives illustrated in the internal CSR scenario as less visible than those in the external CSR scenario. Then we proceeded to test our moderation hypothesis employing the Model 1 in the PROCESS SPSS Macro (Hayes 2017).[1] The measure of luxury consumption orientation served as the moderator in the relationship between the type of CSR initiative and WTB (see Fig. 6.1).

The results showed that internal CSR initiatives increase WTB compared to external CSR activities. On the contrary, the effect of luxury

---

[1]The model is aimed at testing moderation models in case the moderator is a continuous variable

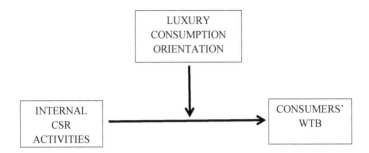

**Fig. 6.1** Proposed moderation model

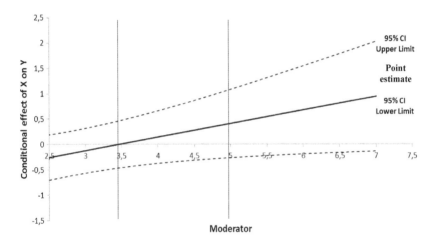

**Fig. 6.2** Johnson-Neyman floodlight analysis for experimental data analysis

consumption orientation did not influence the WTB. Of greater importance, luxury consumption moderates the relationship between type of
CSR initiative and WTB. In particular, the results revealed that internal
CSR initiatives significantly affect WTB, but only for consumers with
low luxury consumption dispositional motivation, namely those with
an internalized motivation (see Fig. 6.2).

Overall, consistent with $H_1$, these results suggest that luxury consumption motivation acts a catalyst for the effect of CSR dimensions
on WTB. The internal CSR dimensions (ethical and economic) showed
a strong effect in the face of internalized consumption motivation,

whereas the external CSR dimensions (legal and philanthropic) showed a stronger effect for consumers with an externalized motivation (see Appendix B for statistical analyses).

## Conclusions and Implications for Theory and Practice

The present chapter examined the CSR initiatives undertaken by four luxury companies: on internal CSR dimensions side, Brunello Cucinelli S.p.A. and Giorgio Armani S.p.A.; on the external CSR dimensions side, Prada and Fendi. The most important conclusion that can be drawn from our case study analysis is that even in a prestige-based sector such as fashion luxury and for highly reputed luxury brands, sustainability can be an important ingredient for success. In other words, luxury brands may embed sustainable values into the core of their branding strategy by pursuing initiatives that align with the well-known CSR framework (Carroll 1979, 1991). Indeed, all four luxury brand cases presented in this chapter demonstrate that such pursuit does not imply a dilution of luxury brands' inherent prestige, tradition and quality, but to instead illuminate their positive contributions to the communities and societies in which they operate.

Additionally, we performed an empirical, experimental analysis about the differential effectiveness of internal and external CSR activities on consumers' WTB products from luxury brands engaging in those activities. The study demonstrated that internal CSR activities (i.e., those in the economic and ethical domains) enhance WTB more than external CSR activities (i.e., those in the legal and philanthropic domains). Importantly, however, this effect has resulted to be significant only for consumers who buy luxury items for internalized motivations, thus for expressing their individual style and tastes, and not for externalized motivations, thus for socially positioning themselves. More specifically, results have shown that for consumers who buy luxury goods mainly for externalized motivations (status seeking and ostentation), the relationship between CSR activities and WTB was not significant, while it was significant for consumers who buy luxury goods mainly for internalized motivations.

Overall, this research helps to advance current knowledge about luxury and CSR in some important ways. First and foremost, against the backdrop of a great number of studies documenting the incompatibility between luxury and sustainability, our study is one of the first attempts to empirically test if and how luxury firms' CSR initiatives might receive consumers' approval. Second, our research offers a rethinking of the four dimensions of the Carroll's CSR model, mainly by connecting said dimensions with luxury goods' perceptions (i.e., the distinction between external and internal dimensions). This model may be particularly useful for future studies of luxury goods. Using this distinction, we were able to show that consumers with internalized motivation to luxury consumption are more likely to favor initiatives belonging to internal rather than external CSR dimensions, while such a preference does not manifest for consumers with externalized motivations to luxury consumption. Overall, therefore, these findings demonstrate that consumers might not all have similar reaction to CSR initiatives undertaken by luxury brands.

From a managerial perspective, our results suggest that, when implementing their CSR actions, luxury companies should consider them in light of their visibility to consumers. In particular, managers should be aware that customers who mainly buy luxury products for their inherent quality (rather than for what they symbolize to others) tend to respond favorably to internal CSR activities (i.e., those related to the economic or ethical dimensions). More specifically, luxury companies that have a customer base mainly made up of consumers driven by a need to abide by their style and taste when buying luxury items should focus on "discrete" CSR initiatives that are not particularly visible to others. Therefore, our findings are particularly useful to luxury companies that want to develop their sustainability in mature markets, which tend to prioritize internalized luxury consumption compared to emerging markets (Nancy and Aaron 1998). More generally, our research suggests luxury companies to segment consumers based on their luxury consumption motivations and to engage in those CSR initiatives that are likely to encounter the favor of the most prevalent segment of their customer base.

Despite the merits of our investigation, further studies are needed to identify the underlying mechanisms and boundary conditions for the relationship between internal CSR activities and consumers' reactions. Additional studies might focus analyzing post-purchase consumer behavior, including the effect of CSR activities on customer engagement. Moreover, researchers could focus on external CSR activities and their potential role in influencing customers' engagement with luxury brands. More specifically, future work could focus on identifying and exploring conditions under which external CSR activities might be beneficial for consumers. Finally, future studies might investigate other factors related to consumers or even to the type of luxury product analyzed that could moderate the effect of CSR initiatives on consumers' responses.

# Appendix A: Experimental Study Text

*Incipit.* Thank you for your participation! In this survey we are interested in studying how people feel in certain situations. All your responses will remain anonymous and confidential. Please read the instructions on the screen carefully, as you will be asked to do different things throughout the survey. We would like to emphasize that there are no right or wrong answers, as we are simply interested in your opinions.

When you are ready to begin, please click> in the bottom right to proceed.

*Q1.* Please indicate on a scale from 1 to 7 why you would buy a luxury product:

(1) Mainly for an "internal" motivation, related to my individual style and my taste;

(7) Mainly for an "external" motivation, related to my economic and social status

*Experimental Scenario Internal CSR.* SHINE is a luxury brand that has recently developed the following initiatives, an ethical and an economic one.

- Concerning the ethical initiative, the company offers to its employees a series of working benefits for them and their children.
- Concerning the economic initiative, the company has bought a software able to optimize the manufacturing process thus reducing internal production costs.

*Experimental Scenario External CSR.* SHINE is a luxury brand that has recently developed the following initiatives, a philanthropic and a legal one.

- Concerning the philanthropic initiative, the company has donated money to help the building of a new pediatric hospital.
- Concerning the legal initiative, the company has acquired a certification attesting the traceability of its raw materials, thus having now the opportunity to put this certification on the label of its products.

*WTB.* Now please indicate, on a scale from 1 to 7 (1 = Strongly disagree; 7 = Strongly agree), your level of agreement with the following statements regarding your intention to buy a jacket from the brand previously mentioned, after knowing the initiatives this brand has developed:

*WTB_1.* I would purchase the jacket from this brand. (1 = Strongly disagree; 7 = Strongly agree)

   *WTB_2.* I would consider buying a jacket from this brand. (1 = Strongly disagree; 7 = Strongly agree)

   *WTB_3.* The probability that I would consider buying a jacket from this brand is high. (1 = Strongly disagree; 7 = Strongly agree)

*Man_Check.* On a scale from 1 to 7 (where 1 = "Not at all" and 7 = "Very much"), to what extent do you perceive as visible and observable from outside the company (that is from people who are not part of the firm, such as consumers) the initiatives developed by the brand and previously described?

(1 = Not at all; 7 = Very much)

*Incipit.* Now we are interested in learning more about you. Please note that all the answers you provide will be kept anonymous.

*Age* What is your age?

*Gender* What is your gender?

*Debriefing.* This is the end of the study. Thank you for your participation!

The objective of this research was to identify how the presence of activities related to corporate social responsibility influences consumers' willingness to buy luxury products.

If you have any comments regarding this research, please share your thoughts with us below.

# Appendix B: Experimental Study Results

In order to check our manipulation we conducted an analysis of variance (one-way ANOVA) on the manipulation check score, in which the type of CSR initiative (0 = internal, 1 = external) served as the independent variable. Results indicated that the manipulation was successful at 10% of significance level, meaning that on average participants recognized internal CSR initiatives scenario as less visible as those in the external CSR initiatives scenario ($M_{internalCSR} = 4.31$, $SD = 1.56$; $M_{externalCSR} = 4.74$, $SD = 1.52$; $F(1,157) = 3.00$; $p = .08$).

Then we proceeded to test our hypothesis. We dummy-coded the CSR variable (0 = internal CSR condition, 1 = external CSR condition) and employed Model 1 in the PROCESS SPSS Macro (Hayes 2017). The measure of luxury consumption orientation served as the moderator in the relationship between the type of CSR initiative and WTB. The results showed a significant and negative main effect of type of CSR initiative on WTB ($b = -.92$; $p = .03$), which suggests that internal CSR initiatives (coded as 0) increase WTB compared to external CSR activities (coded as 1). On the contrary, the effect of luxury consumption orientation on WTB was not significant ($b = .001$; $p = .99$).

Of greater importance, the interaction between type of CSR initiative and consumers' luxury consumption orientation was significant ($b = .27$; $p = .03$).

In order to more closely inspect the effect of the CSR initiative type on WTB at different levels of the moderator, we employed the Johnson-Neyman "floodlight" approach (Spiller et al. 2013) aiming at deeper exploring the moderation relationship. The results revealed a significantly negative effect of type of CSR initiative on WTB for luxury consumption orientation values lower than 1.30 ($b_{JN} = -.58$, SE = .29, 95% confidence interval: $-1.15$; $-.001$, see Fig. 6.2), but not higher values. This suggests that internal CSR initiatives significantly affect WTB, but only for consumers with low luxury consumption dispositional motivation, namely those with an internalized motivation.

# References

Achabou, Mohamed Akli, and Sihem Dekhili. 2013. "Luxury and Sustainable Development: Is There a Match?" *Journal of Business Research* 66 (10): 1896–1903.

Amatulli, Cesare, Matteo De Angelis, Michele Costabile, and Gianluigi Guido. 2017. *Sustainable Luxury Brands: Evidence from Research and Implications for Managers.* Palgrave Advances in Luxury Series. London: Palgrave Macmillans.

Amatulli, Cesare, and Gianluigi Guido. 2012. "Externalised vs. Internalised Consumption of Luxury Goods: Propositions and Implications for Luxury Retail Marketing." *The International Review of Retail, Distribution and Consumer Research* 22 (2): 189–207.

Amatulli, Cesare, Gianluigi Guido, and Rajan Nataraajan. 2015. "Luxury Purchasing Among Older Consumers: Exploring Inferences About Cognitive Age, Status, and Style Motivations." *Journal of Business Research* 68 (9): 1945–1952.

Atwal, Glyn, and Alistair Williams. 2009. "Luxury Brand Marketing— The Experience Is Everything!" *Journal of Brand Management* 16 (5–6): 338–346.

Bansal, Pratima, and Kendall Roth. 2000. "Why Companies Go Green: A Model of Ecological Responsiveness." *Academy of Management Journal* 43 (4): 717–736.

Bhattacharya, Chitra Bhanu, and Sankar Sen. 2004. "Doing Better at Doing Good: When, Why, and How Consumers Respond to Corporate Social Initiatives." *California Management Review* 47 (1): 9–24.

Carroll, Archie B. 1991. "The Pyramid of Corporate Social Responsibility: Toward the Moral Management of Organizational Stakeholders." *Business Horizons* 34 (4): 39–48.

Carroll, Archie B. 1979. "A Three-Dimensional Conceptual Model of Corporate Performance." *Academy of Management Review* 4 (4): 497–505.

Cook, Thomas D., Donald Thomas Campbell, and William Shadish. 2002. *Experimental and Quasi-Experimental Designs for Generalized Causal Inference.* Boston: Houghton Mifflin.

Cristini, Hélène, Hannele Kauppinen-Raisanen, Mireille Barthod-Prothade, and Arch Woodside. 2017. "Toward a General Theory of Luxury: Advancing from Workbench Definitions and Theoretical Transformations." *Journal of Business Research* 70: 101–107.

Davies, Iain A., Zoe Lee, and Ine Ahonkhai. 2012. "Do Consumers Care About Ethical-Luxury?" *Journal of Business Ethics* 106 (1): 37–51.

De Angelis, Matteo, Feray Adıgüzel, and Cesare Amatulli. 2017. "The Role of Design Similarity in Consumers' Evaluation of New Green Products: An Investigation of Luxury Fashion Brands." *Journal of Cleaner Production* 141: 1515–1527.

De Barnier, Virginie, Sandrine Falcy, and Pierre Valette-Florence. 2012. "Do Consumers Perceive Three Levels of Luxury? A Comparison of Accessible, Intermediate and Inaccessible Luxury Brands." *Journal of Brand Management* 19 (7): 623–636.

Delmas, Magali A., and Vanessa Cuerel Burbano. 2011. "The Drivers of Greenwashing." *California Management Review* 54 (1): 64–87.

Dodds, William B., Kent B. Monroe, and Dhruv Grewal. 1991. "Effects of Price, Brand and Store Information on Buyers' Product Evaluations." *Journal of Marketing Research* 28 (8): 307–319.

Fionda, Antoinette M., and Christopher M. Moore. 2009. "The Anatomy of the Luxury Fashion Brand." *Journal of Brand Management* 16 (5–6): 347–363.

Fletcher, Kate. 2013. *Sustainable Fashion and Textiles: Design Journeys.* Abingdon: Routledge.

Gershoff, Andrew D., and Judy K. Frels. 2015. "What Makes It Green? The Role of Centrality of Green Attributes in Evaluations of the Greenness of Products." *Journal of Marketing* 79 (1): 97–110.

Griskevicius, Vladas, Joshua M. Tybur, and Bram Van den Bergh. 2010. "Going Green to Be Seen: Status, Reputation, and Conspicuous Conservation." *Journal of Personality and Social Psychology* 98 (3): 392.

Han, Young Jee, Joseph C. Nunes, and Xavier Drèze. 2010. "Signaling Status with Luxury Goods: The Role of Brand Prominence." *Journal of Marketing* 74 (4): 15–30.

Hayes, Andrew F. 2017. *Introduction to Mediation, Moderation, and Conditional Process Analysis: A Regression-Based Approach.* New York: Guilford Publications.

Janssen, Catherine, Joelle Vanhamme, Adam Lindgreen, and Cécile Lefebvre. 2014. "The Catch-22 of Responsible Luxury: Effects of Luxury Product Characteristics on Consumers' Perception of Fit with Corporate Social Responsibility." *Journal of Business Ethics* 119 (1): 45–57.

Kapferer, Jean-Noël. 2010. "All That Glitters Is Not Green: The Challenge of Sustainable Luxury." *European Business Review* 2: 40–45.

Langenwalter, Gary A. 2009. "Planet First." *Industrial Management* 51 (4): 10–12.

Lochard, Cécile, and Alexandre Murat. 2011. "*La nouvelle alliance, Luxe et Développement durable.*" Éditions d'Organisation Groupe Eyrolles, Paris, 217p.

Luchs, Michael G., Rebecca W. Naylor, Julie R. Irwin, and Rajagopal Raghunathan. 2010. "The Sustainability Liability: Potential Negative Effects of Ethicality on Product Preference." *Journal of Marketing* 74 (5): 18–31.

Luo, Xueming, and Shuili Du. 2015. "Exploring the Relationship Between Corporate Social Responsibility and Firm Innovation." *Marketing Letters* 26 (4): 703–714.

Maignan, Isabelle, and Odies Collins Ferrell. 2001. "Corporate Citizenship as a Marketing Instrument-Concepts, Evidence and Research Directions." *European Journal of Marketing* 35 (3/4): 457–484.

Nancy, Y. Wong, and C. Ahuvia Aaron. 1998. "Personal Taste and Family Face: Luxury Consumption in Confucian and Western Societies." *Psychology & Marketing* 15 (5): 423–441.

Nueno, Jose Luis, and John A. Quelch. 1998. "The Mass Marketing of Luxury." *Business Horizons* 41 (6): 61–68.

Pino, Giovanni, Cesare Amatulli, Matteo De Angelis, and Alessandro M. Peluso. 2016. "The Influence of Corporate Social Responsibility on Consumers' Attitudes and Intentions Toward Genetically Modified Foods: Evidence from Italy." *Journal of Cleaner Production* 112: 2861–2869.

Spiller, Stephen A., Gavan J. Fitzsimons, John G. Lynch, JR., and Gary H. McClelland. 2013. "Spotlights, Floodlights, and the Magic Number Zero: Simple Effects Tests in Moderated Regression." *Journal of Marketing Research* 50 (2): 277–288.

# 7

# Luxury Perfume Brands and Millenial Consumers

Aileen Stewart and Lindsey Carey

## Introduction

Perfume, scent or fragrance, all terms that consumers associate with a desirable, chic, fashionable and exciting product that stimulates the senses and provides an evocative and special choice. Chemistry, art or illusion perfume generates strong consumer responses, with floral, oriental, wood or fresh scents all being created by the industry (Carey et al. 2016).

Perfume is regarded as a personal product with consumers forming significant attachments to their chosen fragrance, "*When a woman buys perfume, she buys much, much more than simply fragrant fluids. The perfume image, its promises, its scent, its name and package, the company*

A. Stewart (✉) · L. Carey
Glasgow School for Business and Society, Caledonian University,
Glasgow, UK
e-mail: a.stewart3@gcu.ac.uk

L. Carey
e-mail: l.carey@gcu.ac.uk

© The Author(s) 2020
I. Cantista and T. Sádaba (Eds.), *Understanding Luxury Fashion*,
Palgrave Advances in Luxury, https://doi.org/10.1007/978-3-030-25654-8_7

*that makes it, the stores that sell it – all become a part of the total perfume product"* (Cant et al. 2009, p. 192). Brand attachment therefore is of importance for any branded perfume brand.

Chanel No. 5 is over 90 years old and yet it is still the no1 fragrance brand although there are over 300 new fragrances being launched every year (Khanom 2016). However, the fine fragrance or luxury segment of the market experienced a decline of sales in the last year, as consumers seek lower prices, although the usage of perfume remains high. Luxury perfume brands are experiencing a more challenging environment and are seeking to expand more lucrative consumer segments (Libby 2016). Millennials are recognised as the next dominant market segment offering marketers new opportunities (Bowen and Chen McCain 2015). Additionally, symbolism is at the forefront of luxury fragrance research as perfume is, by its very nature, an accessible symbol of the luxury brand it represents (Aaker 1997; Rambourg 2014).

Finally, loyalty to a specific perfume has also traditionally been a characteristic of this market (Albert and Merunka 2013) However, while the perfume industry is at the apex of new sales and marketing approaches, new consumers, new communication formats and new entrants to the marketplace, is placing 'change' at the forefront of the industry (Euromonitor 2017). At the frontline of these changes to consumer perfume sales, are fragrance consultants. With direct contact to the consumer, these 'brand ambassadors' have invaluable information on consumer attitudes towards fragrance purchases.

This research employs qualitative methods of data collection and analysis that are non-quantitative and seeks to explore social relations, with generated data describing reality as experienced by the respondents. As such, the study utilises interviews with ten specialist sales consultants and four industry professionals who are experts in fragrance business strategy as well as industry data and reports to investigate how the luxury perfume industry is responding to the new challenge, through Consumer Brand Relationship (CBR), brand loyalty and communication strategies, of connecting to the lucrative Millennial segment.

Results highlight a number of key concepts; customer segmentation within the fragrance industry, behavioural differences between age groups in-store, brand familiarity, Paradox: promoting customer loyalty within the fragrance market, Importance to Millennials, changing market, lifestyle tribes, emotional attachment, millennial consumer self-concept, fragrance markets focus on younger consumers, motivations for purchasing fragrance and influence of peers in buying decisions. Conclusions form these identified that Millennial consumers buying habits are different from other generations and that brand loyalty factors are changing from traditional product driven markets to 'lifestyle tribes' where emotion and hedonic factors are more important.

## Perfume Trends and the Luxury Perfume Market

The history of fragrance is well documented with evidence of essential oils being use as far back as 2000 BC. However, it wasn't until the 14th century where Queen Elizabeth of Hungary commanded the development of a personal scent. This saw the creation of scented oils with an alcohol solution and was ultimate known throughout Europe as 'Hungary Water' (Perfume Society 2016). The early twentieth Century saw fashion designers recognised the connection between fashion, fragrance and the brand. Charles Fredrick Worth, the 'father' of haute couture was the first Fashion House to recognise the importance of its luxury brand name with his protégé Paul Poiret who, on establishing his own Fashion House, created and launched the first fashion branded perfume, Rosine in 1911 (Pouy 2007). Today, the luxury fashion brands use this brand extension format as a way to expand their 'core' business and to generate significant profit (Albrecht et al. 2013). Consequently, consumers are now familiar with the large luxury Fashion House's fragrances, with many creating iconic brand statuses of their own e.g. Chanel No. 5 and Miss Dior (Drylie-Carey and Stewart 2018).

As a group, Western Europeans are recognised as the largest and most valuable consumer group for the fragrance industry. However, currently this market is an ageing population with many consumers described as 'habitual consumers who repeat purchase' (Amatulli et al. 2016). As a result, fragrance brands are being challenged to discover and develop new and interesting ways to connect with younger consumers, who they hope will experiment and purchase multiple fragrances for different occasions (Mintel 2016; Khanom 2016). The past decade has seen a plethora of celebrity branded fragrances e.g. Beyoncé and Rihanna being created to stimulate and connect to new consumer groups. However, this market has stalled with fragrances in this market generating a falling market share (Euromonitor 2017). It appears consumers no longer wish to emulate or connect to their celebrity idols through their choice of fragrance. The exception to this however, is that of younger consumers who, while they too don't want to emulate their celebrity favourites, want to be part of a 'lifestyle tribe' that is seen to build and develop a connection. Particularly successful celebrities and brands of this nature have been Zoella the digital influencer, pop princess and social media star Ariana Grande and retailer brands such as, Hollister and Victoria's Secret (Euromonitor 2017; Euromonitor International 2012).

However, the fragrance market relies on premium or luxury branded products being sold to those consumers with the highest disposable incomes (Amatulli et al. 2016; Euromonitor International 2012). Although, this does not preclude mass market consumers, with many buying, what are termed, 'entry level' luxury branded products with fragrance being seen as a comparatively inexpensive way to own designer goods (Mintel 2016). As Euromonitor indicates, "*A significant proportion of respondents claimed to regularly buy themselves small treats on the basis that they 'deserve them.' This reflects the well-documented 'lipstick effect' theory that women often forego extravagant purchases in times of recession, such as cars, holidays and kitchens, and instead splurge on small luxuries to boost their morale, such as cosmetics or fragrances*" (Euromonitor International 2012).

Luxury branded fragrances form part of this 'small treats' market and allow consumers the hedonistic experience of luxury branded products without the expense of higher priced items. This consumer spending practice was recognised during the most recent global recession, which began at the end of 2007 and ended in 2009. This is now ten years ago however, economic conditions have been slow to recover, with businesses now recognising this practice as a means of monitoring consumer spending (Euromonitor 2017; Butler 2017). Most recently, the boss of John Lewis, recognised the return of the' lipstick effect' *"with a rise in sales of beauty products heralding a consumer squeeze"* (Butler 2017).

A review of the fragrance industry highlights, after a small decline in spending during 2015 and 2016, the industry is once again on the rise, albeit modestly with a +0.7% increase, although luxury branded perfume has experienced a further small decline (Euromonitor 2017; Khanom 2017). This indicates a change in attitude i.e. Richmond identified that the *"luxury cachet, aspirational appeal and emotional connection with consumers have all ensured that fragrances remain a dressing table staple"* (Butler 2017; Richmond 2012). However, while there may be a small decline in luxury perfumes being evidenced, this hasn't changed the importance of fragrance with 85% of UK female consumers using perfume as part of their daily grooming routine and being responsible for over two-thirds of the total sales of fragrances in the UK. With approximately 300 new fragrances being launched on a yearly basis, a degree of saturation can be seen (Khanom 2016; Butler 2017). However, a change in the marketplace can be evidenced, with consumers no longer relying on luxury brands or celebrity endorsed products but are instead engaging with 'High Street' retail branded fragrances e.g. Babe Power by Missguided, recognised as the fastest selling scent by the Fragrance Shop, one of the UK's leading fragrance retailers and H&M's '*Conscious*' Perfume oil, also being received positively (Khanom 2017). This change is significant, as on closer examination the demographic that are making this change are seen to be young consumers aged 16–24s (Khanom 2017). This also explains the interest by the luxury brands to engage with this audience e.g. in 2016 Chanel launched Chanel No. 5 L'Eau, aimed at younger consumers and featured Lily-Rose Depp in its promotional campaign (Khanom 2017).

As such, all sectors of the market are seeking to target younger consumers who are forming their opinions, making multiple purchases, creating personal scent, and have a higher disposable income as they are yet to take on the responsibilities of home buying or providing for dependents. Hence, the Millennials market, in particular females, is of significant interest to brands, marketers and academics alike.

# The Millennial Consumer and Perfume Consumption

The segmentation of consumers has generated a large variety of research with demographics, geographic, psychographics, Attitudes, Interests, and Opinions (AIO's) and behaviours all being used as a way of dividing and targeting specific consumers to fulfil their needs and wants in a more targeted manner. The most recognised method by both academia and business is to group consumers by generation in terms of past, present and future buying behaviour (Gardiner et al. 2014). Groupings of Baby Boomers, Generation X, Generation Y and Generation Z are now recognised as popular marketing terms.

There are many and often conflicting views of the age span each of these cohorts comprises. However, generally Baby Boomers are consumers born after the Second World War until the early 1960's (54–62 approx.), Generation X, those born mid 1960's until the late 1970's (38–53 approx.), Generation Y born between 1980 until 2000 (17–37 approx.) and finally Generation Z born from 2000 onwards (16 and under) (Carpentera et al. 2012). Each of these segments is of significant interest to marketers and have formed many academic studies, particularly Baby Boomers and Generation X as these segments have grown up and have experienced different life stages.

Generation Y, or 'Millennials' are the next generational segment to reach adulthood and to connect with brands and marketing techniques. This generation is also the first to have grown up with or experienced technology and interconnectivity as the norm (Carpentera et al. 2012). As such, they connect and experience marketing communication in a completely different manner than the generations that have gone before them.

Millennials have been labelled with contrasting characteristics; self-centred, disloyal and lazy on one hand and tech-savvy, environmentally conscious, entrepreneurial and innovative on the other and who, as a group, spend more than previous generations (Greenberg 2011; Lodes and Buff 2009). However, studies suggest that characteristics contrast due to the group still developing and maturing (Howe and

Strauss 2000; Foscht et al. 2009; Manpower 2016). Hence, classifying Millennials as the one homogenous group is difficult, posing new challenges for marketers and brands who want to connect with them.

Nevertheless, consensus can be found in their love of technology, with their multi-tasking environment of smart phones, laptops, tablets and gaming consoles all playing a significant part in their lives, often simultaneously. As a result, Millennials are comfortable communicating via e-formats, social media, creating and posting information online, with the demand for information 'right here right now' expected (Butler 2017; Barghi et al. 2010).

# Consumer Brand Relationship (CBR) and Brand Loyalty

Rissanen and Luoma-Aho identified just how difficult it is to engage and retail to Millennial consumers, when they recognised that *"self-branders were motivated by identification with an organisation, brand or product, therefore representing a fertile base for long-lasting relationships, benefiters were solely after material gain and not interested in building a relationship. In fact, benefiters would often disengage as soon as their material needs were met"* (Khanom 2017; Rissanen and Luoma-Aho 2016). While, this short attention span can be seen negatively, millennial consumers are good communicators, using social media to spread word rapidly, allowing brands to connect in a faster more direct manner (Richmond 2012; Phau and Cheong 2009).

Hence, for marketers and branders engaging and retaining Millennial consumers is complex and a contrast to engaging with more brand loyal older generations (Young and Hinesly 2015). Millennial consumers connect and utlise different brands/products to create their own look rather than a homogenised version that brand loyal consumers, who attach the one or few brands do e.g. seeking a variety of perfumes to suit different occasions (Greenberg 2011; Giovannini et al. 2015). Therefore, one of the most important elements brands endeavouring to connect with this consumer group can do, is to concentrate on building meaningful relationships that create a 'tribal' community (Carpentera et al. 2012; Rissanen and Luoma-Aho 2016).

Perfume brands currently deploying this tactic are 'Zoella' and 'Scentbird', an online luxury perfume brand subscription service. Beyond the context of branding, Bowlby indicates, when humans form connections, attachment and love, loyalty ensues (Bowlby 1979). Hence, if brands can create and shape relationships with consumers, a pattern of loyalty develops.

As an area of academic study, Consumer Brand Relationship (CBR) first emanated as an area of research from Fournier's (1998) seminal paper (Greenberg 2011; Fournier 1998). The research identified the concept of brands building relationships with consumers. Additionally, it was found that through repeat connections, between brands and consumers, the consumers found a channel for self-identity. Hence, CBR goes beyond consumers selecting particular products/brands but denotes that consumers are building a 'lifestyle' by the product/brand choices they make and the connections they form with them. Ralph Lauren is the classic 'lifestyle' fashion brand however, new product targeted perfume brands such as, Escentric Molecules are offering younger consumers different options.

It is these connections that builds the equity of a brand, with several authors Aaker (1997), Jevons et al. (2005) and (Keller et al. 2011) recognising strong CBR with increased brand equity i.e. the added value, be it financial or emotionally, the use of a brand makes to a product/service. As such, the importance of relationship building between brand and consumer and the value this brings to both parties is evident. More recently, Fetscherin and Heinrich (2015) presented a meta-analysis of research, spanning many versions of the CBR concept, from brand attachment, brand passion, brand love and brand romance amongst others in so doing, establishing the depth, breadth and importance of the subject area for all market sectors.

Additionally, studies by Nobre and Brito (2010) and Neudecker et al. (2013) presented conceptual models and theories indicating a multi-faceted nature to CBR with many different factors; consumer personality, brand personality and partner quality, all identified as dimensions of CBR (Carpentera et al. 2012). Expanding this further, Neudecker et al. (2013) suggests the linear approach, recognised within the traditional consumer purchase decision-making process, is altered due to this multi-dimensional nature of CBR (Lodes and Buff 2009). Therefore, a range of both rational and emotions needs are experienced when considering CBR with brands needing to consider all factors when establishing CBR strategies.

Granot et al. reiterates this connection between consumer decision making and CBR. Their study revealed that female consumers, use the brand as a fundamental element of the retail decision-making process, with three key themes emerging; emotional (brand), service (retail environment) and experiential (shopping and consumption), all factors associated with fragrance purchases (Howe and Strauss 2000; Granot et al. 2010). However, this study relies on consumers displaying loyalty to their chosen brands, recognising it is difficult to form a relationship where only one party is committed (Granot et al. 2010).

Earlier in the chapter one of the characteristics associated to Millennial consumers was disloyalty, as a result the development of CBR with millennials must be viewed differently, creating a different challenge for marketers. Nevertheless, this doesn't mean Millennials are a 'lost cause' with Hwang and Kandampully (2012) finding that brand loyalty improves for this group through emotional aspects such as, self-concept connection, emotional attachment, and brand love. In these terms, Millennials form brand attachments through sensory or hedonic factors rather than traditional cognitive factors such as brand trust or source credibility and with luxury brands being viewed differently too, it offers significant insight to this group of consumers.

Hwang and Kandampully (2012) also found *"that younger consumers form brand love as they perceive that a brand expresses an important part of their selves"*. With many perfume brands using 'love' e.g. Chanel, Allure and Dior, J'Adore, as a communication strategy, perfume brands are perfectly positioned to connect to Millennial consumers. Hence, the formation of brand attachment and loyalty goes far beyond the product for Millennials, encompassing service, be it in store or online, where they seek friendly staff who connect to their emotional needs (Foscht et al. 2009; Beauchamp and Barnes 2015).

## Brand Attachment

Brand attachment is defined as *"having positive feelings of affection, passion, and connection for a brand"* (Thomson et al. 2005, p. 80). Brand loyalty, on the other hand is viewed as consumers preferring branded products or services over other brands and demonstrating repeat purchases of these (Foscht et al. 2009; Zhang and Feng 2017). As such, brand loyalty and brand attachment can both be associated to psychological constructs and with Qing et al. (2015) identifying that deeper brand attachment correlates directly to stronger brand loyalty and an increase in purchase price, it is easy to ascertain how brand attachment and brand loyalty encourages consumers to purchase premium priced luxury brands.

Several authors, Park et al. (2010) and Zhang and Feng (2017), have also suggested that brand attitude also plays a role, but that significant difference exist between attitude and attachment i.e. attitude relies on purely logical constructs while attachment is both logical and emotional. As such, the use of brand attitude can be regarded as a poor indicator of consumer behaviour towards brands and when testing 'true' brand behaviour brand attachment should be considered as the way to predict brand loyalty and purchase intention (Park et al. 2010).

Thomson et al. (2005), Holt (2004, 2005) support this by indicating that strong brand loyalty is directly linked to consumers who experience emotional attachment to a brand. Hence, if brands can develop and connect to consumers on an emotional level strong and lasting bonds develop. Bowlby was the first to recognised that emotional attachment determines how a consumer interacts with and forms a relationship with a brand (Bowlby 1979). With Zhang and Feng (2017) concluding, emotional satisfaction can be viewed as a psychological reaction on the part of the consumer when their 'needs' are met or more likely surpassed. Hence, emotional connections encourage consumers to purchase, as a result brands endeavour to create emotional triggers to develop consumer attachment and brand 'love'.

Consequently, the creation and development of brand 'love' has become an important marketing tool for all brands. Researchers too, consider it to be an area of interest, Albert and Merunka (2013), have identified that a consumer's belief of brand reliability links directly to the development of brand love (Foscht 2009).

Trust is also recognised as a significant aspect of brand relationship and is often seen to connect to brand love. Trust has been identified as having three dimensions (honesty, reliability and altruism), which are recognised to heighten feelings towards a brand. However, the third factor, 'altruism' "recognised as the brands willingness to take consumers' interests into account" appears not to generate an emotional connection of love for the brand (Albert and Merunka 2013; Manpower 2016).

However, conceptual differences between love and trust have been proven: *"love is a feeling the consumer develops toward the brand, whereas trust is rooted in the consumer's expectations about the brand's honesty, altruism and reliability"* (Albert and Merunka 2013, p. 263; Manpower 2016). As such, brands should endeavour to generate feelings of love in conjunction aspects of reliability and honesty to create strong CBR.

Personification of the brand i.e. the brand is associated with human attributes is the most commonly used technique, whereby consumers can associate with non-physical human characteristics created for the brand Nobre and Brito (2010) and Keller et al. (2011). For consumers, brand personality allows them to form associations, impressions and preferences for brands such as Chanel; evoking glamour, style and upper social class. However, Malär et al. (2011) identifies that emotional brand attachment increases for consumers when self-congruence with a brand occurs.

Furthermore, brands that connected with the 'actual' self-generated higher levels of emotional attachment, with an even more pronounced increase when the consumer was involved with the product or displayed public self-consciousness. While those connecting with ideal self-congruence generated lower attachment, suggesting perfume brands should connect with consumers actual selves rather than ideal selves. This is encouraging as, identified earlier, Millennials or *"self-branders were motivated by identification with an organisation, brand or product"* and as such identifies how brands can better connect with this generation (Rissanen and Luoma-Aho 2016, p. 504).

Orth et al. (2010) discovered that brand attachment is influenced by how a consumer interacts with a brand's personality and how, considering Aaker's brand personalities, this can be a conduit through which consumers demonstrate self-expression (Aaker 1997; Rissanen and Luoma-Aho 2016). Time is also associated with consumers forming strong emotional attachments. Thomson et al. (2005) identified that consumers form strong bonds with only a few perfumes over their life time, despite the large number of scents experienced. However, Millennials are at the beginning of their life's journey hence, perfume brands should seek to connect to this group as early and form memorable meaningful relationships as soon as possible.

Schindler and Holbrook reinforces this concept by suggesting that brands and products fixed during sensitive or pivotal periods of life, are recalled, or continued as brand preferences throughout adulthood, indicating the importance of connecting to consumers at an age when they are forming their own opinions and developing their own self-identity (Matthews 2009). As Matthew's (2009) fragrance industry report highlights, relationships with fragrances are lifelong, with fragrance brand switches considered a major change rather than a parenthesis.

Thus, the aim of the study sought to investigate how the perfume and in particular, luxury perfume industry, is responding to this new challenge and communicating with the lucrative Millennial segment, through brand relationship, attachment and loyalty.

## Methodology

A qualitative method employs methods of data collection and analysis that are non-quantitative and seeks to explore social relations. Generated data describes reality as experienced by the respondents of the study (Adams et al. 2014). This study sought the views of 'brand ambassadors', who have invaluable information on consumer attitudes, loyalty and brand relationship towards fragrance purchases, to generate the 'reality' of the perfume industry.

Ten specialist sales consultants and four industry professionals, who are experts in the perfume industry, as well as fragrance business strategy, were interviewed to capture meaningful and relevant data. Face to face (in person) semi-structured interviews were deployed with the specialist sales consultants. While, due to location and time challenges, a semi-structured telephone interview was used for the industry professionals. Both methods allowed specific topics to be addressed while affording the freedom to explore areas of interest or uniqueness within each interview.

All participants were selected through convenience sampling through contacts with the sales consultants working in a number of major UK based perfume retailers e.g. The Fragrance House, The Perfume Shop, House of Frasers, Boots and Passion for Perfume. The industry specialists too, came for a variety of companies all holding senior positions e.g. Head of Corporate Communications, Managing Director, Regional Manager, and Marketing Manager. Grounded theory analysis (as described by Easterby-Smith et al. (2015)) was carried out using the prescribed seven-stage process on the transcripts with four themes emerging.

The themes reflected themes that emerged from the interviews by all the participants and addressed topics associated with the research such as, segmentation differences, brand attachment, loyalty and attachment to fragrance. Key concepts were also established within the themes to provide greater depth and meaning.

# Findings and Conclusion

The purpose of the research was to investigate the views of perfume industry experts on the changing format of the industry in relation to Millennial consumers and the changing formats this brings in relation to CBR, brand attachment and loyalty. The key themes which emerged from this research are presented in the Table (7.1).

# Predictor Factors and Facilitators of Fragrance Purchasing for Millennial Women

The first key concept to emerge from the research was the recognition of customer segmentation within the fragrance industry. Gardiner, Grace and King highlight generational segmentation as a recognised format

Table 7.1 Thematic representation of data

| Themes | Key concepts |
|---|---|
| Predictor factors and facilitators of fragrance purchasing for Millennial women | Customer segmentation within the fragrance industry |
| | Behavioural differences between age groups in-store |
| | Brand familiarity |
| | Paradox: promoting customer loyalty within the fragrance market |
| Celebrity Branding | Importance to Millennials |
| | Changing market |
| | Lifestyle tribes |
| Importance of attachment towards fragrance brands | Emotional attachment |
| | Millennial consumer self-concept |
| Factors influencing consumer innovativeness | Fragrance markets focus on younger consumers |
| | Motivations for purchasing fragrance |
| | Influence of peers in buying decisions |

by business to group consumers. The perfume consultants and industry professionals underline that age was an important factor when targeting and selling to consumers (Gardiner et al. 2014; Barghi et al. 2010).

> Our customers can be categorised into sections, we have our 'average' older consumer who is above 60 years of age. She often has grown up children and grandchildren and likes to get a bargain and enjoys her fragrance. The next category would be 45-55 years old who is slightly more affluent enjoys designer brands such as Calvin Klein, especially if she can get it at a lower price. Finally, we have younger consumers who are looking for the newest trendy fragrance. (Industry Specialist)

Hence, grouping consumers by age is a key business practice in the fragrance industry. However, caution should be observed when categorising consumers.

> It depends on the person, you can't generalise it into an age group, I don't think. (Sales Consultant)
> It doesn't always depend on the age group, we have a wide selection of fragrances so we have some fragrances that any age group might come in and buy. (Sales Consultant)

Furthermore, while generational segmentation is a universal method of identifying and targeting consumers, personal attitudes, interests' and opinions should also be considered. Distinct behavioural differences between age groups in-store were also observed.

*More mature consumers prefer a heavier fragrance while younger ones generally go for a sweet or fruity fragrance.* (Sales Consultant)

However, while the scent itself offers differentiation between generations marketing also plays a significant role. Highlighting Bowen and Chen McCain who suggest Millennials are being recognised as the next dominant market segment offering marketers new opportunities (Bowen et al. 2015; Rissanen and Luoma-Aho 2016).

*Younger people can also go for a specific type of fragrance, it can depend on how it is marketed. A younger customer may go for a younger fresher fragrance because it is from a pop star or model.* (Sales Consultant)

Scent and marketing were not the only differentiators with individual customer service being important to mature consumers too. Millennials however, did not value this factor aligning with the 'disloyal' personality trait recognised by Greenberg and Lodes and Buff who, in part, found Millennials to be self-centred, disloyal and lazy (Greenberg 2011; Lodes and Buff 2009; Rissanen and Luoma-Aho 2016).

*Mature consumers like one to one customer service … years, whereas young customers will chop and change between brands and don't care where they shop.* (Industry Specialist)

However, while disloyalty was observed as a factor for many millennial consumers personal connection to scent was observed, which may be explained by Howe and Strauss, Foscht et al. and Manpower who suggest that characteristics of this generation are still developing and maturing (Howe and Strauss 2000; Foscht et al. 2009; Manpower 2016).

*It could be that a twenty-year-old might come in and ask for Nina Ricci because her Grandmother wore it and she absolutely adores the fragrance because of this. It's down to individual personality.* (Sales Consultant)

The industry professionals did recognise millennial consumer individuality however, the over-riding belief was that this was not common-place.

*You are a lot more subject to change when your younger I think. Young consumers are yet to find their signature scent.* (Industry Specialist)

Consequently, what could be regarded as disloyalty is more likely to be consumers experimenting as a way of finding their own preferences.

*All age groups have some sort or attachment with a fragrance that they have had in the past and it brings back memories, because all fragrances do I think …I think it is loyalty to their brands and their fragrance.* (Sales Consultant)

As Hwang and Kandampully found brand loyalty improves for Millennials through emotional aspects such as, self-concept connection, emotional attachment, and brand love, with sensory or hedonic factors being the most important factors for them (Hwang and Kandampully 2012). Bednarz, Beauchamp and Barnes (2015) too, highlight the formation of brand attachment and loyalty for Millennials where Millennials go beyond the product to appreciate service, where they seek friendly staff who connect to their emotional needs.

Consequently, brand loyalty requires further consideration when connecting to Millennial consumers and with Hwang and Kandampully finding *"that younger consumers form brand love as they perceive that a brand expresses an important part of their selves"*, it is crucial for brands to find ways to connect to this consumer group (Hwang and Kandampully 2012).

# Celebrity Branding

To date the use of celebrity endorsements or celebrity branded fragrances has been used as the principal method of connecting to millennial consumers.

*Younger consumers are more celebrity led, they go with the fashions, whatev-er's new, whatever's out, whoever's the face of it.* (Sales Consultant)

*Younger consumers are more likely to seek out new product launches, espe-cially the celebrity ones that are coming out they are influenced by adverts, magazines, TV programmes and fast-moving fashion.* (Sales Consultant)

The past decade has seen a plethora of celebrity branded fragrances e.g. Beyoncé and Rihanna being created to stimulate and connect to new consumer groups (Euromonitor 2017). This connection was evidenced by the sales consultants who linked celebrity perfumes with young consumers.

*Young consumers are influenced by adverts; I think celebrity culture has a lot to do with it, the next top model or who's on the telly the most.* (Industry Specialist)

*Young consumers are more likely to come in for celebrity perfumes especially if they have a favourite artist or actor.* (Sales Consultant)

However, as Khanom (2017) indicates Millennial consumers are no longer relying on luxury brands or celebrity endorsed products but are instead engaging with 'High Street' retail branded fragrances e.g. Babe Power by Missguided and H&M's 'Conscious' Perfume oil, marking a changing market format. Consequently, the luxury brands are endeav-ouring to engage with this audience through promotional campaigns for new 'fresh' fragrances targeting younger consumers e.g. Chanel No. 5 L'Eau, featuring Lily-Rose Depp in its promotional campaign (Khanom 2017). The industry highlights this change too.

*Celebrity fragrances they are one hit wonders. Justin Bieber was so big at Christmas but not much has been sold after this. Last year it was Katy Perry but nobody stocked it after Christmas. They have a short time span.* (Sales Consultant)

This correlates to the Millennial characteristics and the view that they now no longer wish to emulate their celebrity favourites, preferring a 'lifestyle tribe' created and fuelled by social media stars such as, digi-tal influencer Zoella and pop and social media princess Ariana Grande.

Popular retail brands who create this essence of belonging and 'cool' have also proved to be successful, for example, Hollister and Victoria's Secret (Euromonitor 2017). As such, the emotional connection generated by tribal marketing is altering perfume brand attachment.

> *As you get older you're more reluctant to change in comparison to being younger. It's not a big deal because they are not attached to it in any way they just buy it because you like it and its new. You are a lot more subject to change when your younger I think.* (Sales Consultant)

This suggests that Millennials lack connection and loyalty to perfume brands, seeking newness over attachment and loyalty.

## Importance of Attachment Towards Fragrance Brands

Thomson et al. (2005) and Zhang and Feng (2017) highlight that attachment and loyalty are both psychological led constructs for consumers, with consumers preferring one brand over another and developing personal connections to a brand, which in turn generates repeat purchases. This appears not to be the case for Millennial consumers who prefer newness.

> *Young consumers are easily influenced by the next fashion ... we have young consumers coming in purely because they like the design of the bottle, or it has a free bag along.* (Sales Consultant)

Holt (2004) highlighted how important brand loyalty and attachment are, indicating that strong brand loyalty is directly linked to consumers who experience emotional attachment to a brand and with Qing et al. (2015) identifying that deeper brand attachment correlates to stronger brand loyalty and an increase in purchase price, it is evident why brands are keen to create consumer attachment. While a lack of attachment was observed, this was not the consensus by all industry professionals, with one of the Industry Specialists suggesting that all customers…

*can become emotionally attached to a smell.* (Industry Specialist)

This however, was not the popular view of Millennial consumers with a superficial attachment proposed. This view implies that smell is of little consequence for younger consumers and that style over substance is more important.

*Every fragrance aimed at the young market competes not on smell but the image, bottle and free gift.* (Industry Specialist)

Hence, the perfidious nature of the Millennial consumer and their demand for newness, creates an unpredictable market with significant challenges for the industry. As a result, perfume brands must connect at a 'deeper' level with young consumers i.e. if brands can create an emotional trigger, consumers will develop brand 'love' and a lasting bond. For Millennial consumers who are regarded as narcissistic on the one hand but environmentally conscious and innovative on the other connecting to their self-concept is vital (Albert and Merunka 2013).

However, millennial consumers appear to be no different in their relationship with their chosen fragrances, seeing them very much as an extension of their own self-concept.

*Brand image and personality is a really big thing for younger consumers, it represents who they are.* (Industry Specialist)
    *I think a lot of consumers see their perfume as an extension of themselves, especially the couture brands such as Chanel and Dior. They are buying into the lifestyle of it.* (Industry Specialist)

Additionally, Malär et al. (2011) found brands who connect with the 'actual' self rather than the 'ideal' self, generated higher levels of emotional attachment, with an even greater increase when the consumer was involved with the product or displayed public self-consciousness and with Rissanen and Luoma-Aho (2016) observing, Millennials or 'self-branders' are motivated by identification with an organisation, brand or product, establishing an interesting insight into connections with this consumer group (Giovannini et al. 2015).

*You do sometimes get that customer who sees the brand as a lifestyle but I think that is dying out now.* (Sales Consultant)

Interaction between brand personality and the consumer has also been found to increase brand attachment (Phau and Cheong 2009; Orth 2010). While Aaker (1997) highlights that brand personalities provide a conduit for self-expression for consumers and this was found to be the case for perfume.

*I think your perfume is part of who you are as a person. It is part of your personality and what kind of person you are.* (Sales Consultant)
   *I would class perfume as an extension of who I am as a person and lots of customers do too.* (Sales Consultant)

Thomson et al. (2005) furthers this by suggesting only a few perfumes generate strong bonds over a consumer's life time. Schindler and Holbrook (1993) also indicates brands that connect during sensitive or pivotal periods of life, such as, at a young age when they are developing their own identity. As such, Millennial consumers are at a key life stage, finding their own self-identity and offers the industry an ideal consumer group to focus on.

## Factors Influencing Consumer Innovativeness

Bowen and Chen McCain (2015) recognise Millennials as the next dominant market segment. The fragrance market is no exception to this…

*A lot of fragrances are aimed at a younger market because they have greater disposable income and therefore have a lot of choice between classic brands and new celebrity ones.* (Industry Specialist)

Interestingly Khanom (2016) recognised Millennial consumers are engaging with 'High Street' retail branded fragrances such as, Babe Power by Missguided and H&M's 'Conscious' Perfume oil and with

Libby (2016) indicating that the luxury segment of the market is experiencing a decline, it highlights a more challenging environment for this marketplace. Although, the usage of perfume remains high and as such, the luxury perfume brands are developing and promoting new fragrances and new editions of classics to target the younger market (Libby 2016).

> *For example, with the new Calvin Klein Shock its whole brand image is targeted at a young consumer.* (Sales Consultant)
> *New Editions of classic fragrances are very popular. Yves Saint Laurent's Parisienne is … really popular with young consumers from 18 up to late thirties.* (Sales Consultant)

However, the luxury brands may not be fully understanding this new young consumer as celebrity endorsement, without the creation of a 'lifestyle tribe' is still being used as a method of communication.

> *Kate Moss is the face of Parisienne and this makes it really popular with younger consumers.* (Sales Consultant)
> *Younger faces such as Kiera Knightly for Coco Mademoiselle are being used for to attract younger consumers.* (Sales Consultant)

Hence, the luxury perfume brands need to consider the Millennial consumers motivation to purchase perfume.

> *A lot of young consumers buy the perfume just because they want the bag but they may not like the perfume. It's easier to sell when a free gift is offered. Often, they will buy the perfume with a free gift, keep the gift for themselves and give the perfume as a present to their sister or friend.* (Sales Consultant)

Euromonitor (2017) however, indicates that 'lifestyle tribes' are the most important aspect of this group of consumers with instant communication and reassurance being sought from social media platforms. The significance of this was recognised by way of peer influence.

> *I think younger consumers are influenced by their peers.* (Industry Specialist)

Understanding advertising and communication techniques are also crucial as there is a misconception that millennials rely on technology, meaning traditional marketing channels are irrelevant however, Millennials are more likely to engage with traditional methods than older consumers (Bednarz-Beauchamp and Barnes 2015). As such, traditional communication methods should be considered as appropriate methods to reach this consumer group. However, the industry professionals recognised while traditional communication methods do work, when connecting to Millennial consumers appropriate channels need to be used.

> *Depends what kind of TV programme they are advertised during for example you wouldn't find Chanel advertising during Big Brother.* (Sales Consultant)
> *Young consumers are likely to read More or Heat magazine and see perfumes being advertised in there, particularly celebrity ones.* (Sales Consultant)
> *I think seventeen to early thirties are heavily influenced by marketing, advertisements on the television and magazines. I think they have a lot more disposable income.* (Industry Specialist)

Hence, by considering communication format, timing and location, fragrance brands can connect and market their new products to Millennial consumers using familiar and traditional methods.

## Conclusions

The branded fragrance industry has come a long way from Paul Poiret's Rosine with the luxury Fashion Houses' utilising perfume as the dominant brand extension. Consumers have enjoyed engaging with these products as an entry to desirable luxury products and while this market remains significant changes have been seen.

Millennial consumers and their buying habits are at the heart of this change with considerable differences between generations being observed. While older generations appreciated individual customer service and remained loyal to a perfume brand and sales consultants too,

Millennial consumers were not viewed as such, with their fickle behaviour resulting in fluctuating purchase behaviour of both perfume brands and locations.

However, while this could be viewed as disloyalty, when age is considered this inconsistency is more closely associated to consumers of this age experiencing their formative years when they are experimenting with the aim of finding their own signature scent. Consequently, loyalty, which is established at this age, appears to come from brands that can generate an emotional attachment through hedonic factors and brand love lacking the nostalgia that older consumers possess.

Celebrity perfumes have, in recent years, formed an important part of the industry targeting, in particular, young consumers. However, this research discovered that the attraction of celebrity endorse perfumes is lessening with 'lifestyle tribes' now more important. Hence, luxury perfume brands need to consider this communication strategy more closely rather than relying on young celebrities to endorse their new younger perfumes.

Furthermore, the type of communication strategy the luxury branded perfumes generate requires further consideration, as while instance connection through social media platforms was found to be important, traditional communication methods were also found to be just as important to Millennial consumers. Hence, for any perfume brand wishing to form a consumer brand relationship, attachment and loyalty with Millennial consumers, a more holistic communication strategy, one which connects through instant digital formats, by lifestyle tribe and through emotional and hedonic connections, needs to be adopted.

# References

Aaker, Jennifer L. 1997. "Dimensions of Brand Personality." *Journal of Marketing Research* 34 (3): 347–356.

Adams, John, Hafiz T.A. Khan, and Robert Raeside. 2014. *Research Methods for Business and Social Science Students.* New Delhi: Sage.

Albert, Noel, and Dwight Merunka. 2013. "The Role of Brand Love in Consumer-Brand Relationships." *Journal of Consumer Marketing* 30 (3): 258–266.

Albrecht, Carmen-Maria, Christof Backhaus, Hannes Gurzki, and David M. Woisetschläger. 2013. "Drivers of Brand Extension Success: What Really Matters for Luxury Brands." *Psychology & Marketing* 30 (8): 647–659.

Amatulli, Cesare, Antonio Mileti, Vincenzo Speciale, and Gianluigi Guido. 2016. "The Relationship Between Fast Fashion and Luxury Brands: An Exploratory Study in the UK Market." In *Global Marketing Strategies for the Promotion of Luxury Goods*, 244–265. Pennsylvania: IGI Global.

Bardhi, Fleura, Andrew J. Rohm, and Fareena Sultan. 2010. "Tuning in and Tuning Out: Media Multitasking Among Young Consumers." *Journal of Consumer Behaviour* 9 (4): 316–332.

Beauchamp, Michelle Bednarz, and Donald C. Barnes. 2015. "Delighting Baby Boomers and Millennials: Factors That Matter Most." *Journal of Marketing Theory and Practice* 23 (3): 338–350.

Bowen, John T., and Shiang-Lih Chen McCain. 2015. "Transitioning Loyalty Programs: A Commentary on 'The Relationship Between Customer Loyalty and Customer Satisfaction'." *International Journal of Contemporary Hospitality Management* 27 (3): 415–430.

Bowlby, John. 1979. *The Making and Breaking of Affectional Bonds*. London. Tavistock Publications.

Butler, Sarah. 2017. "'The Lipstick Effect': Britons Treat Themselves as Budgets Tighten." *The Guardian*. https://www.theguardian.com/business/2017/jul/15/the-lipstick-effect-britons-treat-themselves-as-budgets-tighten Accessed on 9 August 2017.

Carey, Lindsey, Aileen Stewart, and Susan Walkinshaw. 2016. "Luxury Perfume Brands: Consumer Brand Relationship and the Mature Consumer." Paper Presented at the 5th Global Fashion Conference, Sweden.

Cant, M.C., J.W. Strydom, C.J. Jooste, and P.J. du Plessis, eds. 2009. *Marketing Management*, P192. Cape Town: Juta and Company.

Carpentera, Jason, Marguerite Moore, Anne Marie Doherty, and Nicholas Alexander. 2012. "Acculturation to the Global Consumer Culture: A Generational Cohort Comparison." *Journal of Strategic Marketing* 20 (5, August): 411–423.

Drylie-Carey, Lindsey, and Aileen Stewart. 2018. "Mature Consumers' Relationship with Their Perfume." *Revista Mediterránea de Comunicación* 9 (1): 363–370. https://doi.org/10.14198/MEDCOM2018.9.1.22.

Easterby-Smith, Mark, Richard Thorpe, and Paul R. Jackson. 2015. *Management and Business Research*. London: Sage.

Euromonitor, 2017. "Bitter Sweet: The Smell of a Paradigm Shift in the Global Fragrance Market." https://www.euromonitor.com/bitter-sweet-the-smell-of-a-paradigm-shift-in-the-global-fragrance-market/report. Accessed on 5 September 2017.

Euromonitor International. 2012. "Global Buying Behaviour in the Recession." https://blog.euromonitor.com/global-buying-behaviour-in-the-recession/. Accessed on 28 August 2017.

Fetscherin, Marc, and Daniel Heinrich. 2015. "Consumer Brand Relationships Research: A Bibliometric Citation Meta-Analysis." *Journal of Business Research* 68 (2): 380–390.

Foscht, Thomas, Judith Schloffer, Cesar Maloles III, and Swee L. Chia. 2009. "Assessing the Outcomes of Generation-Y Customers' Loyalty." *International Journal of Bank Marketing* 27 (3): 218–241.

Fournier, Susan. 1998. "Consumers and Their Brands: Developing Relationship Theory in Consumer Research." *Journal of Consumer Research* 24 (4): 343–373.

Gardiner, Sarah, Deborah Grace, and Ceridwyn King. 2014. "The Generation Effect: The Future of Domestic Tourism in Australia." *Journal of Travel Research* 53 (6): 705–720.

Giovannini, Sarah, Yingjiao Xu, and Jane Thomas. 2015. "Luxury Fashion Consumption and Generation Y Consumers: Self, Brand Consciousness, and Consumption Motivations." *Journal of Fashion Marketing and Management* 19 (1): 22–40.

Granot, Elad, Henry Greene, and Thomas G. Brashear. "Female Consumers: Decision-Making in Brand-Driven Retail." *Journal of Business Research* 63 (8): 801–808.40.

Greenberg, Karl. 2011. "Study: Gens X, Y Rely on Research, Less on Loyalty." *Mediapost*, February 7. Available at https://www.mediapost.com/publications/article/144338/study-gens-x-y-rely-on-research-less-on-loyalty.html. Accessed 3 September 2017.

Holt, Douglas B. 2004. *How Brands Become Icons: The Principles of Cultural Branding*. Boston: Harvard Business Press.

Holt, Douglas B. "14 How Societies Desire Brands. 2005." *Inside Consumption: Consumer Motives, Goals, and Desires*, p. 273.

Howe, Neil, and William Strauss. 2000. *Millennials Rising: The Next Great Generation*. New York, NY: Vintage Books.

Hwang, Jiyoung, and Jay Kandampully. 2012. "The Role of Emotional Aspects in Younger Consumer-Brand Relationships." *Journal of Product & Brand Management* 21 (2): 98–108.

Jevons, Colin, Mark Gabbott, and Leslie de Chernatony. 2005. "Customer and Brand Manager Perspectives on Brand Relationships: A Conceptual Framework." *Journal of Product & Brand Management* 14 (5): 300–309.

Keller, Kevin Lane, M. G. Parameswaran, and Isaac Jacob. 2011. *Strategic Brand Management: Building, Measuring, and Managing Brand Equity.* Pearson Education India.

Khanom, Roshida. 2016. *Fragrances-UK-August 2016.* UK: Mintel. Available From https://Academic.Mintel.Com/Display/748733/?__Cc=1. Accessed on 5 September 2017.

Khanom, Roshida. 2017. *Fragrances-UK-August 2017.* UK: Mintel. Available from https://store.mintel.com/fragrances-uk-august-2017. Accessed on 5 September 2017.

Libby, Charlotte. 2016. *Prestige Beauty-UK-December 2016.* UK: Mintel. Available From http://Store.Mintel.Com/Uk-Prestige-Beauty-Market-Report. Accessed on 6 September 2017.

Lodes, Megan, and C. L. Buff. 2009. "Are Generation Y (Millennial) Consumers Brand Loyal and Is Their Buying Behavior Affected in an Economic Recession? A Preliminary Study." *Journal of Academy of Business and Economics* 9 (3): 127–134.

Malär, Lucia, Harley Krohmer, Wayne D. Hoyer, and Bettina Nyffenegger. 2011. "Emotional Brand Attachment and Brand Personality: The Relative Importance of the Actual and the Ideal Self." *Journal of marketing* 75 (4): 35–52.

Manpower. 2016. "Facts, Figures: 'Millennial Careers: 2020 Vision'." *Global Report.* Available at http://www.manpowergroup.com/wps/wcm/connect/660ebf65-144c-489e-975c-9f838294c237/MillennialsPaper1_2020Vision_lo.pdf?-MOD=AJPERES. Accessed 28 August 2017.

Matthews, Imogen. 2009. "Women's Fragrance Buying Habits Revealed." France: Esprit. Retrieved from https://www.yumpu.com/en/document/view/3247276/womens-fragrance-buying-habitsrevealed-givaudan. Accessed 28 August 2017.

Neudecker, Niels, Oliver Hupp, Alexandra Stein, and Harald Schuster. 2013. "Is Your Brand a One-Night Stand? Managing Consumer-Brand Relationships." *Marketing Review St. Gallen* 30 (6): 22–33.39.

Nobre, Helena, and Carlos Brito. 2010. "Brand Relationships: A Personality-Based Approach." *Journal of Service Science & Management* 3: 206–217.

Orth, Ulrich R., Yonca Limon, and Gregory Rose. 2010. "Store-Evoked Affect, Personalities, and Consumer Emotional Attachments to Brands." *Journal of Business Research* 63 (11): 1202–1208.

Park, C. Whan, Deborah J. MacInnis, Joseph Priester, Andreas B. Eisingerich, and Dawn Iacobucci. 2010. "Brand Attachment and Brand Attitude Strength: Conceptual and Empirical Differentiation of Two Critical Brand Equity Drivers." *Journal of marketing* 74 (6): 1–17.

Perfume Society. 2016. "The Perfume Society: Explore—History." Available at https://perfumesociety.org/discover-perfume/an-introduction/history/. Accessed on 3 September 2017.

Phau, Ian, and Edith Cheong. 2009. "How Young Adult Consumers Evaluate Diffusion Brands: Effects of Brand Loyalty and Status Consumption." *Journal of International Consumer Marketing* 21 (2): 109–123.

Pouy, Jean-Bernard. 2007. *Perfume a Global History*. Paris, France: Somogy Art Publishers.

Rambourg, Erwan. 2014. *The Bling Dynasty: Why the Reign of Chinese Luxury Shoppers Has Only Just Begun*. Singapore: Wiley.

Richmond, Alexandra. 2012. "Men's and Women's Fragrances-UK-September 2012." Mintel. Available from http://reports.mintel.com/display/590313/. Accessed on 3 September 2017.

Rissanen, Hilkka, and Vilma Luoma-Aho. 2016. "(Un) Willing to Engage? First Look at the Engagement Types of Millennials." *Corporate Communications: An International Journal* 21 (4): 500–515.

Schindler, Robert M., and Morris B. Holbrook. 1993. "Critical Periods in the Development of Men's and Women's Tastes in Personal Appearance." *Psychology & Marketing* 10 (6): 549–564.

Thomson, Matthew, Deborah J. MacInnis, and C. Whan Park. 2005. "The Ties That Bind: Measuring the Strength of Consumers' Emotional Attachments to Brands." *Journal of Consumer Psychology* 15 (1): 77–91.

Yao, Qing, Rong Chen, and Xiaobing Xu. 2015. "Consistency Between Consumer Personality and Brand Personality Influences Brand Attachment." *Social Behavior and Personality: An International Journal* 43 (9): 1419–1427.

Young, Amy M., and Mary D. Hinesly. 2015. "Identifying Millennials' Key Influencers from Early Childhood: Insights into Current Consumer Preferences." *Journal of Consumer Marketing* 29 (2): 146–155.31.

Zhang, Yueli, and Feng Liu. 2017. "The Formation of Brand Loyalty: A Partial Dual-Factor Explanation." *Journal of International Consumer Marketing* 29 (4): 239–249.

# 8

# The Evolution of the Chinese Luxury Fashion Consumer: An Interpretive Study of Luxury Value Perceptions

Patsy Perry, Liz Barnes and Tiantian Ye

## Introduction

The evolution of Chinese luxury fashion consumers has been nothing short of dramatic. From the conspicuous nature of their first luxury fashion purchases and predilection for imitating their Western peers, they have evolved into discerning, brand-literate shoppers with an appreciation of the aesthetics of luxury fashion. This chapter takes an interpretivist approach to understand the evolution of the Chinese luxury consumer, focusing on how contemporary Chinese consumers conceptualise luxury fashion consumption, as an imported phenomenon, from their own experiences, against a backdrop of increasing luxury democratisation. It begins

P. Perry (✉) · T. Ye
Fashion Business & Technology, Department of Materials,
The University of Manchester, Manchester, UK
e-mail: patsy.perry@manchester.ac.uk

L. Barnes
School of Fashion, Manchester Metropolitan University, Manchester, UK
e-mail: l.barnes@mmu.ac.uk

© The Author(s) 2020
I. Cantista and T. Sádaba (eds.), *Understanding Luxury Fashion*,
Palgrave Advances in Luxury, https://doi.org/10.1007/978-3-030-25654-8_8

175

with an overview of the development of the luxury fashion market in China, since the first Western brands entered in the 1990s, to the more recent democratisation and dilution of luxury with the launch of accessible lines such as ready-to-wear, shoes and handbags, and the rise of luxury online, witnessed by several major e-commerce launches as well as experimentation across social media marketing, social commerce, omnichannel and direct-to-consumer, making luxury widely accessible. It also explores the evolution of the characteristics of the Chinese luxury consumer, from their initial conspicuousness and lack of brand loyalty to a highly diverse demographic with fragmented tastes and preferences, indicating that consumer pluralism is a key theme in China's rapidly changing luxury goods landscape. However, the key to understanding luxury consumption in China lies in the very origin of this consumer pluralism—what does luxury mean to the Chinese consumer today?

Chinese consumers are relative newcomers to the world of luxury fashion, compared to their Western peers who grew up in social environments where the idea of luxury was securely established. Highly diverse and fragmented tastes and preferences in China indicate that consumer pluralism is a key theme in the luxury goods landscape (Liu et al. 2016), one that is constantly made more acute by the evolution of the concept of luxury itself. Today, the unique aura of luxury fashion has been diluted, especially within categories such as ready-to-wear, shoes and handbags. The democratisation of luxury increases the volume of sales by adopting 'abundant rarity' as a strategy and expanding product portfolios (Kapferer 2012). Most luxury fashion (mass-produced ready-to-wear and accessories inspired by the aesthetic classics of haute couture) is positioned in an intermediate and relatively accessible level of the luxury hierarchy scale, with only 25% of luxury fashion brands classified as 'absolute luxury' (D'Arpizio 2016). This widening accessibility is clearly seen in the rise of online retailing and social media marketing, which allow anybody to purchase and associate with luxury brands. Yeoman and McMahon-Beattie (2006) termed the 'luxurification of society' as the consuming of affordable luxury products that meet aspirational needs. More recently, luxury and non-luxury collaborations, such as Louis Vuitton and Supreme's capsule collection, represent the fusion of highbrow elite culture and streetwear, creating a new dimension of luxury democratisation which acknowledges the purchasing power of younger generations, and also pays tribute to youth culture. Luxury sacrifices some of its cultural privilege to embrace this highly promising consumer group, and to encourage an earlier start to luxury consumption in the consumer lifespan. Through the process of authenticating the imported phenomenon of luxury fashion consumption, Chinese consumers incorporate socio-cultural references into their understanding.

## The Development of China's Luxury Fashion Market

China's luxury fashion market is relatively young, as Western luxury fashion brands, such as Armani, Dior, Ermenegildo Zegna, Fendi and Versace, did not enter mainland China until the 1990s. In fact, China did not begin its journey to consumerism and tourism until Mao's Cultural Revolution ended in 1978 and the Open Door economic liberalisation policy of the late 1970s enabled it to break away from its previous Communist isolation and attract foreign capital and knowledge to support economic, industrial and social development. Previously, China was a closed society: from the inception of the People's Republic in 1949 until the end of the Cultural Revolution in 1978, bourgeois lifestyles were prohibited and all members of society were a part of the proletariat. When Deng Xiaoping came to power, the country was opened up to the outside world and its planned economy was reformed to a free-market one to boost economic development and raise national incomes. The reform policies also contributed to China's transformation from a production to a consumption-focused economy, creating a rising middle class willing and able to purchase Western luxury brands as desirable symbols of success and affluence (Bonetti et al. 2016). As entrepreneurial activity and financial success were encouraged under the reformed system, possessing visible luxuries became a way for Chinese consumers to compensate for their previous state of extreme thriftiness (Rucker and Galinsky 2008). By 2012, China overtook Japan to become the world's biggest luxury market (Caïs 2018) and by 2017 accounted for almost one-third of the global luxury market in terms of spend (McKinsey & Co. 2017) with further growth predicted to reach 40% of the global luxury market by 2024 (Boston Consulting Group 2018).

During the early stages of internationalisation of Western luxury brands, the China market entry strategy was to target affluent tourists and businessmen by opening boutiques in the shopping arcades of five star hotels, partly due to foreign investment restrictions but also because the shopping mall concept did not exist in China (Chevalier and Lu 2010). The luxury image of high end hotels, such as the Peninsula Palace in Beijing, provided positive associations for appropriate upscale positioning of the foreign brand in the Chinese market (Bonetti et al. 2016). Later, department stores were opened in Tier 1 cities such as Beijing and Shanghai, and wholesale arrangements set up with local distributors. More recently, foreign luxury brands opened extravagant flagship stores in Chinese capital cities, then dedicated diffusion brand stores in key capital cities and then key provincial cities (Moore et al. 2010). Relaxation of foreign investment policies enabled the expansion of high-end shopping malls developed with foreign partners, which could provide a suitably prestigious environment for international luxury brands to open standalone mono-stores. For example, a store in Shanghai's famous Plaza 66 shopping mall ("home to luxury since 2001") clearly signifies that a brand is luxury (Kapferer 2014a). However, the Chinese government's 2013 anti-corruption crackdown on lavish gift giving, a slowing economy as a result of the global financial crisis and the 2015 devaluation of the yuan created a volatile and challenging luxury market (Bonetti et al. 2016; Bain 2018). In recent years the market has recovered and seen increased purchasing within China, rather than abroad (D'Arpizio and Levato 2018), as a result of lower price differentials between Chinese mainland and overseas markets due to a realignment of price points by luxury brands (Guarino 2015), and the government's crackdown on the grey market daigou channel (purchases by a Chinese person overseas on behalf of a customer in mainland China) in order to boost internal consumption. Increased customer reach as a result of online retailing and expansion of physical stores beyond key capital cities also supports further growth in luxury consumption. Furthermore, a number of domestic brands have entered China's luxury fashion market, promoting new concepts of Asian luxury, for example Shang Xia's approach to reviving Chinese craftsmanship or Icicle's philosophy of living in harmony with nature.

In recent years, the sector has seen widespread democratisation and dilution of luxury with the launch of accessible lines such as ready-to-wear, shoes and handbags, and the rise of luxury online, with several major launches on Chinese e-commerce platforms, as well as experimentation across social media marketing, social commerce, omnichannel and direct-to-consumer, making luxury widely accessible. Going forward, the influence of digital is expected to permeate every purchase (D'Arpizio and Levato 2018). Even though media censorship hinders Chinese consumers from being fully engaged with global consumer communication platforms, widely used domestic social media, along with technological advances in communication platforms, provide the opportunity for the digital isation of fashion marketing communications in China (Liu et al. 2018). WeChat has become the leading online platform for luxury brands to connect with Chinese consumers, provide brand and product information, and encourage followers to share online posts (Liu et al. 2018). Many foreign brands, including Louis Vuitton, Gucci, Burberry and Fendi, have opened WeChat online shops that allow anybody to purchase and associate with their brands. Through such widely accessible platforms, Chinese consumers have been able to accelerate their fashion knowledge.

There has clearly been a swift and dramatic evolution of luxury fashion in China since its inception in the 1990s, and in the next section we consider the evolution of the Chinese luxury consumer's characteristics, from initial conspicuousness and lack of brand savviness to a highly diverse demographic with fragmented tastes and preferences.

# The Chinese Luxury Fashion Consumer

For many years, Chinese luxury consumers were portrayed as big spenders on big brands. There is no doubt that collectivism is deeply rooted in Chinese culture, and the idea of the collective group drives many consumers to follow certain patterns in their purchasing and fashion habits. However, this cultural relic is not the only factor driving China's luxury fashion market today. Modern Chinese consumers now demonstrate highly diversified tastes and shopping preferences that are not only different from their Western peers, but also from the tastes of previous generations. The Chinese luxury fashion market has been revitalised by younger and digitally savvy consumers (Liu et al. 2016) and highly educated, youthful and brand-conscious fashion innovators (Zhang and Kim 2013), who are less likely to be restrained by traditional cultural values and social norms.

Western consumerism and materialistic urban lifestyles are considered elements of advanced living (Eckhardt et al. 2015). Materialism, the belief that the pursuit and ownership of possessions are linked to happiness and perceptions of success (Belk 1985), can explain why Chinese luxury consumers were initially drawn to famous brands and loud signals. Levels of materialism vary according to cultural and economic conditions, but tend to be highest in markets where there has been rapid and recent socio-economic and cultural change, as this is the key way in which consumers can demonstrate their success and status in society (Kamal et al. 2013). Thus, for many years, affluent Chinese consumers were known for their preferences for loud and highly conspicuous product designs, which enabled them to impress others by displaying their wealth noticeably (Eckhardt et al. 2015; Zhan and He 2012). They lacked knowledge of the hierarchy of luxury brands, were not able to distinguish between different brands and consequently were not brand loyal (Kapferer 2014b).

Over the past decade however, Chinese luxury consumers' knowledge and tastes have evolved significantly. Tier 1 cities (Beijing, Shanghai, Guangzhou and Shenzhen) in particular have witnessed rapid development in luxury consumers' tastes and sophistication in recent years, to a point where Chinese consumer behaviour became comparable with that of consumers in mature markets (Liu et al. 2016). As they become more sophisticated and discerning, their preferences change from highly conspicuous consumption to a taste for quieter and more exclusive pieces (Bonetti et al. 2016; Eckhardt et al. 2015) and a greater focus on intrinsic value (Kapferer 2014b). Unique products are usually novel, scarce and utilised by a limited number of consumers (Tian et al. 2001), and may be treated as an investment (Watson and Yan 2013). In luxury fashion, unique products include items made from exotic materials, involving atelier craftsmanship, runway pieces with limited production, and limited editions or tailor-made goods. Consumers are driven by their motivation to disassociate themselves from the crowds, and purchasing unique products is one solution. The gravitation towards a more understated, discreet look also brings greater diversity in preferred brands and a shift towards emerging and less ubiquitous brands (Bonetti et al. 2016). Newer and aspirational brands including Stella McCartney, Alexander McQueen, Jimmy Choo and Balenciaga became as desirable as the traditional established market leaders Louis Vuitton, Dior and Hermès (Bain & Co. 2015). The two-tier society (the 'haves' and 'have-nots') in Veblen's arguments has therefore been transformed into a highly complex consumer world (Han et al. 2010). Conspicuousness still exists, but it is now characterised by diverse signals in different consumer groups or sub-cultures. In the 'old-luxe' age, marketing and advertising campaigns targeted only an exclusive consumer group, and the advertisers and the luxury consumers shared similar values. However, the 'new' concept of luxury represents a diluted exclusivity being compensated by an abundant rarity and by marketing and branding activities creating emotional connections with luxury consumers. Highly diverse and fragmented tastes and preferences in China indicate that consumer pluralism is a key theme in the luxury goods landscape (Liu et al. 2016), one that is constantly made more acute by the evolution of the concept of luxury itself.

## Conceptualising Luxury Fashion Value: A Chinese Perspective

Consumer value can be defined as the consumer's "interactive, relativistic preference and experience in consumption" (Holbrook 2005, p. 46). Luxury marketing requires consumers to perceive sufficient value in the item to compensate for the high price point (Tynan et al. 2010). Perceived luxury value is made up of its social signifier function and its personal or hedonic component, which can be presented respectively as 'luxury for others' and 'luxury for oneself' (Kapferer and Bastien 2009). Consumer value can be further conceptualised into four dimensions of financial, functional, personal (hedonic) and social (conspicuous) value (Shukla and Purani 2012; Hennigs et al. 2012). Consumption is highly symbolic and diversified in different cultural settings, and the concept of luxury varies across time, geography and culture, as people in disparate global marketplaces define luxury differently (Wiedmann et al. 2007; Yeoman and McMahon-Beattie 2006). More recently however, Hennigs et al. (2012) argued that global luxury consumers generally possess similar values regardless of country of origin, although the relative importance of value dimensions varies across cultures. The following sub-sections review the literature on the four dimensions of luxury value and consider its application to the Chinese context.

## Financial Value

The financial dimensions of luxury's consumer value revolve around their direct monetary aspect (Hennigs et al. 2013). There is a direct link between financial value perception and quality perception, since the relationship between price and perceived quality is theoretically positive (Parguel et al. 2016). However, this relationship can be influenced by the prior information held by consumers, so that consumers with limited knowledge and experience about a product or brand may have a stronger tendency to use price to assess its quality (Okonkwo 2014).

As luxury brands were originally associated with the aura of exclusivity and rarity, prestige prices have become one of luxury's most important indicators (Shukla and Purani 2012). However, price perceptions can vary across geographic and cultural boundaries. Kapferer and Laurent (2016) found that in the same product category, the perceived minimum price of luxury differed by over 40% across different countries. Such geographic differences in luxury price perception may indicate difficulty in objectively conceptualising luxury. As the definition of luxury is highly subjective, it can vary from individual to individual, and even from one life-stage to another. For instance, a young person may consider a Louis Vuitton wallet a lavish treat, but may see it as a fairly ordinary item later on in life, when his or her financial status is stronger. Therefore, the process of conceptualising luxury is influenced by an individual's life experiences and by the social context he or she finds themselves in.

Today, Chinese luxury consumers are widely recognised as amongst the world's top spenders, even though China was historically a nation of savers (Wang and Lin 2009). Although the one-party system with its highly-controlled political ideology is still a key feature of modern China, society has clearly moved on from communist-era thriftiness as it embraces the culture of consumerism. However, thriftiness can still be seen in the resourcefulness of Chinese consumers who use daigou third-party overseas shopping services to purchase luxury products and avoid import tariffs of up to 60% (Reuters 2016). The huge contradiction between today's spending patterns and the stereotypical perception of the Chinese as prudent points to the tensions between traditional values and lesser-known dynamics of the socio-economic environment. Chen and Lamberti's (2015) study on Chinese upper-class value perceptions showed a significant leap from general preconceptions regarding their understanding of luxury's financial value. Their findings revealed that elite shoppers recognised premium prices as a tool used to position luxury in the market and were willing to pay these higher prices in order to maintain the exclusivity of their purchases. With higher purchasing power and stronger brand awareness, consumer perceptions of luxury fashion's financial value are evolving and are being transformed from a search for bargains to a balance between exclusivity and value-for-money.

## Conspicuous Value

One of luxury's most critical values is its ability to visibly signal and convey its associations of social and financial privilege (Holt et al. 2004). Veblen defined conspicuousness in luxury consumption as "the purchase of expensive goods to wastefully display wealth rather than to attempt to satisfy more utilitarian needs of the consumer, for the sole objective of gaining or maintaining higher social status" (cited in Eckhardt et al. 2015, p. 807). Under the new paradigm of luxury democratisation, the market has become less status-driven as the concept of luxury has been 'normalised' (Kastanakis and Balabanis 2014). Consequently, research on conspicuous consumption requires a more in-depth examination of contextual characteristics (Wilcox et al. 2009).

Chinese consumers' conspicuous value perception of luxury consumption is highly related to the concept of face (Thompson 2011), which can be defined as the recognition by others of an individual's social standing and position (Lockett 1988). The concept of face reflects an individual's personal efforts to acquire wealth, position and power. As Chinese culture is collectivist and places value on interpersonal relationships, gaining face enables followers to move higher up the status ladder (King and Myers 1977) by achieving validation from other in-group members. Chinese culture thus encourages consumers to engage in certain buying patterns, making them more likely to over-consume luxury goods as a way of joining elite society. In the early years of China's consumerism revolution, luxury lovers would rush to buy prestige brands with prominent logos. After experiencing long-term deprivation from the state's ideological control on consumption, modern Chinese consumers adopted consumerism as a form of self-compensation (Rucker and Galinksy 2008). Chadha and Husband's (2006) five-stage model maps the evolution of luxury culture in Asia against the different levels of economic development, from an initial stage of poverty and subjugation, to the showing-off stage, to the final stage of becoming more confident and discerning. As conspicuous luxury goods trickle down to lower classes over time, the elite is forced to select even more exclusive inconspicuous items (Han et al. 2010) to maintain their status. Inconspicuous alternatives can benefit sophisticated customers by limiting or preventing imitation by lower social groups (Hebdige 1999), allowing them to show off their superior tastes and distinguish themselves from lower status consumers (Eckhardt et al. 2015). When more people own conspicuous luxury brands, the signalling ability of such goods becomes diluted, and there evolves an increased desire for sophistication and subtlety in design in order to further distinguish oneself for a narrow group of peers, evidenced in a shift away from loud, visible brand signals to niche, highbrow choices (Eckhardt et al. 2015). For example, as Louis Vuitton handbags became increasingly commonplace and popular among aspirational consumers, such as young office workers, affluent luxury consumers moved onto more exclusive or bespoke items (Willett 2015) in order to stand out from the crowds.

## Functional Value

Functional value refers to the useful dimension of products (Tynan et al. 2010) or the consumer's rational motivation in consumption (Shukla and Purani 2012). Functional value emanates from luxury's quality value, including delicacy and craftsmanship, alongside its uniqueness value in terms of product rarity and exclusivity (Chen and Lamberti 2015). However, with the increasing democratisation of luxury fashion, there has been an erosion of rarity and exclusivity (Kapferer 2012). Therefore Chen and Lamberti (2015) proposed a further dimension of usability value, which includes innovativeness, aesthetics and durability, to reflect the emerging trend of luxury brands seeking to create an emotional attachment with consumers, rather than focusing on promoting product exclusivity.

As foreign brands gravitate towards the digital sphere, Chinese social media platform WeChat has become the leading online platform for luxury brands to connect with Chinese consumers, provide brand and product information, and encourage followers to share online posts. Accordingly, fashion knowledge has accelerated amongst Chinese consumers and enabled them to develop stronger capabilities to evaluate the functional value of luxury products. Cross-cultural research by Shukla et al. (2015) showed that Chinese consumers value the functional perspective of luxury more than other Asians. As they gain experience and knowledge, they become more individual-oriented in their appreciation for unique products (Chen and Lamberti 2015; Zhan and He 2012). Chinese consumers are now moving from imitation to differentiation in their fashion consumption behaviour, thanks to increased fashion knowledge and brand literacy.

## Hedonic Value

Hedonic consumption refers to "those facets of consumer behaviour that relate to the multisensory, fantasy and emotive aspects of the product usage experience" (Hirschman and Holbrook 1982, p. 92). The hedonic value of consumption has been well documented in luxury consumption research, and it is long accepted that "one buys luxury goods primarily for one's pleasure" (Dubois and Laurent 1996, p. 472). The underlying consequence of luxury consumption is the sense of enjoyment and indulgence of an expensive yet non-essential item (Lu 2008) which offers high levels of symbolic and emotional or hedonic values (Tynan et al. 2010). However, China is typical of a collectivist culture, where interdependence, emotional control and moderation discourage individuals' hedonic consumption motivations (Yu and Bastin 2010) and the traditional Confucian principle of self-discipline acts as a strong restraint against those promoting Western hedonism (Wang and Lin 2009).

Nevertheless, hedonic values are stimulated in China through media communications which target younger generations and urban professionals. These include print media, commercials and Western films, where the frequent appearance of foreign brands are seen as indicators of hedonic values (Thompson 2011). Hedonic consumption is also encouraged by luxury branding and marketing practices, for example the widely adopted practice of experiential marketing in luxury retailing whereby luxury brands aim to embed value in personalised experiences created through active consumer participation. Utilising multiple stimuli to activate consumer participation and connection by incorporating aesthetic, entertainment, educational and escapism elements, they aim to foster hedonic consumption (Atwal and Williams 2009). Due to the relatively low brand awareness and loyalty of Chinese consumers, luxury brands have utilised multiple marketing strategies to increase the level of brand recognition, for example exhibitions and flagship stores where consumers can engage in a holistic sensational luxury experience and be driven to hedonic consumption (Liu et al. 2016).

To summarise, China's socio-cultural environment influences consumers in their perception of the four value dimensions of luxury fashion consumption. These collectivist socio-cultural effects on Chinese consumers' value perceptions emanate not only from the current economic context of a socialist free-market economy with Chinese characteristics, but are also due to historical memories of extreme thrift and Confucian ideals, with a unique definition of elitism, as well as consumers' aspirations to be 'modern' and 'Western.' Consumers and the world of fashion are connected by radical socio-cultural transformations that affect both (Hui 2014), therefore research on Chinese luxury consumer behaviour should revolve around a contextual understanding of socio-cultural influences. To achieve a more holistic understanding of socio-cultural influences, the impact of traditional Chinese culture must be considered, alongside the fast pace of modernisation to which Chinese consumers are also exposed (Zhang and Kim 2013), and critically reviewing these cultural tensions can contribute to understanding the on-going dynamics of the evolution of Chinese luxury consumers. As noted by Hennigs et al. (2012, p. 1019), there is a need in dynamic global marketplaces "to understand why consumers buy luxury goods, what they believe luxury is and how their perceptions of luxury value affect their purchase behavior as well as considering and distinguishing cultural influences". This is particularly relevant as luxury fashion evolves, now representing a diluted exclusivity compensated for by abundant rarity, which is achieved through marketing and branding activities aiming to create emotional connections with luxury consumers (Kapferer 2012). There is also a methodological opportunity to take a qualitative approach to explore the luxury fashion as a cultural phenomenon from the perspectives of the consumers who determine the market dynamics of contemporary China, which could appreciably deepen understanding of underlying consumer motivation and reveal new market dynamics.

# Methodology

Consumer reality is constantly changing and is influenced by external social and cultural factors. To understand contemporary Chinese consumer values, the essential structure and components of the lived consumer experience need to be clarified. Assuming consumer reality to be subjective, socially constructed, self-evolved, multiple, holistic and contextual (Holstein and Gubrium 1994), an interpretivist approach was taken as a means to generate rich, lived experiences from the data. In many Chinese luxury consumption studies, the Chinese luxury consumer is stereotyped as a passive adopter of Western luxury concepts. However, in this study, consumers' proactive role is acknowledged in terms of how they may be able to reinvent luxury value from their experience. By capturing lived and contextual consumer experiences, a richer and more authentic research outcome is achieved, which complements the generalisations of quantitative approaches. As the consumer is the central constructor of the consumption experience, this inquiry engages in reflexive reasoning and reflects on the origins of their experiences (Holstein and Gubrium 1994).

Using Bevan's (2014) phenomenological interview technique, as followed in previous luxury fashion research (e.g. Tynan et al. 2010; Dion and Arnould 2011; Liu et al. 2016), one-to-one depth interviews were conducted with ten Chinese luxury fashion consumers in 2017. One-to-one interviews ruled out the effects of envy, which could play on emotions in a group discussion, and which in the case of Chinese consumers especially, could cause loss of face. Phone interviews enabled the recruitment of participants from different residential areas to enhance the diversity of the sample pool. They were conducted in Chinese and lasted an hour on average, with some extending to 90 minutes, plus further follow-up communication by email where necessary. Interviews were recorded with interviewees' consent and participants were assured of anonymity and confidentiality.

The purposive sample consisted of eight female and two male consumers, including affluent students and professionals who had achieved financial success in non-manufacturing businesses, such as art or finance. These contemporary consumers may have different lifestyles and consumption experiences to the previous generation of affluent Chinese consumers, whose money may have come from property development or the energy business. The respondents self-identified as luxury consumers, had permanent Chinese residency and above-average household incomes, and who were willing to share their personal experiences and perceptions of luxury fashion consumption. Most were in their twenties or thirties and resided in Tier 1 cities such as Shanghai and Beijing, and other economically developed regions such as Hubei and Zhejiang. Others lived in Tier 3 cities, selected to uncover the diverse and dynamic nature of reality in Chinese luxury consumption. Although Tier 1 cities such as Beijing and Shanghai are well-known for their luxury retail offering, today's luxury consumers may also come from less-developed cities or areas. Table 8.1 displays the respondent profiles.

The interview topic guide included several broad questions to generate relevant consumer experiences, followed by probing questions to elicit further detail, as shown in Table 8.2.

The voice recordings were transcribed and translated into English to form the data pool for template analysis, following the principles of King (2012) and Braun and Clarke (2006). The a priori template of theory-driven codes generated from the literature review served as a reference for the primary data in terms of the level of intensity or the significance that each code carried. The data analysis was conducted more inductively, by firstly creating rich thematic descriptions of each interview, coding the data and generating potential emerging themes,

**Table 8.1**   Respondent profiles

| Participant ID | Occupation | Age | Gender | Residential area | Annual household income (RMB) |
| --- | --- | --- | --- | --- | --- |
| Participant A | Marketing director | 36 | Male | Shanghai | 2,000,000 |
| Participant B | Student | 25 | Female | Hubei | 1,200,000 |
| Participant C | Entrepreneur | 35 | Male | Beijing | 750,000 |
| Participant D | Student | 26 | Female | Zhejiang | 1,000,000 |
| Participant E | Student | 28 | Female | Beijing | 550,000 |
| Participant F | Senior editor | 30 | Female | Beijing | 1,500,000 |
| Participant G | Teacher | 29 | Female | Guangdong | 1,000,000 |
| Participant H | Student | 25 | Female | Sichuan | 2,000,000 |
| Participant I | Writer | 66 | Female | Beijing | 700,000 |
| Participant J | Student | 25 | Female | Zhejiang | 1,500,000 |

The average annual income in China in 2017 was 74,318 RMB (National Bureau of Statistics of China, cited in Statista 2019) although for white collar workers it was 91,284 RMB (Zhaopin 2018, cited in PR Newswire 2018)

**Table 8.2** Interview topic guide

| Broad questions | Probes |
|---|---|
| • Would you like to share the story of your latest purchase of luxury fashion?<br>• What does luxury mean to you?<br>• Tell me why buying luxury fashion makes you feel good? | • Why do you buy luxury fashion?<br>• What is your favourite brand/shop? Tell me about it and why you like it<br>• What makes a brand 'luxury'?<br>• Tell me about how you make the decision to buy luxury fashion products?<br>• You just mentioned that wearing luxury designer clothes helps you fit into your social group. Tell me more about it<br>• What should luxury quality be like?<br>• Have you purchased accessible luxury brands before? What do you think of them? |

reviewing and refining themes, and lastly selecting vivid and compelling extract examples for the final write-up.

# Findings and Discussion

Experienced Chinese luxury consumers not only see luxury fashion as a high-value commodity with added social and psychological value, but also as a form of art. Some respondents valued timeless, iconic styles and fashion designs, rather than novelty or trends. Preference for 'timeless' luxury tastes may be based in the Chinese thriftiness consumption value, and such consumers may be using their cultural knowledge to justify their non-seasonal less-trendy choices of luxury fashion. Respondents tended to perceive the designers behind luxury fashion brands as artists, and therefore the products attached with their names as artworks, not just to be used but also to be appreciated for their aesthetic excellence:

> *My interests in Yohji Yamamoto the brand didn't start with my shopping and picking up this brand on the shop floor. For me, I knew his artistic identity first and I validated him at a spiritual level.* (Participant I)

However, artistic images of fashion designers and their brands are now created by the luxury branding strategy of 'artification', as a means of overcoming the growth dilemma and restoring luxury legitimacy (Kapferer 2014b; Dion and Arnould 2011). Therefore, confusion and distractions are raised in front of consumers. Some younger participants' ideas of 'fashion as art' could be constructed or manipulated by luxury's branding and marketing communication activities:

> *I still remember the film about Chanel and I've even got the soundtrack on my phone … She represents the modern female who can achieve success without compromising gender roles, social classes. The film intensified my interest towards Chanel the brand. When I am using a Chanel bag, I think I can be the next 'new' female.* (Participant F)

Luxury's democratisation differentiates contemporary luxury from the traditional, old-luxe concept, and its evolution has visibly expanded the market size of luxury fashion, but several respondents expressed confusion and even denial towards the idea of 'accessible luxury':

> *I believe these two are very different concepts. Accessible luxury doesn't belong to real luxury. It is situated between fast fashion and luxury.* (Participant B)
> *I am not paying £300 for a Coach bag… Pricewise it's not a big spend but neither is it a bargain. The design is neither forward nor classy. I don't understand what kind of need can be satisfied by Coach… You are not buying because it's cheap.* (Participant D)

The 'aspirational realm' emerged from the data, extending understanding of Western frameworks (e.g. Shukla and Purani 2012). Respondents saw luxury fashion as a symbol of the West but also the 'art of life' that they should aspire to. Modern luxury consumers play two roles simultaneously, as adopters of Western concepts and re-inventors of long-forgotten traditional fine-living philosophies. Pioneering luxury fashion consumers have rediscovered the consumption activity with a more philosophical, metaphysical and intellectual meaning that resonates with traditional Confucian philosophy. For example, Participant Y felt that "*luxury fashion's design has to be original and unique. And it should also achieve some spiritual highness"*. Participant F felt that *"the value of luxury fashion is beyond items"* and that *"luxury is endorsed by the spirit of devotion through the process of making and by the pursuit of ultimate beauty."* Both statements echo how traditional Chinese educated elites (scholar-bureaucrats) appreciated luxury—by its artistic excellence and its philosophical references.

Four-dimensional luxury value perceptions are grouped under the theme 'instrumental realm' of luxury value, as the direct value that consumers can perceive or achieve in luxury consumption (Hennigs et al. 2013; Vigneron and Johnson 2004). The sub-themes in this instrumental realm present a set of values emanating from the joint influences of luxury's democratisation and China's socio-cultural context.

## Financial Value

Although participants were earning competitive salaries or were supported by their wealthy parents, they still kept within their (generous) budgets, and were unlikely to purchase luxury products impulsively. That respondents mainly invested in handbags and shoes can be used as evidence that Chinese consumers are strongly aware of pricing in luxury but want their money to be well spent. Participant B explained that *"a Louis Vuitton bag for 10,000 RMB is good value"*. Chinese consumers can be better described as looking for value-for-money in luxury fashion consumption, as opposed to being 'bargain hunters'. However, when explaining her luxury fashion journey, Participant H acknowledged that when she was living overseas where luxury goods prices were cheaper than in China, she *"ended up buying loads because they are cheap"* as she felt that *"the more I bought, the more I saved"*, explaining her excessive luxury consumption in terms of saving money. But with greater experience and knowledge, 'bargains' become off-putting to more discerning consumers. Heavy discounts contaminate the brand's prestigious image in the consumer's mind, as Participant D explained: *"Those luxury fashion brands that always end up in [the] sale, I don't recognise them as true luxury"*. Similarly, Participant A felt Prada's less expensive products tarnished the brand's overall exclusive and elite image: *"I fell in love with*

*Prada before, but it didn't last. Prada's product range is too wide. Anyone can afford a Prada product. It put me off. For me luxury means that not everyone can afford it.*" This reveals the intertwined effects between financial value and conspicuous value: Chinese luxury consumers prefer brands whose price is well-perceived, so that they can achieve the rewards of conspicuous value. Chinese luxury consumers' price-sensitivity can be redefined in terms of value for money, rather than in terms of seeking discounts or bargains.

## Conspicuous Value

Chinese consumers' traditional preference for mainstream luxury brands, such as Chanel, Louis Vuitton and Gucci, came from their conspicuous value as a display of financial capital and social identity. This is particularly significant in a society where financial success is encouraged (Thompson 2011) and where people are judged on their looks.

> *People are really judgmental about what you are wearing ... people will judge your social status by your look.* (Participant C)

Participant A similarly justified his purchases of Dior suits for work, as his job role effectively made him the 'face' of the brand in China:

> *My job was socialising with people. And what you wear and how you look, your tastes directly affect how people perceive your professionalism... You need the right things to enhance your image.* (Participant A)

Chinese consumers' luxury consumption is still motivated by conspicuous value, especially for consumers who are on the lower-to-middle levels of the social or career ladder. But once individuals achieve higher social status, they feel less needy of the conspicuous value of luxury fashion, as stated by Participant I:

> *For people like me, who has already achieved success in my professional area, I don't need any validation from others.* (Participant I)

There is a sense of a journey, as the same participant acknowledged her changing taste as she moved along the learning curve and became more discerning towards lesser-known brands:

> *I was quite keen on well-known luxury brands because they can bring social recognition, along with the self-satisfaction. I don't deny there was a feeling of showing off. I wanted people to know exactly what I was wearing or using. However, the more I know about what the story behind each luxury good is, and the more luxury products I have, the less interest I have in well-known brands, like Louis Vuitton.* (Participant I)

Similarly, Participant C preferred more radically designed brands such as Maison Margiela and Comme des Garçons, although previously had been a fan of Gucci, Versace, Louis Vuitton and Armani. This shows how conspicuous value evolves over time: as the signalling ability of more commonly owned goods becomes diluted, an increased desire for sophistication and subtlety in design allows the more educated consumer to distinguish themselves with niche, highbrow choices (Eckhardt et al. 2015). In addition, a new dimension of conspicuous consumption in the display of the user's cultural capital emerged from the data, which relates to their appreciation of luxury fashion's aesthetic qualities. Thus, Participant A distinguished those who are merely wealthy from those who are wealthy and have taste:

> *Chinese people's aesthetics remains in its infant stage. For me, there are different rich people in society. First it's the rich vulgar. They only have money. They can buy all the luxury they want but they don't have taste.* (Participant A)

## Functional Value

Participants valued craftsmanship and excellent materials. Participant I was really impressed by the *"perfection"* of luxury. They would examine the product material and the product finish, including stitches (Participant D) or the texture and quality of the leather (Participant H, Participant B). Three participants identified three key words (originality, innovativeness and uniqueness) that exist in the realm of usability value, which was first identified by Chen and Lamberti (2015) as product innovativeness, aesthetics and durability. Usability value is different from the concept of novelty in design; while novelty is driven by newness, originality, innovativeness and uniqueness are driven by a holistic appreciation of luxury fashion's aesthetic superiority in design, and serve to "*show personality*" (Participant A), "*social image*" (Participant F) or "*personal style*" (Participant H). Chinese luxury consumers' increased knowledge has made them more critical and demanding of product offerings. Functionality in luxury fashion has moved beyond the measure of good quality and now has a more hybrid meaning, which encompasses the excellence of both the material quality and non-material-oriented aesthetic innovation, thus redefining the meaning of functionality in luxury fashion.

## Hedonic Value

Participants' expressions of hedonic value were identified in two perspectives: 'joy from others' and 'joy from self'. Supporting Vigneron and Johnson's (2004) research that found hedonic-driven consumers are less susceptible to interpersonal influences and are more role-relaxed and individualistic, some participants indicated that hedonic reward came from within themselves, rather than from other-oriented conspicuousness. Participant I had developed a preference for less well-known brands that would not be recognised by the masses:

> *It comes from inner joy. The joy comes from me using the bag. So the charm of luxury comes from the self-satisfaction, rather than from recognition from others … You know, no one recognises those niche luxury fashion brand. So the joy comes from within yourself.* (Participant I)

An interesting dynamic from the cross-pollination of hedonic consumption with a collectivist cultural background, here termed as 'joy from others', emerged from the data. Participant C spoke of the "*joy of sharing and discovery*", or the recreational pleasure of shopping with like-minded friends with whom he could share his thoughts and ideas about

**Table 8.3** Final thematic template

| Main themes | Sub-themes | |
|---|---|---|
| 1. Luxury fashion concept | 1.1 Anti-trend | |
| | 1.2 Fashion as art | |
| | 1.3 Confusion of democratisation | |
| 2. Instrumental realm | 2.1 Financial | 2.1.1 Accessories as priority |
| | | 2.1.2 Knowledge-bound |
| | | 2.1.3 Value-for-money |
| | 2.2 Conspicuous | 2.2.1 Financial privilege |
| | | 2.2.2 Cultural privilege |
| | | 2.2.3 Social identity |
| | 2.3 Functional | 2.3.1 Craftsmanship |
| | | 2.3.2 Material |
| | | 2.3.3 Usability |
| | 2.4 Hedonic | 2.4.1 Joy from others |
| | | 2.4.2 Joy from self |
| 3. Aspirational realm | 3.1 A Western symbol | |
| | 3.2 Art of life | 3.2.1 Luxury fashion as art |
| | | 3.2.2 Reviving Chinese traditional luxury value |

the aesthetics of luxury fashion. This finding expands our understanding of how collectivist consumers interact within a social group, which may not only generate potential peer pressure but also creates opportunities for extra peer validation, which contributes to achieving hedonic rewards.

The final thematic template in Table 8.3 presents a summary of the data analysis: the first main theme of how consumers conceptualise luxury fashion was identified from the literature but its sub-themes emerged from the data. The second main theme and first order sub-themes were identified from the literature review, but the second order sub-themes emerged from the data. The third main theme (aspirational realm) represents luxury fashion's indirect value, which emerged entirely from the data.

# Conclusion

Consumption is not only a commercial activity, but also a cultural and social one. Chinese consumers characterise luxury four-dimensionally in financial, conspicuous, functional and hedonic terms (Shukla and Purani 2012; Shukla et al. 2015; Chen and Lamberti 2015), but also imbue luxury fashion with a unique contextual value that reflects the socio-cultural realm of their world. The conceptualisation of luxury is thus situated between China's ancient cultural heritage and consumers' unconscious and spontaneous identity-seeking activities on the one hand; while on the other, it lies in Western influences and the evermore consumerism-oriented society that is hidden beneath the jargon of the socialist free-market economy, albeit with Chinese characteristics. Chinese luxury fashion consumption also involves Chinese characteristics of dual identities—one identity serves to increase consumers' competitiveness in their social life, the other serves as an aspirational tool to enable them to achieve a better self. Figure 8.1 suggests a contextualised extension to the four-dimensional Western framework of luxury consumer value to reflect the aspirational realm for Chinese luxury fashion consumers.

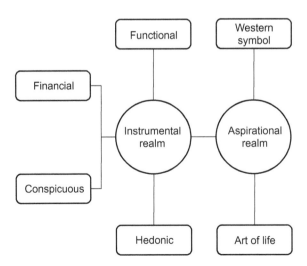

**Fig. 8.1** Empirical framework of Chinese luxury fashion consumer value

The empirical framework confirms that conspicuous, functional, financial and hedonistic values are the four vital aspects of luxury value formation (Shukla and Purani 2012), but also suggests a new aspirational realm of consumer value, reflecting the social evolution from isolation to globalisation and a cultural renaissance of Chinese traditional values. Luxury fashion symbolises a Western lifestyle, perceived as more modern and advanced. Beyond materialistic indulgence, luxury fashion also offers a form of spiritual enlightenment, in terms of elegant living through fine goods and an appreciation of aesthetics—the so-called 'art of life'. The empirical analysis gives insight into how China's unique cultural background can construct consumer value and lead consumers to reinvent the value of luxury fashion consumption.

# References

Atwal, G., and A. Williams. 2009. "Luxury Brand Marketing—The Experience Is Everything!" *Journal of Brand Management* 16 (5): 338–346.

Bain & Co. 2015. "Luxury Goods Worldwide Market Study: Fall-Winter 2015." Available at http://www.bain.com/publications/articles/luxury-goods-worldwide-market-study-winter-2015.aspx. Accessed on 28 February 2019.

Bain, C. 2018. "What's Really Driving China's Big Luxury Rebound." Available at https://qz.com/1302063/chinas-luxury-spending-rebound/. Accessed on 28 February 2019.

Belk, R.W. 1985. "Materialism: Trait Aspects of Living in the Material World." *Journal of Consumer Research* 12 (3): 265–280.

Bevan, M.T. 2014. "A Method of Phenomenological Interviewing." *Qualitative Health Research* 24 (1): 136–144.

Bonetti, F., P. Perry, and J. Fernie. 2016. "The Evolution of Luxury Fashion Retailing in China." In *Luxury Fashion Retail Management*, edited by T.-M. Choi and B. Shen, 49–70. Singapore: Springer.

Boston Consulting Group. 2018. "The Key Trends for the Luxury Goods Industry in 2018." Available at https://www.bcg.com/d/press/20february2018-altagamma-true-luxury-global-consumer-insight-184693. Accessed on 28 February 2019.

Braun, V., and V. Clarke. 2006. "Using Thematic Analysis in Psychology." *Qualitative Research in Psychology* 3 (2): 77–101.

Caïs, C. 2018. "Stirring Dragon: The Rise of Chinese Luxury Brands." Available at https://www.forbes.com/sites/forbesagencycouncil/2018/11/26/stirring-dragon-the-rise-of-chinese-luxury-brands/#2c2cf7b6ebc5. Accessed on 28 February 2019.

Chadha, R., and P. Husband. 2006. *The Cult of the Luxury Brand: Inside Asia's Love Affair with Luxury.* London: Nicholas Brealey International.

Chen, S., and L. Lamberti. 2015. "Entering the Dragon's Nest: Exploring Chinese Upper-Class Consumers' Perception of Luxury." *Qualitative Market Research: An International Journal* 18 (1): 4–29.

Chevalier, M., and P. Lu. 2010. *Luxury China: Market Opportunities and Potential.* Singapore: Wiley.

D'Arpizio, C. 2016. "Altagamma 2016 Worldwide Luxury Market Monitor". Available at https://altagamma.it/media/source/ALTAGAMMA%20WW%20MARKETS%20MONITOR%202016.pdf. Accessed 28 February 2019.

D'Arpizio, C., and F. Levato. 2018. "Altagamma 2018 Worldwide Luxury Market Monitor." Bain & Co.

Dion, D., and E. Arnould. 2011. "Retail Luxury Strategy: Assembling Charisma Through Art and Magic." *Journal of Retailing* 87 (4): 502–520.

Dubois, B., and G. Laurent. 1996. "The Functions of Luxury: A Situational Approach to Excursionism." In *NA-Advances in Consumer Research*, edited by K.P. Corfman and J.G. Lynch Jr., vol. 23, 470–477. Provo, UT: Association for Consumer Research.

Eckhardt, G.M., R.W. Belk, and J.A. Wilson. 2015. "The Rise of Inconspicuous Consumption." *Journal of Marketing Management* 31 (7–8): 807–826.

Guarino, P. 2015. "Could Global Pricing Alignment Backfire?" Available at https://www.businessoffashion.com/articles/opinion/op-ed-could-global-pricing-alignment-backfire. Accessed on 28 February 2019.

Han, Y.J., J.C. Nunes, and X. Drèze. 2010. "Signaling Status with Luxury Goods: The Role of Brand Prominence." *Journal of Marketing* 74 (4): 15–30.

Hebdige, D. 1999. "The Function of Subculture." In *The Cultural Studies Reader*, edited by A. During, 441–450. London: Routledge.

Hennigs, N., K.P. Wiedmann, C. Klarmann, S. Strehlau, B. Godey, D. Pederzoli, A. Neulinger, K. Dave, G. Aiello, R. Donvito, K. Taro, J. Taborecka-Petrovicova, C. Rodrıguez Santos, J. Jung, and H. Oh. 2012. "What Is the Value of Luxury? A Cross-Cultural Consumer Perspective." *Psychology and Marketing* 29 (12): 1018–1034.

Hennigs, N., K.P. Wiedmann, S. Behrens, and C. Klarmann. 2013. "Unleashing the Power of Luxury: Antecedents of Luxury Brand Perception and Effects on Luxury Brand Strength." *Journal of Brand Management* 20 (8): 705–715.

Hirschman, E.C., and M.B. Holbrook. 1982. "Hedonic Consumption: Emerging Concepts, Methods and Propositions." *Journal of Marketing* 46 (3): 92–101.

Holbrook, M.B. 2005. "Customer Value and Autoethnography: Subjective Personal Introspection and the Meanings of a Photograph Collection." *Journal of Business Research* 58 (1): 45–61.

Holstein, J.A., and J.F. Gubrium. 1994. "Phenomenology, Ethnomethodology, and Interpretive Practice." In *Handbook of Qualitative Research*, edited by N.K. Denzin and Y.S. Lincoln, 262–272. Thousand Oaks: Sage.

Holt, D.B., J.A. Quelch, and E.L. Taylor. 2004. "How Global Brands Compete." *Harvard Business Review* 82 (9): 68–75.

Hui, C. 2014. "Mao's Children Are Wearing Fashion!" In *The Changing Landscape of China's Consumerism*, edited by A. Hulme, 23–55. Oxford: Chandos Publishing.

Kamal, S., S.-C. Chu, and M. Pedram. 2013. "Materialism, Attitudes, and Social Media Usage and Their Impact on Purchase Intention of Luxury Fashion Goods Among American and Arab Young Generations." *Journal of Interactive Advertising* 13 (1): 27–40.

Kapferer, J.-N. 2012. "Abundant Rarity: The Key to Luxury Growth." *Business Horizons* 55 (5): 453–462.

Kapferer, J.-N. 2014a. "The Future of Luxury: Challenges and Opportunities." *Journal of Brand Management* 21 (9): 716–726.

Kapferer, J.-N. 2014b. "The Artification of Luxury: From Artisans to Artists." *Business Horizons* 57: 371–380.

Kapferer, J.-N., and G. Laurent. 2016. "Where Do Consumers Think Luxury Begins? A Study of Perceived Minimum Price for 21 Luxury Goods in 7 Countries." *Journal of Business Research* 69 (1): 332–340.

Kapferer, J.-N., and V. Bastien. 2009. "The Specificity of Luxury Management: Turning Marketing Upside Down." *Journal of Brand Management* 16 (5–6): 311–322.

Kastanakis, M.N., and G. Balabanis. 2014. "Explaining Variation in Conspicuous Luxury Consumption: An Individual Differences Perspective." *Journal of Business Research* 67 (10): 2147–2154.

King, N. 2012. "Doing Template Analysis." In *Qualitative Organizational Research*, edited by G. Symon and C. Cassell, 426–450. London: Sage.

King, Y.C., and J.T. Myers. 1977. "Shame as an Incomplete Conception of Chinese Culture: A Study of Face." Chinese University of Hong Kong, Social Research Center.

Liu, S., P. Perry, C. Moore, and G. Warnaby. 2016. "The Standardization-Localization Dilemma of Brand Communications for Luxury Fashion Retailers' Internationalization into China." *Journal of Business Research* 69 (1): 357–364.

Liu, S., P. Perry, and G. Gadzinski. 2018. "The Implications of Digital Marketing on WeChat for Luxury Fashion Brands in China." *Journal of Brand Management.* https://doi.org/10.1057/s41262-018-0140-2.

Lockett, M. 1988. "Culture and the Problems of Chinese Management." *Organization Studies* 9 (4): 475–496.

Lu, P.X. 2008. *Elite China: Luxury Consumer Behavior in China.* Singapore: Wiley.

McKinsey & Co. 2017. "Chinese Luxury Consumers: More Global, More Demanding, Still Spending." Available at https://www.mckinsey.com/business-functions/marketing-and-sales/our-insights/chinese-luxury-consumers-more-global-more-demanding-still-spending. Accessed on 28 February 2019.

Moore, C.M., A.M. Doherty, and S.A. Doyle. 2010. "Flagship Stores as a Market Entry Method: The Perspective of Luxury Fashion Retailing." *European Journal of Marketing* 44 (1/2): 139–161.

Okonkwo, U. 2014. *Luxury Fashion Branding: Trends, Tactics, Techniques.* Basingstoke: Palgrave Macmillan.

Parguel, B., T. Delécolle, and P. Valette-Florence. 2016. "How Price Display Influences Consumer Luxury Perceptions." *Journal of Business Research* 69 (1): 341–348.

PR Newswire. 2018. "China White-Collar Average Salary Dips in the First Quarter of 2018." Available at https://www.prnewswire.com/news-releases/china-white-collar-average-salary-dips-in-the-first-quarter-of-2018-300622146.html. Accessed on 28 February 2019.

Reuters. 2016. "China's Grey Luxury Market Threatened by New Tax Regime." Available at http://fortune.com/2016/04/03/chinas-grey-luxury-market-taxes/. Accessed on 28 February 2019.

Rucker, D.D., and A.D. Galinsky. 2008. "Desire to Acquire: Powerlessness and Compensatory Consumption." *Journal of Consumer Research* 35 (2): 257–267.

Shukla, P., J. Singh, and M. Banerjee. 2015. "They Are Not All Same: Variations in Asian Consumers' Value Perceptions of Luxury Brands." *Marketing Letters* 26 (3): 265–278.

Shukla, P., and K. Purani. 2012. "Comparing the Importance of Luxury Value Perceptions in Cross-National Contexts." *Journal of Business Research* 65 (10): 1417–1424.

Statista. 2019. "Average Yearly Wages in China from 2008 to 2017 (in Yuan)." Available at https://www.statista.com/statistics/743522/china-average-yearly-wages/. Accessed on 28 February 2019.

Thompson, M. 2011. "Chinese Hedonic Values and the Chinese Classical Virtues: Managing the Tension." *Journal of Management Development* 30 (7/8): 709–723.

Tian, K.T., W.O. Bearden, and G.L. Hunter. 2001. "Consumers' Need for Uniqueness: Scale Development and Validation." *Journal of Consumer Research* 28 (1): 50–66.

Tynan, C., S. McKechnie, and C. Chhuon. 2010. "Co-creating Value for Luxury Brands." *Journal of Business Research* 63 (11): 1156–1163.

Vigneron, F., and L.J. Johnson. 2004. "Measuring Perceptions of Brand Luxury." *Journal of Brand Management* 11 (6): 484–506.

Wang, C.L., and X. Lin. 2009. "Migration of Chinese Consumption Values: Traditions, Modernization, and Cultural Renaissance." *Journal of Business Ethics* 88 (3): 399–409.

Watson, M.Z., and R.N. Yan. 2013. "An Exploratory Study of the Decision Processes of Fast Versus Slow Fashion Consumers." *Journal of Fashion Marketing and Management* 17 (2): 141–159.

Wiedmann, K.-P., N. Hennigs, and A. Siebels. 2007. "Measuring Consumers' Luxury Value Perception: A Cross-Cultural Framework." *Academy of Marketing Science Review* 11 (7): 1–21.

Wilcox, K., H.M. Kim, and S. Sen. 2009. "Why Do Consumers Buy Counterfeit Luxury Brands?" *Journal of Marketing Research* 46 (2): 247–259.

Willet, M. 2015. "Louis Vuitton Is Now a 'Brand for Secretaries' in China." Available at https://www.businessinsider.com/louis-vuitton-losing-sales-in-china-2015-2?r=US&IR=T.

Yeoman, I., and U. McMahon-Beattie. 2006. "Luxury Markets and Premium Pricing." *Journal of Revenue and Pricing Management* 4 (4): 319–328.

Yu, C., and M. Bastin. 2010. "Hedonic Shopping Value and Impulse Buying Behaviour in Transitional Economies: A Symbiosis in the Mainland China Marketplace." *Journal of Brand Management* 18 (2): 105–114.

Zhan, L., and Y. He. 2012. "Understanding Luxury Consumption in China: Consumer Perceptions of Best-Known Brands." *Journal of Business Research* 65 (10): 1452–1460.

Zhang, B., and J.H. Kim. 2013. "Luxury Fashion Consumption in China: Factors Affecting Attitude and Purchase Intent." *Journal of Retailing and Consumer Services* 20 (1): 68–79.

# Part IV

## Case Studies: Brand Building and Communication

# 9

# Speedy Tuesday: Omega's Adoption of Communication 4.0

## François H. Courvoisier and Claire Roederer

## Introduction

Omega is one of the 18 watch brands of the Swatch Group, located in Biel, Switzerland, which is the most important watch producer worldwide with a turnover of 8 billion Swiss francs. Omega is a brand of "accessible luxury", i.e. with an average selling price about 6000 Swiss francs for the standard models; most of the Omega watches are mechanical, which means hand or automatic winding. The brand Omega has four product lines called Speedmaster, Seamaster, DeVille and Constellation.[1] Traditionally, advertising of Omega products is made

[1]For more details, see www.omegawatches.com.

F. H. Courvoisier (✉)
HES-SO//Haute Ecole de Gestion Arc, Neuchâtel, Switzerland
e-mail: francois.courvoisier@he-arc.ch

C. Roederer
EM Strasbourg Business School, Laboratoire Humanis,
Strasbourg, France
e-mail: claire.roederer@em-strasbourg.eu

© The Author(s) 2020
I. Cantista and T. Sádaba (eds.), *Understanding Luxury Fashion*,
Palgrave Advances in Luxury, https://doi.org/10.1007/978-3-030-25654-8_9

by print ads in newspapers and magazines and distribution of watches takes place through own specialized boutiques and multibrand retailers.

At noon (Bienne, Switzerland time) on January 10, 2017, at Swatch Group's headquarters, the Omega watch brand sold 2012 copies[2] of a limited edition of the "Speedmaster Speedy Tuesday" (a replica of the iconic watch worn by NASA's Apollo program astronauts) via Instagram in 4 hours 15 minutes and 43 seconds. Usually retailed in bricks and mortar stores, the brand thus drew "closer" to its customers by proposing an interactive commercial activity on its website… It convinced 2012 people to participate, generating a business turnover estimated at more than 12 million Swiss francs in just over 4 hours. On July 10, 2018, a "Speedy Tuesday 2" operation was organized, again with 2012 pieces offered at 6350 Swiss francs for an exclusive "Ultraman" model in reference to the eponymous Japanese series.[3] This time, the limited edition sold out in 1 hour 53 minutes and 17 seconds (Maillard 2018), twice as fast as the "Speedy Tuesday 1" operation, leaving several thousand of the brand's fans on a waiting list… While limited series are an old device, often used in the world of watchmaking, Speedy Tuesday operations, combining limited series and social media commerce, are symptomatic of profound changes in the way brands communicate and market their products directly to their consumers.

The present research, based on a case study and interviews with experts, aims to understand how communication codes and the emergence of *social commerce* impact the marketing strategies of iconic brands such as Omega. In our theoretical framework, we use the brand's experience to understand what is at work in terms of co-creation between lovers of the iconic model Speedmaster and Omega. Our findings allow us to observe what we suggest calling a morphing form of communication and distribution channels that results from these

---

[2]See Box 9.1 below: Tuesday May 29, 2012, Robert-Jan Broer published his first post about the Omega Speedmaster.

[3]Ultraman is a fictional superhero and is the first *tokusatsu* hero launched by Tsuburava Productions in Japan. Ultraman first appeared as the titular character alongside his human host Shin Hayata in the 1966–1967 Japanese television series, "Ultraman", which ran for 39 episodes.

efficient and ephemeral operations based on limited series developed by and for a community of fans, and marketed via social networks.

# Theoretical Research Framework

## The Web 4.0 as a Communications and Social-Commerce Space

Driven by the digitalization of communications and the rapid development of social networks (Zorik and Courvoisier 2018), some brands are devising new ways to reach their loyal customers, often fans and collectors, in the luxury watch sector. Generally, they do this via their bricks and mortar distribution networks by attracting customers through a classic *pull*-type advert, including ads in the trade and consumer press and urban signage.

In the 2000s, interactive web 2.0 led to the rise of blogs and forums, as well as social platforms such as Facebook, YouTube, Instagram, Pinterest and Twitter. These platforms led brands to review their communication strategies and start real conversations with the market. Marketing 3.0 then put the sharing of values between communities, collaboration, and the quest for meaning at the heart of marketing strategies. Marketing 4.0, while remaining resolutely collaborative in the search for values and meaning, relies on the increased use of customer data (*Big data*) to predict and anticipate consumption (Kotler et al. 2016).

This web evolution has witnessed the rapid development of *social commerce* (or s-commerce), an innovative form of electronic commerce (e-commerce) that combines social interactions and user contributions on social media to boost online shopping. As an emerging phenomenon, social commerce has been the subject of a growing number of academic papers over the past ten years (Alalwan et al. 2017).

From a business perspective, the use of media and social networks appears to be a useful communications and sales strategy through targeting existing customers or winning new ones (Lin et al. 2016).

Marketing 4.0 is part of the experiential marketing and co-creation movement (Roederer and Filser 2015) as well as that of tribal marketing (Cova and Cova 2002): it involves reaching consumer targets with strong common interests, and seeking memorable experiences (Marion 2003).

## The Dilemma of Luxury Brands

Luxury brands also look for ways they can make use of web 4.0 and social media. Many still hesitate to be too accessible on platforms that have become central to the lives of many consumers, for fear of diluting their image and positioning that until now has been based on exclusivity, inheritance and uniqueness (Pentina et al. 2018). However, some brands such as Vuitton, Chanel and Burberry have opted for an active presence on social media to get closer to certain targets, such as millennials (Quach and Traichon 2017), who help to create the brand's story by sharing their emotions and experiences.

## Brand Experience

We can define brand experience as a series of interactions between a person and the brand in various consumption situations, generating value and making sense for the individuals who experience them (Roederer and Filser 2015). At the risk of being overused, the term 'experience' should be reserved for interactions that are sufficiently memorable for the client to remember, whether positively or negatively. This definition is based on the idea that the experience is not "the" product or "the" service, but the consumer interacting with "the object of his or her desire" which can be a product, a service or a mix of both, in a specific situation, that is to say circumscribed to a place and a moment. It is this assemblage of elements and the interactions between the elements of the assembly that create the experience. Once the interaction is over, the positive or negative memory of the experience remains.

In the watch industry, the experience provided by the Omega luxury brand is no exception to this interactionist definition of the experience, even if Omega traditionally favors an exclusive and physical distribution network across the globe, in single-brand boutiques and in multi-brand retailers. With an online shop in the US and sustained presence on social networks, including Facebook, Twitter and YouTube, the brand has nonetheless been open to the opportunity of communicating differently and with new targets for several years.

The emergence of web 4.0 has transformed advertising codes in an increasingly "multichannel" distribution context where social commerce is co-created through the experiences that consumers choose to share on social networks. Watch brands, from entry-level to *Haute Horlogerie*, cannot ignore these developments otherwise they risk losing momentum with certain digital savvy consumers who are often the prime target. As the case of Speedy Tuesday clearly illustrates below, it is possible for a "superstar brand" (Brynjolfsson et al. 2010) like Omega to leverage social networks to sell a luxury product by co-creating an exclusive experience with enthusiasts of the brand, in which communication and sales are wholly intertwined, circumscribed in time.

## Choice of Terrain, Objectives and Research Protocol

On the basis of the conceptual framework developed, we adopted a case study approach, basing our analysis on non-directive interviews with Omega's vice-president of communications and public relations (Mr. Jean-Pascal Perret, interviewed in his office, July 4, 2018) and the founder of the Speedy Tuesday community (Mr. Robert-Jan Broer, interviewed per e-mail, November 6 and 9, 2018) to capture their stories and their feedback. In addition, we observed the reactions of some journalists and thought leaders in the watch-related press.

We then conducted a content analysis to process the interviews collected and, in parallel, conducted a literature review to illustrate the communications adopted for the Speedy Tuesday Operation.

**Box 9.1: The Speedy Tuesday case in figures**

On January 10, 2017, the Omega brand sold 2012 copies of a limited edition of the "Speedmaster Speedy Tuesday" via Instagram in just 4 hours 15 minutes and 43 seconds, only available in advance on the official website Omegawatches.com. Usually retailed in bricks and mortar stores, the brand thus drew "closer" to its customers by proposing an interactive market activity on its site… In reducing the psychological distance, the brand promoted concrete awareness (spontaneous purchase and instant pre-order of a limited edition), convincing 2012 people to take immediate action, and generating an estimated turnover of over 12 million Swiss francs in just 4 hours… without compromising the brand identity (luxury, exclusivity that presupposes a certain distance) or its values (performance, innovation).

On July 10, 2018, a "Speedy Tuesday 2" operation was conducted featuring an exclusive "Ultraman" model in reference to the eponymous Japanese series, again with 2012 pieces offered at 6350 Swiss francs. This time, the limited edition found takers in just 1 hour 53 minutes and 17 seconds (Maillard 2018), twice as fast as the "Speedy Tuesday 1" operation, leaving a few thousand fans on a waiting list… As the operation took place in both cases at noon, Bienne time (in Switzerland), American fans were not yet up and many Asians were already asleep…

It is not easy to evaluate the number of members of the Speedy Tuesday virtual community (the fans of the Omega Speedmaster watch) since it is not formally constituted and is active on different channels and social networks[4]: the Fratellowatches website, Facebook (2800 members in March 2019) and Instagram, on which the hashtag was used 152,000 times (March 2019). A post published by Robert-Jan Broer, founder of the community, generates more than 10,000 views! "The typical community member profile is a 35- to 55-year-old male, casual or regular buyer, although more and more women are contributing photos and stories. The socio-demographic profiling of these people is not very important and in any case, they do not want it" (Broer 2018).

---

[4]See Box 9.2 below: the origin of the Speedy Tuesday community.

# Results of the Analysis

## The Birth of a Community

### Original Heroic Figures

When we reconstruct the genesis of the Speedy Tuesday operation, two key figures emerge; first, the president of Omega Watches (one of Swatch Group's 18 brands), Raynald Aeschlimann, who quickly saw the potential and understood the value of social networks to bring the brand's customers together. For a global brand such as Omega, being able to get away from geographical constraints by offering platforms based on a shared passion represented a new vision, subsequently turned into a business opportunity, but also a new interpretation of the brand's customer as an active, collaborative and creative person.

The second figure at the center of the Speedy Tuesday adventure is that of Robert-Jan Broer, a Dutch journalist, founder and host of the Fratellowatches.com website and at the origin of the Speedy Tuesday community established in 2012. Robert-Jan embodies a new posture and a new era of watchmaking opinion leaders: he is both a journalist and a lover of the brand, who put his clear understanding of digital codes at the service of his passion. In this way, he invented a new practice, halfway between journalism and the digital age collection, becoming a community leader and an influencer. His actions and enthusiasm drew the Omega brand to him.

---

**Box 9.2: Portrait of the founder of Speedy Tuesday**

Robert-Jan Broer

Born in 1977 in a family already in love with beautiful watches like Omega Speedmaster, Robert-Jan Broer has written articles on watchmaking for over 20 years. Active in online watch communities since 1998, he created the Fratellowatches.com website in 1994. He explains his passion for Speedmaster watches in a video published by Hodinkee (https://www.hodinkee.com/articles/robert-jan-broer-omega-speedy-tuesday-watch-video).

---

> **The origins of the Speedy Tuesday community**
>
> After Robert-Jan posted a photo of one of his Speedmaster watches on Facebook using the expression "Speedy Tuesday", and following the positive reaction from many followers, he decided to use it as a "working title" for a recurring subject on Fratellowatches.com. "Tuesday, May 29, 2012 I published the first Speedy Tuesday article, followed by many more over the following weeks and years. In the meantime, the #speedytuesday hashtag has been used over 21,000 times on Instagram by Speedmaster fans worldwide" (Broer 2018). In addition, Robert-Jan has organized informal Speedy Tuesday meetings where Speedmaster fans can meet face to face and chat about their passion. In 2013, Omega became interested in the community and, together with Robert-Jan, organized the first official Speedy Tuesday event near Amsterdam, in the visitor center of the European Space Agency, because of the link with the historic moon landing, Apollo 11 in 1969. In 2014 there was a new joint operation in a shop in Amsterdam to present the novelties of the year. However, the real collaboration began in 2016, when Robert-Jan met Raynald Aeschlimann at a dinner party. The latter quickly seized the opportunity to collaborate with the community, and "the idea of developing an exclusive Speedmaster for fans was put forward. This watch was then launched following the close involvement of Robert-Jan with Omega's development team" (Broer 2018).

## Praxeological Dimension and Co-creation of the Experience

Between 2012 and 2017, the community using the #speedytuesday hashtag was built through feed sent to the Instagram network. Little by little, the phenomenon gained momentum and many people around the world began using #speedytuesday to publish their Speedmaster posts and photos. It is a small, fast-paced community that regularly streams content and breathes life into the Speedy Tuesday community. The contributions (generally photos of the watches worn, or presented in a personal environment) are central to the sharing of the consumer experience, and reflect the praxeological dimension of the experience.

The co-creation mechanism promoting the product and creating a link between enthusiasts was one of the key drivers of Speedy Tuesday: indeed, many of Omega's Speedmaster model fans had been identified for decades and were already offered the very first limited series in the 1970s.

For the record, the Speedmaster is one of the icons of Swiss watch-making, as it was selected by NASA in the 1960s for the Apollo astronauts, and worn by the first men to set foot on the moon, Neil Armstrong and Buzz Aldrin on July 21, 1969. However, the forms of co-creation by the brand's aficionados, made possible via social net-works, and the shared enthusiasm of the community are new in their intensity. Thus the launch of both Omega Speedy Tuesday limited edi-tions triggered 152,000 publications on Instagram in March 2019.

While the #speedytuesday hashtag has been used on multiple plat-forms, the main community resides on Instagram, the network most suited to the photos that fans take of their watch. Every Tuesday, they ask each other questions and discuss their watch. The Speedy Tuesday publications remain smaller than those collected by Speedmaster watches alone (336,600 in March 2019), but the community is more involved and engaged than the rest of the watch's fans.

## Hybridization of Shopscapes and New Communication Codes

Compared with the traditional way of "marketing" a new product, the Speedy Tuesday case is based on a hybridization of shopscapes (Appadurai 2015), specific to social commerce, and is characterized by the fact that no investment is made in traditionally paid advertising. In terms of communication, the operation was relayed by Omega on the same day (Tuesday, January 10, 2017 and Tuesday, July 10, 2018) when it published a press release with photos of the limited edition at noon Swiss time, simultaneously translated into several languages, and sent a newsletter to Omega news subscribers.

The information was also published on the brand's social networks (Twitter, Instagram and Facebook), adopting the codes specific to social media, with photos on Instagram corresponding to the *essentially* cate-gory, in other words, a lifestyle form of expression, with an object or a collection of objects placed on a flat surface.

This is clearly a disruption, specific to 4.0 advertising, which inter-twines a lifestyle content with a community made up of the brand's aficionados within a limited timeframe, to whom the role of presenting the product and marketing it (among its members) is devolved to some extent. According to Robert-Jan Broer, the most popular visual on Instagram #speedytuesday since July 2018 is that of the "Ultraman" watch. This makes sense, since it was the most recent buzz product. Apart from this operation, the most popular visuals are those that feature details of the Speedmaster models, zooming in on the dials, the cases, the crowns, etc. Images that are more elaborate or too staged, like the watch placed next to a pair of sunglasses or a valuable fountain pen, are less popular, except for wristshots, in other words, watches worn in close-up on the arm. This probably reflects the mindset of true enthusiasts who are far more interested in the product itself than in its lifestyle environment. On the other hand, the most popular topics published reflect the pride of having bought or received a Speedmaster. Issues of price and increases in market value are also widely discussed. Finally, many members of the community experiment with different bracelets on their Speedmaster and ask what other members think.

Ultimately, we are witnessing a hybridization of communication and distribution channels that serves a time-limited brand experience which draws brand enthusiasts closer to an exclusive product (available in limited series), designed specifically for them (it is named after the Speedy Tuesday community). This scarcity tends to reinforce the collectionism of the fans, and also offers an opportunity for investors who resell their watch with a good margin (up to 100%) after a couple of weeks on specialized websites as chrono24.com. The result speaks for itself; 2012 watches sold the first time in a little over 4 hours, and the second batch in less than 2 hours! At a time of "short-term" with respect to digital and life in general, together with the speeding up of everyday life, the "long-term" of watchmaking is still something consumers care about (Maillard 2018).

## The Brand's Narrative of the Operation

The narrative of the brand's operation is characterized by its emphasis on the symbolic dimension of time. Thus, the community's name refers to the rhythm, the speed (speedy), and a day of the week (Tuesday), the number of watches in the limited series refers to the founding date of the community as explained above and the duration of the sale is known to the nearest second. In a way, we are witnessing the development of a time-coded language for the initiated. In a semiotic reading, we can consider that numbers and letters combine to form coded messages reserved for those in the know… Not only does it reflect a radically modern way of communicating on community-led social networks, but an esoteric dimension also clearly emerges from the operation, basically recreating a form of mythical exclusivity specific to the Omega brand identity. Over and above the commercial aspect, and in line with the vision of the president, Raynald Aeschlimann, the brand above all wants to please the Speedy Tuesday community of fans (Broer 2018) with exceptional models, purchased solely on the basis of photos posted on Instagram and the brand's official website, even though the customers cannot touch the watches before buying them. At the same time, the Speedy Tuesday operations conducted in 2017 and 2018 allowed Omega to relay these original successes on other traditional media, mainly in public relations, attracting the attention of many magazines and specialized watchmaker sites. The value of these media benefits, expressed in terms of advertising space and resonance, far exceeds the cost of a traditional advertising campaign (Perret 2018).

# Theoretical Discussion and Contributions for Marketing

## Towards a Morphing Between the Sales Channel and the Communication Channel

The Speedy Tuesday case expresses what we call morphing[5] between the sales channel and the communication channel, which is at the heart of the new web marketing 4.0 codes, that is to say a form of ephemeral

---

[5]Morphing is a video process that changes (or morphs) images (especially faces), often from a photo, to transform them into something else.

hybridization of sales and communication channels that corresponds to the expectations and lifestyle of a new generation of millennials and people permanently connected to a tribe. These are passionate people who are interested not only in the product and its design (based as much on the watch's mechanical design as its aesthetics), but also in its price, its communication and its distribution, the two latter elements of the classic marketing mix tending to converge clearly thanks to the possibilities of digital tools. The immediacy and punctuality of the operation (online sales via Instagram, a limited series in a limited time) lead to a morphing that can be described as events in the sales and communication channel. This way of operating capitalizes on brand communities and digital communications, without jeopardizing the traditional distribution networks that luxury brands must preserve.

## The Global Dimension: Towards a Specific Geography

For global brands like Omega, communication 4.0 provides a means to remove geographical boundaries, recreating boundaries specific to brand-lover communities, while leveraging and fine-tuning its target communications to make them viral. Apart from the commercial operation, Speedy Tuesday is developing a new episode in the history of the Omega brand and its legendary Speedmaster, introducing a radical and global modernity, co-created around the Speedmaster by the brand and its enthusiasts. Speedy Tuesday offers a story embedded in the most timeless elements of the Omega brand and the Speedmaster models, moving beyond geographical boundaries to shape new experiences underpinned by passion and shared emotion.

## The Energy of Desire and Marketing 4.0

To understand how digital technology is transforming consumer desire, Kozinets et al. (2016), informed by the work of Deleuze and Guattari, define desire not as a state of want, but as a flow of energy. Arrangements or systems that connect objects, their representations and different forms of Internet user participation thus form 'desire networks'. In the case of Speedy Tuesday, the desire networks at work rely on the power of the attraction of photos featuring the Speedmaster worn on the wrist, discussions between members of the community (private or public participation) and technical comments, right through to the climax consisting of the actual sale of the limited series. As this desire is linked to innovation (Kozinets et al. 2016), the technical specificities of the Speedy Tuesday serve to activate the network dynamics that develop thanks to this incessant flow of sublimated images of the brand, together with articles about the brand posted by social network users.

The marketing 4.0 codes create architectures of desire by proposing assemblies featuring a strong brand and an exclusive experience relayed by highly attractive visual content that stimulates the desire to consume the brand in different ways. The sentiment that the Anglo-Saxons call Fear of missing out, or Fear of missing something (FOMO) reinforces the desire for an exclusive product sold in a limited way at an unexpected moment. It seems that by communicating in a constructive way with the Speedy Tuesday community, the Omega brand has capitalized on these networks of desire, stemming from the combination of a shared passion and the technological potential of digital communications.

# Limitations of the Study, Future Research Avenues and Managerial Implications

Given its exploratory methodology based on interviews and a documentary study, the present case study does not claim to be representative of all commercial operations carried out by watch brands on social networks. However, it is symptomatic of a broadening of global brands' communication strategies, enacted in this case by a seized opportunity following a meeting between the president of Omega and the enthusiastic founder of a specialized watchmaking site.

It was a very meaningful and interesting process to witness from up close, as Omega involved me in every major step. I was also surprised that it is a real passion about Omega. I would think the commercial aspect would be much more important, but Omega wanted us (the community) to be happy in the first place. The commercial success was of course a great plus, but nobody expected it would be this huge at the beginning. I was mainly surprised that so many people bought these watches without even seeing them "in the flesh", they just ordered it based on pictures we took and that Omega took. (Broer 2018)

This limitation suggests future research opportunities both for global brands and for newcomers, who not only seek to sell their products via digital channels, but can also use them to obtain crowdfunded resources. The field is open for further research on new marketing 4.0 codes (striking types of message, millennial-specific language, eye-catching visuals…) that can be adopted to boost brand awareness and subsequent commercial success.

For Omega, the question now is whether to launch a Speedy Tuesday 3 operation or not. Is the community created by Robert-Jan Broer still 'hungry'? Would the thousands of disappointed Speedy Tuesday operations 1 and 2 hopefuls (because they were not connected, lived in another time zone or did not apply in time) bite the hook of a new operation, eagerly awaiting the next calendar month with a Tuesday 10th? Does the Omega brand risk turning off its customers with a marketing operation that is too predictable or repetitive? In terms of managerial implications, we do not believe this type of "guerilla marketing" operation has run out of steam yet, provided it can always surprise with an unusual and exclusive model, offered at an unexpected moment through a media familiar to the target. Studies have also shown that the appetite of watch collectors for limited series and exclusive models is generally insatiable (Courvoisier 2018). In addition, the media impact on dedicated watchmaking sites, such as Worldtempus or Watchonista, as well as in the specialized press, make it a powerful means of communication and far cheaper than conventional advertising.

# References

Alalwan, Ali Abdallah, Nripendra P. Rana, Yogesh K. Dwivedi, and Raed Algharabat. 2017. "Social Media in Marketing: A Review and Analysis of the Existing Literature." *Telematics and Informatics* 34 (7): 1177–1190. http://dx.doi.org/10.1016/j.tele.2017.05.008. Accessed on 3 May 2019.

Appadurai, Arjun. 2015. *Après le colonialisme, les conséquences culturelles de la globalisation*. Paris: Payot.

Broer, Robert-Jan. 2018. *Correspondance per e-mail* with François H. Courvoisier, 6–9 November.

Brynjolfsson, Eric, Yu Hu, and Michael D. Smith. 2010. "Long Tail vs. Superstars: The Effect of Information Technology on Product Variety and Sales Concentration Patterns." *Information Systems Research* 21 (4): 736–747.

Courvoisier, François H. 2018, January. "Marketing de la rareté: production de séries limitées et de pièces uniques dans l'horlogerie de luxe." In *Proceedings of the 16th International Conference Marketing Trends*. Paris: ESCP Europe.

Cova, Bernard, and Véronique Cova. 2002. "Tribal Marketing: The Tribalisation of Society and Its Impact on the Conduct of Marketing." *European Journal of Marketing* 36 (5/6): 595–620.

Kotler, Philip, Hermawan Kartajaya, and Iwan Setiawan. 2016. *Marketing 4.0: Moving from Traditional to Digital*. Hoboken, NJ: Wiley.

Kozinets, Robert, Anthony Patterson, and Rachel Ashman. 2016. "Networks of Desire: How Technology Increases Our Passion to Consume." *Journal of Consumer Research* 43: 659–682.

Lin, Xiaolin, Yibai Li, and Xuequn Wang. 2016. "Social Commerce Research: Definition, Research Themes and the Trends." *International Journal of Information Management* 37: 190–201.

Maillard, Serge. 2018. "Instagram, le temps court et le temps long." *Europa Star Première* 20 (4): 3.

Marion, Gilles. 2003. "Le marketing « expérientiel »: Une nouvelle étape? Non, de nouvelles lunettes." *Décisions Marketing* 30: 87–91.

Pentina, Irina, Véronique Guillioux, and Anca Cristina Micu. 2018. "Exploring Social Media Engagement Behaviors in the Context of Luxury Brands." *Journal of Advertising* 47 (1): 55–69.

Perret, Jean-Pascal. 2018. *Interview at Omega* with François H. Courvoisier, Biel (CH), 4 July.

Quach, Sara, and Park Traichon. 2017. "From Connoisseur Luxury to Mass Luxury: Value Co-creation and Co-destruction in the Online Environment." *Journal of Business Research* 81: 163–172.

Roederer, Claire, and Marc Filser. 2015. *Le marketing expérientiel. Vers un marketing de la cocréation.* Paris: Vuibert.

Zorik, Kalust, and François H. Courvoisier. 2018. *Marketing horloger: l'intelligence digitale.* Le Mont-sur-Lausanne: Editions Loisirs et Pédagogie.

# 10

# Brand Building: The Case of Collaboration Between Javier Carvajal and Loewe

Eugenia Josa, María Villanueva
and Isabel Cantista

## Introduction

The retail world has changed significantly over the past years. Sale space evolution, the spread of shopping centres associated to recreation and leisure, urban renewal of large avenues full of retail stores or the concern for sustainability are some of the factors that have driven the evolution

E. Josa (✉)
ISEM Fashion Business School, University of Navarra, Madrid, Spain
e-mail: eugenia.josa@isem.es

M. Villanueva
School of Architecture, University of Navarra, Pamplona, Spain
e-mail: mvillanuevf@unav.es

I. Cantista
Faculty of Economics and Business Studies, University Lusíada Norte, Porto, Portugal
e-mail: icantista@por.ulusiada.pt

© The Author(s) 2020
I. Cantista and T. Sádaba (eds.), *Understanding Luxury Fashion*,
Palgrave Advances in Luxury, https://doi.org/10.1007/978-3-030-25654-8_10

of traditional stores. There has been an increasing concern regarding their brand image in order to become more attractive to the consumer.

Architecture has always been captivated by fashion, but at the same time has advocated against it. Like architecture, fashion is a physical expression of the culture of an era: both turn imagination into material form. These realities are offered to people, either for living or as clothing, and through them to represent their own identities (Marenco Morés 2007, p. 17). The strong attraction between fashion and architecture can be seen as a clear sign of time. However, as shall be argued below, it's not a recent phenomenon; since long ago fashion designers have relied on architects to magnify the image of their brands (Bingham 2005, p. 7).

The importance of architecture in the world of fashion has already been noted in some examples from the past. The Au Bon Marché was founded in 1838 and the store as the first department store in the world opened its doors in 1867 emerging from the annexation of neighbouring buildings which were coherently enhanced through the work of the architects Alexandre Laplanche (1839–1910), Louis-Auguste Boileau (1812–1896) and his son Louis-Charles (1873–1914) and also by the engineer Eiffel (1832–1923) who planned the inside structure that would include the staircases at the centre of the store. And if we still had any doubt about the role that such stores—and particularly 'Au Bon Marché'—had on society, one simply has to read Émile Zola's novel, 'Au bonheur des Dames' (1883), inspired precisely by the Bon Marché.

The potentially ephemeral value of a store that could diminish its interest from a strictly architectural perspective is overcome when one considers the dimension of brand building. The brand is a relevant asset created with the long-term in mind, a driving force that is worth much more than the collection or range of products found in a store at any given moment. The influence of the fashion brand identity is clear, namely in the product policy, since, despite the continuous sequence of collections, aesthetics and other values may be identified and lead the market to make the distinction between a Chanel or a Loewe bag.

Collaboration between fashion brands and architects has been on the increase since the 1980s (Kirby and Kent 2010; Manuelli 2006, p. 7) examples of which are the Koolhaas stores for Prada or Renzo Piano for Hermès. This kind of collaborative work is especially noticeable in the flagship stores, where the aim is not only to sell but also the aim of communicating the brand's values, providing greater reasons for the customer—who is increasingly online—to physically visit the store and be engaged in a more holistic experience of the brand (Manlow and Nobbs 2013).

# Case Study

This study will analyse the factors that should be taken into account in store design, according to the criteria applied by Javier Carvajal when designing and constructing Loewe's sale spaces. The success that they evidenced in the 60s and the advance in the evolution that they provided to the brand are considered values to highlight in the field of commercial establishment design.

The work the architect created for Loewe involves a more comprehensive and complete approach to that inherent to architectural project. His work for the brand went beyond the design of the store in Madrid, becoming an integral operation of store openings that reflected the new image that Carvajal projected for the company. The new design affected Loewe's whole structure, positioning the brand in a new way, taking it into modernity and linking it closer to the Spanish culture and, at the same time, remaining faithful to the company's heritage of craftsmanship and expertise. In this case the architect's role affected all aspects of design; he even came up with a collection of products to sell in the stores.

Nowadays the project is still alive; Carvajal's work has been recovered and is contemplated as Loewe's most iconic moment. In this way, at the very end of 2013, Jonathan Anderson arrived to Loewe as the new creative director and proposed to give to the brand "*a new injection of modernity and culture consciousness*" like Loewe mentioned. In order to do this, the designer proposed to carry out a project close to the one of the 50s, 60s and 70s. Anderson's work aims to perform a redefinition of the whole image of the brand identity, based on a review of all contributions of that time at different levels. Behind this new project, emerges the wish to take Loewe's image into the future.

In this way, the work of the architect Javier Carvajal is considered a more holistic and interdisciplinary undertaking than the accomplished as of that time. Therefore, the analysis of the work performed by the architect for the Spanish brand assumes a particular relevance.

# Methodology

In this study we have adopted a qualitative approach in order to develop an in-depth understanding of the design and architecture of the Loewe stores and the ways in which they contribute to brand identity. How Denzin and Lincoln (Kirby and Kent 2010, p. 432) analyse "the combination of multiple methodological practices, empirical materials, perspectives, and observers in a single study is best understood then, as a strategy that adds rigour, breadth, complexity, richness and depth to any inquiry".

The case was developed through interviews and documentation. The study and redrawing of the original graphic documentation of the projects has turned out to be a key element in the process of obtaining deeper knowledge of the commercial premises. This work has allowed us to analyse the examples made by Javier Carvajal, extracting a series of guidelines based on the process of architectural design along with elements that encompass visual merchandising.

It is necessary to present and analyse the proposal of the study of the analysis of stores that will be applied to the selected cases. This model will allow us to thoroughly understand the stores, beyond their visual and image aspects. The undertaking of reworking the architecture projects in order to accurately know the diverse aspects that have been fundamental in the configuration of each store.

The redrawing of the plans and sketches is presented as a key element since it will allow this "deep knowledge" that goes beyond the visual and allows for the discovery of the measurements of things and their inner relation (alignments, relations, geometries, proportions, etc.).

This study undertakes the study of the relationship between architecture and fashion, emphasizing the role of the architect in the process of designing stores. Likewise, it is intended to analyse the way in which both disciplines, architecture and visual merchandising, coexist in the process and the elaboration of the architectural project of the stores. The present analysis is carried out from an architectural perspective, and that, therefore, is filtered by the architect's own and unique vision; a factor that sets it apart from other research related to the design of fashion stores.

The interview was made to Vicente Vela, who worked hand-to-hand with Javier Carvajal.

In the development of this research, we have been able to access the original documentation of the stores that will be studied, through the legacy deposited in the Archive of the University of Navarra, the museum that Loewe has in his factory and the Archive of the Villa de Madrid. As well as the documents found in the London College of Fashion and the RIBA.

It was not possible to observe as the twelve stores projected by Carvajal for Loewe do not exist physically anymore.

## Literature Review

Brand is an important intangible asset for companies. Brands appeared as the signature of the name of who made or produced a given product and thus assumes responsibility for its quality before the customer or purchaser. By revealing the identity or name of somebody who is responsible for the product, trust increases in what is bought and also attributes credibility to the producer.

Presently, brands have assumed a particular importance (Blois 2000, p. 483) because they create a positive image in the consumer's mind, which then leads to a preference, when distinguishing between products that are ostensibly identical, be it in functional or even symbolic terms and thus leading to the acquisition of these goods or services based on this distinction. When such a preference exists, it also increases the equity of a brand (Aaker 1996).

Fashion is an ephemeral phenomenon that changes with the passing of the seasons and the fashion industry seems to relentlessly encourage consumers to own the latest products. As such, fashion embraces the human passion for novelty while simultaneously signalling to others that someone using or owning fashionable products is connected to the moment. They are not only present, but, more importantly, active participants in their historical moment. In this volatile world, stores need to renew themselves and meet the expectations of customers. At the same time, it is recognised that most purchasing decisions are made in the physical store, even now, in the era of the expansion of online commerce (Sääksjärvi and Samiee 2011).

The design and the project value of the architect's work are linked to the role a store performs in terms of appeal and as a shopping experience (Rieunier 2006). Not only do stores need to fulfil their sales functions, they also need to incorporate a series of elements capable of seducing the consumer. In addition to encouraging the consumer to spend more time inside, stores also deliver a brand experience that will contribute to the customer's clear perception of its identity either in cognitive and emotional terms and thus contribute to the attachment to the brand.

In urbanistic terms, by contributing to the design of the city (Kirby and Kent 2010, pp. 432–437). The store or the area in which the stores are found can contribute to the affirmation of the city's character, the *genius loci* of the place, influencing the behaviour of its inhabitants, as mentioned (Rémy 2006, p. 23). In contemporary society, the activity of "going shopping" has a leisure, emotional and social nature. There is a leisure aspect to shopping, when those involved seek to relax and disconnect from day-to-day life, an emotional aspect because this kind of shopping contributes to the construction and expression of individual identity (see the notions of self and self-extended explored by Belk [1988]), and also because these moments are often occasions for interaction, with the stores or retail areas becoming venues for social interaction.

At the same time, architecture, be it in terms of building, remodelling and adaptation of buildings can give a certain visibility to a central thread—the values of the fashion brand—and thus contribute to an image with continuity that emphasises the distinctive role it plays. Kirby and Kent (2010, p. 437) refer to the "sense of permanence in architecture", which contributes to "its visual communicative power". For this to take place, the dialogue between the architect and the brand is fundamental, and this is one of the most important insights which we can gather from the analysis and study of projects that Carvajal created for Loewe.

Visual merchandising emerges as one more element in the work of the architect, since the exterior and interior of the store complete and complement each other. Visual merchandising seeks to optimise the sale point and, according to Kim (2013) has the objectives of creating an agreeable ambience, an effective organisation of in-store merchandise and by doing so, to differentiate brands so that sales increase. The recent study by Park et al. (2015) once again confirms the influence that visual merchandising can have on the brand's image and, ultimately, in the purchasing decisions of consumers.

## Loewe the Brand: Origin and Values

> The German craftsman Enrique Loewe Rossberg arrived in Madrid in 1872. Spain was expanding commercially, so Loewe took this opportunity to settle down in the capital and begin an ambitious commercial project in his specialty of leather craftsmanship. (Hernández Cava 1995, p. 57)

With the brand being targeted at high society, Enrique was impelled to continuously redesign his stores and products. From the very start, architecture was one of the main tools used to constantly improve the company and to create a greater proximity with a distinguished kind of clientele which, from 1905 onwards, included the Royals Don Alfonso de Bourbon and Doña Victoria Eugenia (Hernández Cava 1995; Josa and Villanueva 2014). Being appointed as official supplier of the Royal House, Loewe became a relevant company associated with the cultural change in Spain.

In 1939—coinciding with the end of the Spanish Civil War—Loewe opened a store located in Madrid at Gran Vía 8. This commercial space was designed by the architect Francisco Ferrer Bartolome (Ferrer Bartolomé 1940/1941, pp. 19–22). A year after, he was also responsible for the project of the layout of the store located on Paseo de Gracia (Hernández Cava 1995, p. 109), in the city of Barcelona.

The design of the store windows was one of the most common aesthetic resources exploited by the company. José Pérez de Rozas, Creative Director of the brand between 1945 and 1970 designed them to be exotic, elegant, and above all an imaginative scenery. Pérez de Rozas took delight in demonstrating his creative leadership for the company. His store windows were easily recognisable by the way one could not see the inside of the store, from the street, there were two completely independent spaces: the shop window and the interior of the store. Pérez de Rozas store window design, typically included the bottom of the window being covered with wood, while the back would be covered by curtains creating an enigmatic impression of the shop interior. Within this space we would create a scenery with many other objects apart from the products of the brand, suggesting a story telling approach (Josa and Villanueva 2014).

However, from 1956 onwards, the essence of the company assumed a more modern style. For this task Loewe, collaborated with professionals such as the architect Javier Carvajal and the artist Vicente Vela. These artists became key players in designing a project for the revamped modern image of the Spanish brand (Josa and Villanueva 2016a, p. 121).

The brand wanted to preserve the values of quality and perfect craftsmanship that had characterised its since its origins, while expressing a more modern aesthetic that would carry it into the future.

## Carvajal and Loewe—The 50s

In order to distinguish themselves from other foreign companies that figured among the brand's competition, Loewe needed to create a modern brand that maintained its prestige and exclusivity, associating itself with the image of Spain. Carvajal was able to understand Loewe's needs at the time and provided the company with a thrust towards modernity, through the design and renovation of stores according to the brand's vision (Josa and Villanueva 2016a, pp. 77–93).

The project to give Loewe a modern image is not an isolated case, rather the opposite; it is an integral part of a common strategy in which a group of professionals and businesses were involved, supported by official authorities who sought to promote Spain as a country associated with modernity. This project emerged in the mid-50s with the aim of leaving behind the inevitable crisis that followed the Spanish Civil War. It was the beginning of a new period that urged a renewal and modernization of aesthetics that would contribute to a renewed image for the country.

These years brought collaborations between professionals and Spanish companies seeking to renew their products and eager to embrace new aesthetic and conceptual trends coming from abroad. As a result of this framework, the first institution of Spanish design was created in 1957, the SEDI (Sociedad sobre Estudios del Diseño Industrial—Society for Industrial Design Studies). This association was propelled by the architects Carlos de Miguel, Luis Feduchi and Javier Carvajal, with the collaboration of manufacturing companies such as Loewe, Darro or Plata Meneses (Josa and Villanueva 2016b).

In 1957, the architects Javier Carvajal and José María García de Paredes were responsible for designing the Spanish pavilion at the XI edition of the prestigious Milan Triennial. The architects created an intrinsically Spanish installation inspired by bullrings. To undertake this project, Garcia de Paredes and Carvajal collaborated with other professionals and companies, including Loewe. The brand donated several leather products to the exhibition, for which they were awarded the Silver Medal (Ramirez de Lucas 1957, pp. 43–44).

In both the Spanish Pavilion for the XI Triennial and in the SEDI, Carvajal and Loewe manifested their desire for the renewal of Spain's image and for the adaptation to its newly proclaimed modernity. This collaboration was part of the set of relationships initiated in 1957 by Enrique Loewe Knappe and Javier Carvajal that, like other professionals and commercial entities, joined forces in order to change the images of their businesses, as well as that of their country. Enrique Loewe, in collaboration with Carvajal, revealed an interest in modernizing the company's profile, imbuing its products with a value that went beyond the physical characteristics of the object itself (Josa and Villanueva 2016b).

In 1959, Loewe opened a store on Serrano Street that completely revolutionised the stereotype of other luxury goods establishments (Carvajal 1991, pp. 32–36). This store of Scandinavian influence (Losada 2012, p. 471) was characterized by the order, in its plans and designed sections, and was built with brick, that was painted white and then complimented by the use of walnut wood (Josa and Villanueva 2016a, p. 122).

When Carvajal joined the brand, he invited a young painter, Vicente Vela, to be part of his team. Together, they formed a dynamic team that completely changed the brand; they were able to give expression to the modernity Loewe was looking for.

Vicente Vela's work was essential to the renewal of the brand's image. Vela was contracted to design the store windows, but his talent was rapidly recognised and he ended up collaborating for more than 40 years in the design of Loewe products. *"It was Vela who designed the current Loewe anagram in 1970, which proved to be the driving force for the fame and worldwide recognition of the brand. Until then, Loewe had been identified by an English "L", that Vela replaced by another "L" that was "warmer and more personal" with which he made a stamp to engrave the logo onto leather products.*[1] *On canvas, he mirrored the "L" and created the famous anagram that is widely recognised today Arts"* (Josa and Villanueva 2016a, p. 123).

Loewe's store windows had an artistic dimension that would increase brand notoriety. Examples of the professionals who collaborated with Vela were Pablo Serrano, Arcadio Blasco, Carmen Perujo, Ricardo Mesa, Aurelia Muñoz and Amadeo Gabino.[2] Vela explains that this is what Loewe needed in order to position itself as a modern, cutting-edge brand while, by contrast, the artists considered these collaborations as a mere way of earning some money.[3]

## The Modern World—Nordic Influences

Carvajal's work for Loewe is of great importance as it develops and carries out a project of global identity for the brand. His work transcends the mere award of a project to a client.

This was Carvajal's greatest achievement; stores were not conceived as independent autonomous spaces to be designed, but as part of an integral plan that would redefine Loewe's identity. In this sense, Carvajal's work was a seminal one. He felt the need to design a store that was commercially efficient even before commercial design had become established in Spain and also contributed to the transformation of Loewe stores into a statement about the identity of the brand.

Carvajal designed a total of thirteen stores for Loewe, all of them exhibited a strong personality, were easily recognizable and linked to each other. Showcases, display units and interiors were carefully designed to ensure that the items on display were the centre of attention. Simultaneously, there was a connection between all the stores: the vision of modernity shared by Carvajal and Loewe.

It was important for the stores to express the brand's values leading to a deeper involvement from contemporary consumers. Carvajal's designs were coherent in the way that they expressed the same ideals in different cities or locations.

Nurturing cultural values and Loewe's own roots and tradition provided a strong guiding principle along with a determination to modernize the Loewe brand. Carvajal combined typical Spanish elements with Loewe's own traditions and values in order to create an image for the brand identity subtly updated over time in response to market trends and interpretative leads from its Creative Directors.

In this sense, Carvajal understood the value of craftsmanship of the brand, so he envisioned a combination of the artisan tradition of Loewe with new modern forms from abroad. To implement this modernity, the architect looked to the work of Nordic architects and designers as his references, such as Alvar Aalto, Arne Jacobsen, Hans Wegner or Gunnar Asplund. Interestingly, Jonathan Anderson, Loewe's current creative director, has proposed a review of the firm, based on the work carried out in the 50s, which revives the aesthetics of the Carvajal stores and, consequently, the Nordic influence.

Not only do Carvajal's personal documents indicate the influence Nordic architecture had on him, his designs for Loewe confirm this inspiration, which enabled the firm's modernization that endures to this day. To carry out this study, an analysis of one of the projects undertaken by the architect for the brand was conducted: Loewe's Serrano store. The selection of this architectural piece as an element of analysis is due to its prototypical character, since it contains all the features applicable to other stores designed by Carvajal from 1959 to 1964.

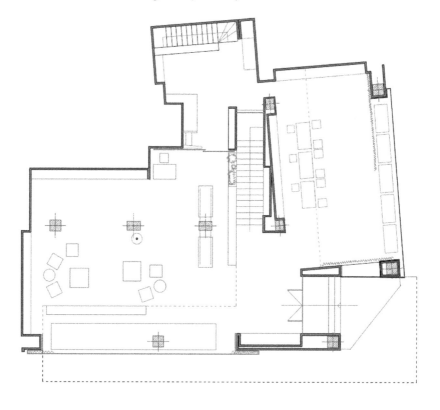

Loewe shop floor sketch, Serrano Street corner with Jorge Juan Street, Architect Javier Carvajal. August 1959. Source: Josa, M.E. (2017) La arquitectura de la tienda: Los casos de Javier Carvajal para Loewe, Doctoral thesis, ISEM Fashion Business School, University of Navarra, Pamplona.

## Form-Space

The architecture of the stores designed by the architect had to fulfil the function and solidity, creating a space with a rigorous and disciplined order, implemented significantly from the plan and the section. But it is specifically through this view, from the section, in which the Scandinavian presence is palpable throughout the entire store, not only in terms of the design of the space (Losada 2012, pp. 469–483), but also with regard to materials and furniture (Josa and Villanueva 2017, p. 93).

The section, thus, becomes one of the indicators that establish a formal connection with Nordic architecture, particularly with Alvar Aalto. The uniqueness of the sculptural form of the Serrano shop evokes the Viipuri Municipal Library project. Viipuri's fundamental and characteristic element is the undulating acoustic ceiling of its conference room (AA.VV. 1948). Formed by wooden slats, this element's function was to allow good acoustic transmission to all areas in this long room. Interestingly, a similar ceiling design was designed by Carvajal (Josa and Villanueva 2017, p. 93).

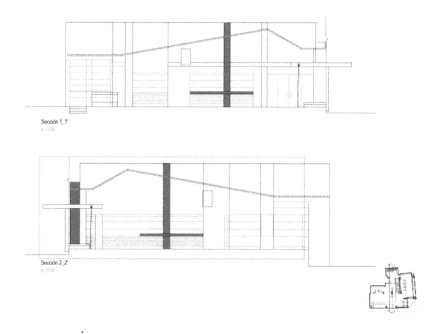

Loewe shop section sketch, Serrano Street corner with Jorge Juan Street, Architect Javier Carvajal. August 1959. Source: Josa, M.E. (2017) La arquitectura de la tienda: Los casos de Javier Carvajal para Loewe, Doctoral thesis, ISEM Fashion Business School, University of Navarra, Pamplona.

In Carvajal's words: *"The influencing factors in the space value of architecture are the light and shadow layout, colour, and even our own expectations determined by the space we just left"* (AA.VV. 1960, pp. 32–36).

Consequently, in Carvajal's draft, both the natural and artificial lighting of its stores were considered essential elements. Carvajal gives especial importance to the light in Barcelona store. The architect creates the circular skylights repeatedly arranged on the two roof planes, creating glare-free lighting at all reading points. The large display space is provided with great luminosity through compound lighting cylinders composed of light and textile. Jacobsen also uses the same type of lights in the SAS Royal Hotel (Jacobsen 2010, pp. 64–89).

On the other hand, Carvajal develops a strategy to extend the Serrano store space outward adopting inspiration from other international works, including those of Nordic style. As Ferrer Bartolomé, Carvajal gave particular importance to window displays, confiding on the integration between outer and interior space, and the establishment of connections with potential customers (Josa and Villanueva 2017, pp. 91–100). This element had already gained prominence in previous Loewe stores, thanks to the design of José Pérez de Rozas (Ferrer Bartolomé 1940/1941, pp. 19–22). Its windows were characteristic because from the exterior one could not see the store interiors; the bottom of the window was covered with wood or curtains to give the interior a mysterious touch (Loewe store exhibition 2014).

Thus, the main change introduced by Carvajal in the Serrano store, and in the later establishments he designed for Loewe, was the window display. "*What the architect provided was a window display with a totally different approach, designed from architecture and for architecture, and that was the renewed image of the 60's*" (Antón 2016, p. 211).

Carvajal's window display acted as and interior claim on the street. Enrique Loewe, who began working in the family business at the time, remembers: "*They had the windows displays open, there was continuity between interior and exterior … The shop was a mystery, and he resolved it*".[4]

This idea of creating continuity between interior and exterior while introducing light was a resource used by modern architects. The use of the so-called 'new materials' provided new capabilities that architecture previously did not have. In this case the use of glass, as independent from the structure, allowed the creation of the extension effect for the space Carvajal designed for Loewe. Although there were many architects who implemented this strategy from Gropius in his Fagus factory, highlighting Arne Jacobsen with his Rodovre Town Hall of 1954–1956 or Munkegaard school, among others. Jacobsen used this effect on many of his projects, creating an indivisible link between the exterior and interior. His work is of great interest because as it will be discussed in the furniture section, it provided inspiration for the Spanish architect in this field as well (Josa and Villanueva 2016b).

## Material

Carvajal's project for Loewe's Serrano store is characterized by the materials and nuanced rationalism of the space. As referred before Scandinavian-influenced white-painted brick for the interior of the establishment and walnut coating of the false ceiling battens resembled the architecture of Aalto. Carpeted floors creating a warmer space. The colours can be seen in the images of Forma magazine, published by Loewe to present their products to its customers (AA.VV. 1963). Oranges, ochres, browns and greens bring colour to the interior space. Fronting the marble, were the glass and neutral tones found in the shop windows (Josa and Villanueva 2017, pp. 91–100).

> The use of brick in Loewe has a double meaning. On the one hand, the use of this material in Spain was very common and reflected the traditional character and craftsmanship the firm desired. But on the other hand, the use of brick was directly linked to Nordic architecture, especially with Alvar Aalto. If his oeuvre is carefully examined, many of his projects were built with this material (AA.VV. 1948) the city of Säynätsalo, the Auditorium in Helsinki and, especially, the home study and experimental house in Muuratsalo where the brick is painted white, like at Loewe, offer just a few examples of the use of this material. (Josa and Villanueva 2017, pp. 91–100)

Fabric is another important element. Carvajal used curtains from ceiling to flor in the stores to provide customers privacy if required. This strategy was also used by Nordic architects on projects such as the Rodovre library or Jacobsen's SAS Royal Hotel, together with Aalto's Viipuri library.

Additionally, marble appears in Carvajal's window as a backdrop, recessed and exempt giving importance to the exposed pieces. Perhaps the best-known example in this respect is the German pavilion designed by Mies van der Rohe, but the Nordic architectural repertoire also offers examples such as the SAS Royal Hotel (Jacobsen 2010, pp. 64–89).

## Design

Following these parameters, Carvajal not only created the ceiling with a structure comprising wooden battens, as we have seen, but also used wood in all fixed and mobile furniture. This resource can be seen in many of the Nordic works of the period, both public and private, designed by both Aalto and Jacobsen.

The store's interior design is particularly striking for its unapologetic modernity. The architect designed a sober commercial space, embellished with materials such as walnut for the interiors and black marble with steel, which accentuated the interior-exterior dynamics. In the interior, one can see the strict order and voluptuousness that comprises the store. The importance of the materials and the nuanced rationalism of the space, created small display areas for the contemplation of the product. A net curtain to veil the window when privacy from the street was desired, a walnut door, marble covering certain walls and violet carpet covering the floor are some of the elements that characterised the space. In the sectioned areas, the ceiling curvature—evoking Aalto and covered by a false ceiling lath—can be perceived (Josa and Villanueva 2016b).

Among the furniture designs created by Carvajal, the chair purposely designed for the Serrano store in 1959 is now historically recognized as the Loewe chair. Built in walnut, with leather straps by Biosca, this piece of furniture epitomised the company's values, hinting at the materials and craftsmanship of the brand and, through its forms, inspiring its modern outlook and brand image project. This modernity was clearly influenced by Nordic design, specifically by the designer Hans Wegner and his most iconic creation in 1949: the rounded chair or simply "the chair" (Josa and Villanueva 2017, pp. 91–100).

Wegner's chair is characterised by a very pure design, as a continuation of traditional Scandinavian forms, built in carefully contoured wood. The seat, made of wood and leather, is fixed over the midpoint of the four rounded legs that, in turn, support the upper part, the curved sculptural backrest with a variable section that characterises this piece. It is this element that reveals the most formal difference with the

Loewe chair. Wegner's backrest piece has a more pronounced curve than that of Carvajal's, which is much flatter.

The approach taken thus included the visible influence of Nordic design, refinement and purity, both in the selection of materials and colour range (glass, walnut, painted white brick) and the conception of other elements in the space (e.g. furniture and lighting) (AA.VV. 1960, pp. 32–36). The exquisite architecture and detailed image obtained when applying these parameters to Loewe's thirteen commercial establishments, acted like a refined packaging in which the brand's products are contained.

Carvajal had thus reflected on the importance of the elements described above (shape-space, material and design) in order to create the brand image and to communicate the vision of modernity the company was pursuing. These aspects were also essential in adding value to the company's exclusive accessories.

Therefore, these ideas ultimately reflect the importance of the outstanding work carried out by Carvajal in the renewal of Loewe's image in a dialogue with Enrique Loewe. The architect knew that the company should cherish its tradition roots while allowing itself to be formally shaped by references from contemporary modern culture giving the brand a distinctive image that would set it apart from other luxury brands.

# Conclusions

It is demonstrated by the study of the stores developed by Carvajal for Loewe that the architect took into consideration the values of the brand that the company wanted to project in the long term. The collaboration between Carvajal and Loewe was decisive in the construction of an image of modernity, while this Spanish luxury fashion brand sought to preserve its original values of artisanal excellence and exclusivity.

This study illustrates how brand identity is crucial to the process of brand building and how brand identity encompasses social and cultural values that may be shared by their own consumers, in this particular case Spanish consumers, or consumers found of Spanish art and culture.

Cultural values also contributed to the strength of the positioning of the brand among other luxury brands.

In practice, this research can provide guidance to fashion companies and especially luxury brands in collaborative projects with architects, emphasising the fact that the outcome of such collaboration should lead to much more than a mere reference in the media, an opportunity to attract attention to the association between a brand and a prestigious architect. The role that fashion companies perform as creators and managers of brands should not be ignored, in fact it should be at the core of the process of collaboration. A vision for the future and the history of the brand provide a starting point in this dialogue. And from this dialogue the store as a cultural expression of the brand may emerge and have a role to play in society.

This case study enabled the identification of key elements that help to materialise brand values inside a store and can provide a reference in the development of architectural projects for brands, particularly for luxury brands, such as Loewe.

At this moment in time, questions of sustainability are becoming increasing urgent and these should be a priority in the Luxury and Fashion business. We hope that this roadmap for dialogue can also contribute to a greater presence of these values in the retail of luxury and fashion brands.

## Notes

1. Interview Vicente Vela, carried by Eugenia Josa at Vicente Vela's workshop (C/Dr. Esquerdo, 163, Madrid) in 19 December 2013.
2. Group of Spanish artists, painters and abstract sculptors, representatives of the avant-garde groups of the 50s and 60s.
3. Interview Vicente Vela, carried by Eugenia Josa at Vicente Vela's workshop (C/Dr. Esquerdo, 163, Madrid) in 19 December 2013.
4. LOEWE, Enrique. 2016. Conferencia Artesanía y Lujo. Tienda Loewe calle Serrano 26, 16 de febrero.

# References

Aaker, David. 1996. *Building Strong Brands*. New York: The Free Press.

AA.VV. 1948. *Design in Sweden Today*. Stockholm: Swedish Institute for Cultural Relations.

AA.VV. 1960. "Instalación y decoración de una tienda en Madrid." *Arquitectura* 16: 32–36.

AA.VV. 1963. "El orden, síntoma del hombre moderno." Forma: Loewe, autumn-winter.

Antón, Javier. 2016. "Javier Carvajal. La Forma de un Lenguaje." PhD diss., University of Navarra, Pamplona.

Belk, Russell W. 1988. "Possessions and the Extended Self." *Journal of Consumer Research* 15 (2): 139–168. Oxford: Oxford University Press. https://www.jstor.org/stable/2489522. Accessed on September 2017.

Bingham, Neil. 2005. *The New Boutique: Fashion and Design*. London: Merrell Publishers.

Blois, Keith, ed. 2000. *The Oxford Textbook of Marketing*. Oxford: Oxford University Press.

Carvajal, Javier. 1991. *J. Carvajal: arquitecto*. Madrid: COAM.

Ferrer Bartolomé, Francisco. 1940/1941. "Tienda de artículos de cuero en una avenida principal de Madrid. LOEWE." *Nuevas Formas* 1: 19–22.

Hernández Cava, Felipe. 1995. "Tiempos de Loewe." In *Loewe 1846–1996*, coords. AA.VV. Madrid: Loewe.

Jacobsen, Arne. 2010. *Arne Jacobsen: muebles y objetos*. Barcelona: Polígrafa.

Josa, Eugenia, and María Villanueva. 2014. "Modernity and Tradition in Loewe. 1959–2013." Paper presented at the Global Fashion Conference: Re-thinking and Reworking Fashion, Gante, November.

Josa, Eugenia, and María Villanueva. 2016a. "Loewe Design Between Modernity and Tradition." In *Fashion Education for the Future: Sustainable Development in Social, Economic, Environmental, Cultural and Geographic Dimensions* (Ebook), 121–126. Sao Paulo: EACH/USP.

Josa, Eugenia, and María Villanueva. 2016b. "Luxury, Tradition and Modernity: Nordic Influences in Loewe Stores." Paper presented at the Global Fashion Conference, Estocolmo, October.

Josa, Eugenia, and María Villanueva. 2017. "La Serrano de Loewe, Javier Carvajal: análisis de proyecto arquitectónico." *ESTOA* 6 (10): 91–100.

Josa, Eugenia, and María Villanueva. 2018. "La tienda como proyecto global: Loewe en Valencia, Arq. Javier Carvajal: Análisis de proyecto arquitectónico." *Constelaciones* 6: 77–96.

Ketchum Jr., Morris. 1948. *Shops & Stores*. New York, NY: Architectural Book Publishing.

Kim, Jong Sung. 2013. "A Study on the Effect That VMD (Visual Merchandising Design) in Store Has on Purchasing Products." *International Journal of Smart Home* 7 (4): 217–223.

Kirby, A.E., and A.M. Kent. 2010. "Architecture as Brand: Store Design and Brand Identity." *Journal of Product & Brand Management* 19 (6): 432–439.

Loewe. 2014. *Fragmentos de una historia 168 años de Loewe*. Exposición Tienda Serrano Loewe, mayo.

Losada, Jorge. 2012. "Realidad e ilusión. Locales comerciales españoles, 1950–1960." PhD diss., University of Navarra, Pamplona.

Manlow, Veronica, and Karinna Nobbs. 2013. "Form and Function of Luxury Flagships: An International Exploratory Study of the Meaning of the Flagship Store for Managers and Customers." *Journal Fashion Mark Manage* 17 (1): 49–64.

Manuelli, Sara. 2006. *Design for shopping: New retail interiors*. London: Laurence King.

Marenco Morés, Claudia. 2007. *From Fiorucci to the Guerrilla Stores. Shop Displays in Architecture, Marketing and Communications*. Milán: Marsilio.

Park, Hyun Hee, Jung Ok Jeon, and Pauline Sullivan. 2015. "How Does Visual Merchandising in Fashion Retail Stores Affect Consumers' Brand Attitudes and Purchase Intention?" *The International Review of Retail, Distribution and Consumer Research* 25 (1): 87–104.

Ramirez de Lucas, Juan. 1957. "Medalla de oro al pabellón de España en la XI Trienal de Milán." *ABC*, 43–44, December 24.

Rémy, Eric. 2006. "Comment thématiser l'offre et théâtriser les lieux de vente?" In *Le Marketing sensorial du point de vente*, edited by Sophie Rieunier. 2nd ed. Paris: Dunod.

Rieunier, Sophie (coord). 2006. *Le Marketing Sensoriel du Point de Vente*. Paris: Dunod.

Sääksjärvi, Maria, and Saced Samiee. 2011. "Relationships Among Brand Identity, Brand Image and Brand Preference: Differences Between Cyber and Extension Retail Brands Over Time." *Journal of Interactive Marketing* 25: 169–177.

Vicente Vela (former Creative Director Loewe 1951?–1985), Interviewed by Eugenia Josa, in Vicente Vela's workshop (C/ Dr. Esquerdo 163, Madrid) 19th diciembre 2013.

# 11

# Rapha: Weaving Story Strands of Luxury

## Catherine Glover

## Setting the Scene

The first place to find Rapha's voice or sense of 'self' is online where an organic search finds weblinks such as 'Rapha® Performance Roadwear' and 'Rapha: The World's Finest Clothing and Accessories' (Google 2017). Its aspirational sensibilities to connect with a global cultural elite can be seen communicated clearly through 'The World's', 'Finest' and 'Performance'. Moving on to the official Rapha website however, the Company webpage acknowledges Rapha's current business in expanded terms:

> Rapha is now more than just a clothing company – in addition to an online emporium of performance roadwear, accessories and publications, the brand includes physical retail locations, luxury travel, and a cycling club with global membership. (2017a)

C. Glover (✉)
Northumbria University, Newcastle upon Tyne, UK
e-mail: catherine.glover@northumbria.ac.uk

© The Author(s) 2020
I. Cantista and T. Sádaba (eds.), *Understanding Luxury Fashion*,
Palgrave Advances in Luxury, https://doi.org/10.1007/978-3-030-25654-8_11

This statement provides an overview of its business empire and reveals its span of lifestyle offerings, multi-media publishing and networked community. Particularly notable is a rare reference to 'luxury', however this is limited to travel. The descriptive noun 'emporium' does add associations of eclectic merchant wares and interestingly derives from the classic stem meaning 'journey' (Oxford University Press 2017a), a neat link to cycling as a mode of transport. If we employ Christopher Berry's (1994) four basic categories of luxury goods to check Rapha's fit, then the goods and services in their statement align to three: clothing ('performance roadwear'), leisure ('cycling club', 'luxury travel') and shelter ('physical retail locations'). Only Berry's fourth category of sustenance is satisfied indirectly, if one is aware that most Rapha retail locations are also clubhouses that contain cafés. Taking this broad view, Rapha can be considered as offering a full palate of universal goods and services to satisfy the luxury needs of a cycling community. Rapha's Company statement though neglects to reveal a meaningful aspect of any modern brand—its culture. The cultural challenges of growing a luxury lifestyle brand are acknowledged by *The Business of Fashion* (2017):

> Ultimately, luxury brands are selling culture—not mere products, but the cultural meaning that has condensed around these products. Yet culture takes time to grow. Building a [brand] with genuine social and cultural capital takes significant time, patience and associated long-term strategy and investment. This is something that aspirants often underestimate.

Simon Mottram, Rapha's CEO and founder, provides clues to his vision, which is imbued with socio-cultural resonance:

> If you take everything out and away from Rapha, all the products, me, the trademark, all the technology, all the Clubhouses, all the staff, loving the sport is the most important thing. … We want to help transform the sport… What that all adds up to is wanting to reach hundreds or thousands or millions of cyclists and take them by the hand, and take them on the most amazing journey through cycling. (2017)

The implicit backstory behind the '… transform the sport…' remark relates to the reputation of professional cycling, which has been negatively affected in recent years with allegations of doping among the highest echelons of the elite rider community. Mottram's motivation to contribute to positive reputation building may reflect his own concerns as a cyclist and his use of the brand to champion a personal goal is clearly in the hope it will resonate with impassioned cyclists globally. Indeed, it provides insight into Mottram's call-to-action communication style which shows purposeful storytelling zeal and his role in Rapha. 'As a storyteller you are a vital force in molding the culture of your organization, community and family' (Simmons 2006, p. 221). Andy Bull labels this mission-focused brand activity 'cause marketing' stating: 'An organization that operates in a particular market, or a particular location, can support causes that concern the community they are seeking to engage with' (2013, p. 69). Whether viewing Mottram's intentions cynically, one can at least trace passion and purpose in his statement, which belies his self-defined role as a 'superpromoter' (Vogelaar 2009) for the sport. He wants to offer the world a transformational experience through cycling (critically, he is not offering transformation through fashion). Pine and Gilmore (2007, p. 47) define transformations as 'effectual outcomes that guide customers to change some dimension of self'.

Using luxury brands to attain a desirable lifestyle is a central component of the modern aspirational way of being and it chimes with the current zeitgeist of the socio-cultural trend of 'wellness' and the personal affordance of self-investment. It is a view reflected by global brand consultancy, Interbrand, which acknowledges the fast evolution of the concept of 'luxury' and proposes that we are now in a new age where brands are becoming a consumer's partner:

In the Age of You, enabled by intelligent infrastructure and powered by big data, the leading brands will develop integrated ecosystems of experiences and reshape the world around us. As people and devices become more connected and everything becomes 'smarter,' businesses are recognising the need to reorganize themselves around 'you'. As a result, each of us will become our own marketplace or 'mecosystem.' As 'intelligent everything' meets the mecosystems of the future, brands will have unprecedented opportunity to create context, creative possibilities, and meaning for individuals—and value for all. And therein lies the challenge. (Robins 2015)

In the Age of You, brands are being required to connect deeply with 'me'. And if both luxury (and its purpose) are dependent on one's context, such as time, location and subjective positional viewpoint (one's selfhood), it seems highly appropriate to base this situated examination of Rapha on *my* own subjective interpretative praxis of the brand (in the mode of Gould 1991; Woodside 2004). As a long-term cyclist with years of commuting experience as well as being an academic with extensive past professional industry experience, I have come into contact with numerous products, retail environments and marketing messages aimed at persuading me to buy new cycling clothing. I have also been responsible as a public relations practitioner for promoting luxury fashion, along with as a design journalist critiquing brand storytelling that aims to sell products and create desire. This places an auto-ethnographic approach at the core of this examination, putting importance on the researcher's perspective (I, me), emphasizing personal storytelling and lending validity to the personal knowing. This auto-ethnographic approach is a valuable contemporary and critical response to alternative traditional, more empirically focused methods. Auto-ethnography can be defined as 'a form of self-narrative that places the self within a social context' (Reed-Danahay 1997, p. 9) and it insists on the use of personal stories, reflections, emotions and experiences, asserting the inevitably subjective nature of knowledge, using subjectivity deliberately as an epistemological resource (Butz and Besio 2009).

So what makes Rapha an instructive luxury case-study worth examining with this self-narrative approach? As a key example brand, Rapha stands out in the marketplace for its beautiful performance fabrics, well-cut and manufactured products and for additionally providing self-realization and 'meaning-making' far beyond the addition to a sartorial wardrobe of another cycling item. Instead, it offers a reflection of personal interests, common stories that reveal collective experiences of cycling, and that stimulate my own recollections of what it takes to power up a mountain when my legs are screaming with pain. One might ask—where is the luxury in that? To clarify a position on luxury, Kapferer and Bastien's (2012) description of luxury as distinct from premium is pertinent here:

Premium means pay more, get more in functional benefits. Luxury is elsewhere: it signals the capacity of the buyer to transcend needs, functions or objective benefits. This is how luxury brands are different from premium or super-premium brands: beyond the experience they bring creative power, heritage and social distinction.

Using this understanding as a basis, we can now consider how Rapha has transformed in such a short period into a rarified luxury lifestyle brand and how this has been communicated through stories.

Stories are commonplace in our culture as instructive vehicles of emotional, moral and causal tales. Contemporary consumer brands use stories frequently as conceptual slogans, such as luxury fashion brand Louis Vuitton, which uses the phrase 'the art of travel' to prompt marketing stories and images synonymous with rarified journeys to an elite global audience. In this instance, storytelling is being used to promote Louis Vuitton's wares by evoking emotional connections that move its audience—a commonplace promotional technique. 'Story was the *original* tool of influence,' states Annette Simmons (2006, p. 230). Rapha certainly complies in this way, by using stories of cycling to create social and commercial influence yet crucially, it does much more, embedding stories at the core of the brand and through the very fabric of its identity, constantly re-defining Rapha and its status as a luxury brand through storytelling. The distinctiveness of the brand's stories seems to be their consistency across all expressions of the brand and this is what we are to interrogate now, using Berry's four categories of luxury goods as a structural framework for the critical textual analysis of Rapha's material goods, services and environments, to ascertain the 'red thread' of luxury that creates a coherent cultural storyworld (Abbott 2008).

## Rapha and Clothing

On the website, Rapha.cc, the range available spans menswear, womenswear and a nominal sample of kidswear. The subcategories vary from cycling kit for when on the bike (bib shorts, tights, jerseys, jackets and gilets) to off the bike (trousers, shirts, tops). The various collections available are distinctive in their purpose, level of performance, price points and promotional pitch. For example, the ethos of the Flyweight collection is communicated through the text 'Using the lightest fabrics for the hottest, most humid days' (2017b), which is placed over an image of four cyclists rounding a corner on a steep incline. The Brevet Collection (2017c) has the text line 'Designed with distance in mind' and an image of two cyclists riding by a river winding through tree-covered mountains. The Classic Collection (2017d) has the text title 'Rapha's Most Iconic Products' with a black-and-white grainy image of a cyclist riding on an empty road. Each collection is a distinctive fashion design story, defined by evocative text and visuals that take a different angle on romance, adventure and purpose on two wheels.

When selecting a clothing sample for analysis, the obvious place to begin is with a cycling jersey—an eponymous item that holds a central place in any cyclist's wardrobe. The Classic Jersey II is Rapha's core product and boasts the longest history. It is available in both men's and women's sizes and the white stripe on the sleeve has become a recognizable brand identifier on the roads of Britain. The product caption selling the men's jersey is a clear example of consumer-focused marketing stating (Fig. 11.1):

A Classic Reborn. The Classic Jersey was Rapha's first ever product. A bold expression of the company's mission to create the world's best cycling apparel, it changed the industry. Predominantly black and cut from an unorthodox merino wool-based fabric, Bicycling Magazine's Editor Bill Strickland declared it the 'best bike jersey the world has ever seen'. Twelve years in the making, Rapha introduces a new generation, the Classic Jersey II. Brought up to speed for 2016, this highly evolved design is cut from a new proprietary merino wool-based fabric, milled to Rapha's exact specification. Called RPM150 (Rapha Performance Merino, the 150 indicates grams per square metre), it is lighter, softer and more breathable than generic merino blends, adaptable to a huge range of conditions. Not stopping at the fabric, the construction of the jersey has also improved with a reworked fit and sections bonded rather than stitched. This reduces weight and bulk even further. (Rapha 2017e)

**Fig. 11.1**   Image from Rapha.cc website, Men's Shop section showing a 'Classic Jersey II' cycling jersey top (2017) (© Rapha—reproduced with permission)

Structured as a short creative vignette, the storied lexicon within this passage belongs to the language of luxury, displaying modern luxe aspirations and qualifiers of luxury (see Kapferer 1997; Barnier et al. 2012). These include: global prestige representing social markers ('best bike jersey the world has ever seen'), heritage and culture attached to Rapha ('a classic reborn', 'changed the industry', 'introduces a new generation'), qualitative hedonistic experience and made to last ('highly evolved design', 'milled', 'bonded rather than stitched' properties of the merino), personalisation services ('adaptable to a huge range of conditions') and its price exceeding mere functional value (£110 in exchange for promise of craftsmanship 'twelve years in the making'). To add to this perception, we know *that* this jersey is a desirable product of universal need to any cyclist through the accreditation from an external media specialist, lending valuable international context and the value added promise of being 'the best'. Altogether, this reinforces the knowledge of luxury as temporal and relational. More information on the jersey is listed under the subtitle 'About the new RPM150 fabric', reinforcing the impression of the preoccupation with quality, not exclusivity, being the contemporary key definer of luxury for consumers globally (Albatross Global Solutions and Numberly 2015, cited by Tesseras 2015). Berry's (1994) says: '… luxury is a question of qualitative refinement rather than quantity' (p. 24) and this caption communicates the message of luxury through adjectival qualities of refinement such as 'highly evolved [design]'. This impression is reinforced offline when physically touching the Classic II jersey, where tacit knowledge and the experience of quality is realized through sensory feedback: the merino fabric feels light, the bonded seams are smooth to the touch and the zip glides with faultless connection and a quiet buzz. It is evident *how* this jersey is luxury by its feel, look and sound, communicating refinement of aesthetic sensibilities and luxurious design.

A second sample of clothing to examine for evidence of luxury indicators is the men's Premium Denim—Slim jeans (see Fig. 11.2), provocatively chosen here for Rapha's labelling of 'premium'. The jeans are part of Rapha's City Collection and come with the tagline: 'For life on and off the bike' (Rapha 2017f). The collection brings Rapha as a sportswear brand into the more traditional realm of fashion clothing and reflects the two contemporary socio-cultural trends of 'wellness' and 'athleisure wear' (the latter defined by Merriam-Webster [2017] dictionary as 'casual clothing designed to be worn both for exercising and for general use' or conversely wearing activewear outside of the gym). The product caption reads:

> The Premium Denim Jeans are designed to be extremely hard-wearing while maintaining optimum stretch for freedom of movement. Made from a solid-colour cotton that is stain resistant and fast-drying, both the fabric and construction have been carefully considered to withstand the rigours of city riding. A reflective Rapha logo is printed inside the

Fig. 11.2   Image from Rapha.cc website, Men's Shop section, showing 'Premium Denim—Slim' jeans (2017) (© Rapha—reproduced with permission)

right leg, while hi-vis piping on the inside seam provides additional on-bike visibility when rolled up. A black cowhide leather patch on the outside waistband has a debossed Rapha logo. The jeans use a proprietary high-stretch 11.4 oz denim, milled specifically for Rapha in Italy. (Rapha 2017g)

Although the caption seems remarkably utilitarian in its listing of functional characteristics, there is subtle evidence of storytelling, with the text implicitly communicating that the jeans are the perfect prop for the typical urban cyclist's transitional experience. It eschews an explicit story of a ride and instead uses provocations of oily, dusty, hazardous journeys evoked through details that rely on the customer's personal knowledge of city cycling, such as needing 'freedom of movement' and 'stain resistant and fast-drying'. Yet is it telling a story of luxury? Kapferer and Bastien's (2012) distinction between a luxury good and a premium one applies here:

> ...premiumness is based on objective superiority when comparing alternatives. The more you pay the more you get. Luxury instead is non-comparable. The pricing power of luxury instead rests on high intangibles, making the brand singular, unique: first and foremost its culture, heritage, then country of origin, exceptional know-how, fame of its clients, and so on. (pp. 47–48)

At first reading, the jeans do seem to fit their premium label as quantitative and qualitative aspects could easily be measured against competitor jeans. Crucially, however, it is the assertions of the culture of cycling, the heritage of Italian production and their exemplary performance that supports that they are, in fact, a luxury item. Tacit understanding of this is likely clear to the consumer who has a propensity for international and urban reference points of excellence and quality, along with fashion, design and sporting know-how. Rapha preoccupations with stealth luxury is evident in the debossed brand logo on the exterior, a covert marque of sartorial distinction. Finally, awareness of exclusivity and provenance as luxury desirables is shown in 'milled specifically for Rapha in Italy'. To reinforce a more empirical argument *that* Rapha jeans are a luxury item can be found supported by external market data. The McKinsey Global Fashion Index (MGFI) is a quantitative benchmark system designed to categorize global fashion companies into six fashion market segments. In their 'State of Fashion 2017' report (2016, p. 40), it features a sales price index (with consideration of local geography) to view a standard basket of goods within each market segment.

The example item is a pair of 'plain men's straight/slim cut jeans (no rips)'. Using this as a relevant comparison analysis tool, the price point of Rapha's Premium Denim—Slim men's jeans is £150 (converting to $190 at time of analysis [Investing 2017]) and this places them in the 'Affordable Luxury' category ($156–$315), not in the lower 'Premium/ Bridge' segment. To reflect briefly on Rapha's rationale for naming their product 'premium', it could denote that their sales lexicon is rooted in the commercial clothing market ('premium' meaning 'relating to or denoting a commodity of superior quality and therefore a higher price', Oxford University Press 2017b). It is also relevant to consider that Rapha consistently uses the words 'apparel' or 'clothing' rather than 'fashion', a deliberate choice of language that contributes to its identity as a brand that places performance-led design at its fulcrum, and pitches style (rather than fashion) as its cultural metronome. Rapha's own lexical preference for premium, however, does not preclude the evidence that we know *how* and *that* its stylish jeans are luxury.

## Rapha and Leisure

The next category for analysis of luxury indicators is that of leisure, explained by Berry (1994) as the effort spent undertaking activities that are a human necessity of living and concerned with bodily and physical satisfactions. Rapha engages with leisure on two social levels: cycling as recreation for amateur riders (Rapha's main customers) and cycling as a professional pursuit (their sponsorship of pro-teams such as Canyon/ SRAM). To recap from earlier, the proposition here is that Rapha uses leisure as the driver to its entire business, casting luxurious goods and services as enabling props for the 'good life'.

The main vehicle for the activation of leisure activities is the Rapha Cycling Club (RCC), which launched in 2015. At the D&AD President's Lecture in London in January 2017, Simon Mottram stated that the RCC had over 9000 members and was aiming for 50,000 within the next five to ten years. On Rapha.cc (2017h), the text claims distinctiveness in its field: 'The Rapha Cycling Club (RCC) is the first cycling club of its kind, an active riding and racing club designed to create a global community of like-minded, passionate road riders.' The RCC here is established as a boutique service, structured as a socio-cultural portal to elite leisure activity. If subscribed to the mailing list, the invitation to join the RCC comes through email, within which it sells the Club with a simple storied pitch: 'All together now, the Rapha Cycling Club' the script reads, accompanied by a photograph showing a band of smiling cyclists wearing Club striped jerseys. Clearly, this content indicates tribal inclusivity through two-wheeled leisure, an offer of how membership access equates to a unique passport to physical and social pleasure through cycling. Mottram himself acknowledges the tribal aspect, having been quoted as saying: 'Cycling is such a sport of tribes' (Lindsey 2017). As a mode of inclusion, the email invitation may not be the typical closed approach of traditional member clubs where an invitation often comes through 'inside' connections. Yet, in many ways, the RCC *is* an elitist, gated community. To join the RCC tribe, a 12-month membership costs £135 (Rapha 2017i) and the Member's webpage acts as a paywall behind which lies the community and leisure services, accessible to those who have the economic capital to afford it and the social and cultural capital to consider it desirable. As a commercial barrier it enforces the impression of Rapha as an 'affordable' luxury brand, with egalitarian roots in social trends such as the 'democratisation of luxury' (Evrard and Roux 2005). The success of the RCC is that it relies on an increasing number of global consumers with high disposable income and the penchant for high prestige luxury symbols and networked communities. Jones identifies these types of protected areas accessed through consumption and economic capital as 'limited-access "electronic communities"' (1999, p. 16). The barriers to join are insurmountable to those who cannot afford it and thus exclusive in their function. Agnès Rocamora discusses social and commercial parameters in the context of luxury fashion noting, 'gates and boundaries are re-embedded on digital platforms, allowing for the reproduction and maintenance of social hierarchies' (2016, p. 210). On Rapha.cc it can be concluded, the digital paywall acts as a technological gatekeeper of aspirational prestige and literally signifies that you are either in or out of the Club. Mottram has taken his activation of socio-cultural tribalism further claiming:

I think Rapha is like a cult, but a good one as well, if you can conjure that idea, and I think that's no bad thing. And if people are in the Club, then they're part of the cult. (2017)

If membership is paid then access into the Club's Member's area or 'cult' host environment, is granted. Tribal connotations can be found infusing all areas and texts, such as the RCC's Terms and Conditions (2017j), of which these are excerpts:

> The RCC motto is *ex duris gloria* ('glory through suffering'). [author's italics]
> The RCC is international in perspective, character and membership.
> The RCC is an inclusive club of like-minded individuals, and members are encouraged to get to know each other both on and off the bike.
> The RCC identity includes RCC typography, RCC stripes & colours and the RCC shield.

Rapha is under fifteen years of age, yet here it is building a myth of a significantly longer heritage and communicating a territorial ambition. The Latin motto and the RCC identity, indicated through colours, type choice and shield, gives the sense of a legacy plumbed for authentic values and ancestral leanings.

The lexicon of social privilege continues (Rapha 2017j) under the Membership sub-header, where the text reads as a code of conduct and meticulous description is given outlining the expected standards of socio-cultural behaviour:

- RCC members will uphold good riding etiquette and camaraderie and abide by the Rapha/RCC ride etiquette rules. Members will greet other riders on the road, wait for dropped riders, and help those in need. …
- The RCC champions the road less travelled and members are encouraged to use the road bike to explore new routes and discover adventures.
- The RCC honours the 'lanterne rouge' in every race; the RCC recognises the suffering needed just to survive.

These are organizing principles that reveal a culturally attuned level of civility, respect and deference—the formal tenets of a philosophy of cycling that Rapha has built into its foundations. It also reveals Rapha's interpretation of authenticity encompassing both the *context* of leisure ('social spins', 'new routes', 'discover adventures') and the *content* of leisure ('road bike', 'lanterne rouge', 'training rides'). The personal, temporal and spatial requirements listed inform and support the new member in conforming to their new consumer brand tribe. In terms of story, 'Championing the road less travelled' is the clue to the RCC's larger meta-narrative as a club of purpose, integrity and Western middle-class values, all activated in the pursuit of an adventurous ideal. This underwrites the sense of luxury, situating Rapha as a label for the bourgeoisie, or in Pierre Bourdieu's terms, their tastes are 'tastes of luxury (or freedom)' (1996, p. 177) rather than necessity, enabled by cultural and economic capital.

The Kit Rules list on the same RCC webpage also reveals cultural and liberal aesthetic persuasions stating, 'The RCC believes in creativity in cycling style, as long as it is done with panache and individuality' (Rapha 2017j). In just a few short words, it communicates to the RCC members the conditionality of how and where style meets performance, revealing the essence and cultish control of this lifestyle brand as it challenges members to indulge in cycling at their leisure while consciously acting as brand ambassadors who exemplify both functional capabilities and aesthetic taste. Pierre Bourdieu comments on taste as a marker of class stating: 'Taste classifies, and it classifies the classifier' (1996, p. 6). Rapha's distinctive air of luxury comes through its penchant for both elite sporting and sartorial flair as displayed on its classifying riders.

On the RCC Membership landing page in the Members section (Rapha 2017i), a looping varied sequence of photographs alternately shows members riding together in Club colours (see Fig. 11.3), a close-ups of individual cyclists or an image of Rapha's own magazine, *Mondial*. Each image is accompanied by a short caption, such as 'Ride With Us', which provides a sense of the dynamic leisure activity of cycling and the social network of the RCC. Underneath, membership benefits are listed under three headers 'Ride', 'Race' and 'Rest', reflecting the benefits of luxury leisure as interpreted by this cycling

**Fig. 11.3**   Image from Rapha.cc website, 'Membership' page (2017) (© Rapha—reproduced with permission)

brand. Examples include '21 RCC chapters in major cities, providing an international riding community', 'Free bike hire on Rapha Travel', 'RCC Race Jersey lifetime crash replacement', 'Monthly socials hosted at Rapha Clubhouses' and 'Priority access to annual sales and select new products'. Words such as 'exclusive', 'limited edition', 'personalised', 'preferential', 'priority access' and 'free' are used, all qualities that underpin the theme of luxurious experience, whether through VIP treatment or complementary services. These are signs of the 'staging of rarity' (Marion 2000, p. 306) and also scarcity, which underpins the perceived elevated value of modern luxury goods and provides the logic of privileged inclusion, thereby engineering the desire to belong.

The link between experience and leisure is a common leitmotif for modern lifestyle brands and Rapha is no exception. End-of-season parties, pop-up events and hard luxury items such as RCC podcasts, RCC smartphone rides app and a 'fleet of high end Canyon bikes and Canyon Commuter bike hire from Clubhouses' exemplify this. With this potent mixture of leisure offerings, Rapha is reflecting clearly the market's current preference for luxury to be inclusive (note, to the 'right' extent, given luxury's relational importance), modern and experiential. In WGSN's *Condé Nast Future Luxury 2016—Key Takeaways* report, it claims these aspects as core contemporary values reflecting:

The traditional perception of luxury as an indicator of status and wealth is questioned, as younger generations are aspiring more to personal expression and seeking brands that share their values. Leading a more refined life centred around culture, travel and wellness gives consumers more cultural cachet than possessing a luxury item, experts at the conference agreed, which is forcing the luxury industry to rethink their positioning, offering and marketing. (Ng 2016)

The relational geographical context of leisurely refinement can be found in its philosophy of 'Local Club, Global Community' (Rapha 2017i). This tagline reflects Rapha's 'glocal' approach, as defined as 'the interpretation of the global and the local, resulting in unique outcomes in different geographic areas' (Ritzer 2006, pp. 337–338). When first joining, new members select their geographical 'Chapter', whether in Europe, North America, Asia Pacific, or the generic option, 'international'. The Rapha's web copy explains:

The RCC is split into chapters located around the world. Each chapter has a unique identity and when you join the RCC you choose the chapter geographically applicable to you. Most chapters are affiliated to a Clubhouse, which will become your base for events and rides. (Rapha 2017k)

The decision to use the word 'chapter' for the local RCC branches is intriguing. One definition of this word is 'the governing body of a religious community or knightly order' (Oxford University Press 2017c). The alignment to a specific chapter is reminiscent of other social clubs, such as American sororities and fraternities. It signifies the active role of the RCC chapter as a social structuring unit for a local community. Each chapter has a text describing its character, riders and ethos, for example:

London is the oldest of the chapters and also one of the largest. It is also a fluid group, with regular faces joining occasional riders for Wednesday hill sessions and Friday social laps of Regent's Park. … These rides are very much about the journey and the chat and will usually involve lunch or a cake stop before heading back to town. … (Rapha 2017l)

The description sells an accessible experience and is weighted semantically to drive inclusive engagement from both novice and experienced riders interested in leisure. It also contains overtones of tribal loyalty, hierarchy and expectations of members' behaviour, as much as what an RCC member can expect if coming along for a ride.

The unique identity of each local chapter is also helped by a distinctive and idiosyncratic graphic logo, or 'emblem' as Rapha calls it. The London chapter emblem, for example, comprises a black crown motif called 'Royal Greenery' and the story behind the design is explained on the website thus:

> For one bloody Tudor ruler an area of isolated farmland on the wrong side of town had instant appeal. In 1538 King Henry VIII seized what is now Regent's Park and added it to his vast collection of hunting chases, which today form London's Royal Parks. 'Old Coppernose' was known to follow a philosophy of working to live, not living to work and most mornings rose late, choosing to spend his day indulging in his favourite pastime rather than get on with the business of governing. It seemed fitting then, to base the emblem for the London chapter of the Rapha Cycling Club (RCC) and its Clubhouses in Soho and Spitalfields, on the emblem of London Royal Parks as a reminder to find time to do what you like best. (Rapha 2017m)

In this paragraph, the key character of King Henry VIII promotes a narrative of refined leisure equating to noble aspirations and the distinctive environs of royal parks evokes socio-cultural privilege. The story and its message resonates for me weeks later, when on a cycle ride of my own in North London, I ride around closed road barriers and into Regent's Park, past the royal crown, sitting atop the gate post. Its gold paint glints in the early morning sunlight and it reminds me of the Royal Greenery motif and the philosophy of mindful leisure, giving me validation that riding urban hills before breakfast is finding personal time to do what I like best. It is also evidence of my subliminal persuasion by the brand and exemplifies that Rapha's influence is not simply the stories it tells, rather that the stories have narrative congruence with my own experience. To sum up, it is 'the cumulative power of [my]…

exposure to the meta-message' (Lakhani 2008, p. 56) that is powerful and mobilizes (Fig. 11.4).

Returning to the Rapha website and app, there can be found numerous storied pitches offering paid for leisure opportunities, most obviously in the travel section where it promotes future rides, events, trips, global training camps, races and tailored holidays. An example of an international trip is the RCC Summit Boulder, a 3-day supported trip

**Fig. 11.4** Photograph of pillar displaying royal insignia and crown, at the entrance to Regent's Park, London (2017)

**Fig. 11.5**   Image of Rapha.cc website, 'RCC Summit Boulder' webpage (2017) (© Rapha—reproduced with permission)

in Colorado, USA, with the cost for a single occupant being £1300 (Rapha 2017n). The web page (see Fig. 11.5) shows a photograph of a dusty road with a backdrop of tree-covered hills and a hazy recession of planes. This promotional copy sets the scene:

> Local guides will lead rides through the old mining camps of Gold Hill, and along the famed Peak to Peak Highway, all supported by follow cars to provide mechanical assistance and ride fuel. Finish your day with some cold Colorado brews while enjoying the company of Summit VIPs and fellow RCC members as you watch the sun tuck behind the Rockies. (Rapha 2017n)

This brief synopsis promises local context combined with the global content of a luxury leisure experience. Descriptive adjectives (such as 'cold Colorado' to qualify 'beer') have been used decisively along with entitled prefixes and abbreviations understood by an international clientele ('Summit VIP') denoting the importance of the conquering endeavour. These move the trip from the realms of the universal need for luxury into the elevated intentional realms of desire. It also communicates the collaborative effort by the brand and the members alike to achieve fulfilment, or physical and bodily satisfaction, through collective immersion in the cultural process of luxury glocalisation. As part of a paid for riding experience, the Summit Boulder trip offers much opportunity for consumer engagement at all levels, for example, it offers collaboration through engendering purposeful activity between clients and support staff/brand (Rapha). Evans and McKee (2010, p. 15) illustrate that structured engagement for consumers increases systematically as the social environment changes from consumption, curation, creation to collaboration, so for the price of £1300, this trip is offering the highest levels of experiential engagement. In 1998, Pine and Gilmore (p. 98) termed contemporary society the 'Experience Economy' explaining: 'An experience occurs when a company intentionally uses services as the stage, and goods as props, to engage individual customers in a way that creates a memorable event.' Pine comments, 'Brands must remember that consumers are looking to become better people. [...] If they are buying physical goods, it's to achieve aspirations, whatever they might be' (Sherman 2016). Simon Mottram commented at the D&AD President's Lecture in London in 2017 that:

> It [cycling] is a social thing, it is a thing you do with friends. You create better relationships on a bike than you do in any other walk of life. I guarantee it almost. .... It offers adventure, discovery, you often see the world, it is something that you can do when you are seventy or you can do when you are seven. And it keeps you fit, and it is generally a good ecological and financial thing to do. It's got everything. (Mottram 2017)

It can be concluded that Rapha package their leisure travel services as the ultimate landscaped stage, with the bicycle and accessories acting as props. Achieving sporting and personal aspirations alongside results in a fulfilling luxury experience and networked community that thousands of international members subscribe to, proving Rapha is achieving a glocality of leisure that is scalable and seemingly authentic.

## Rapha's Shelter and Sustenance

The last two categories of Rapha's portfolio to be considered are shelter and sustenance. A Rapha Clubhouse fits these two categories as both a standalone physical retail space and café. London's Soho is the original, hence its selection for analysis, and it is publicized on Rapha's website in the following terms:

> Rapha's first-ever Clubhouse was launched in 2012 and instantly became a destination for the London cycling community. The location proved so popular that it was expanded in 2014, adding more retail space and a larger café area. The Clubhouse is located a stone's throw from Piccadilly on Brewer Street and is continually vibrant. … Events are a regular feature of the Clubhouse, and visitors could find themselves rubbing shoulders with some of the biggest names in the sport, who will often make a point of visiting when they are in town. (Rapha 2017m)

This is a persuasive blurb and it uses an inviting tone-of-voice and storied approach. On the summer's day that I visit, the door is open with the streets outside humming with taxis, pedestrians and cycle couriers. Immediately inside, there is a horizontal metal rail with hooks for clientele to hang their bikes during their visit; none of the bikes are locked. The atmosphere inside is buoyant, with Rapha staff in branded T-shirts chatting to each other and clients, who are wearing a wide range of business clothing, athleisurewear, performance cycling wear, office shoes, distinctive trainers and cleated cycle shoes. The shop space is visually stimulating with framed photographs of historic riders, newspaper tears and cycling memorabilia hanging from walls and parked at the rear (see Fig. 11.6), a light grey Citroën H-Van. The iconic traditional *voiture balai* or 'broom wagon' holds an iconic and nostalgic place in the history of elite cycling, first introduced to the Tour de France in 1910 for the purposes of collecting overly slow competitors in the mountain stages. Behind the van is a large-scale black-and-white photograph of a snowy mountain pass giving appropriate environmental context. The H-Van is a significant leitmotif of Rapha's alignment to the mythology of cycling (see Barthes 1957) and again signifies cultural acuity. In the main body of the shop, there are orderly racks of clothing, a mannequin display of coloured jerseys (including a signed *maillot jeune*, a King of the Mountains jersey and jerseys from the Rapha current collection), and a traditional glass display case containing perforated leather shoes and wallets, with a classic Peugeot bike balanced

**Fig. 11.6**  Citroën H-Van in Rapha's Soho Clubhouse in Brewer Street, London (2017) (© Rapha—photographed with permission)

on the top. Also on display are Rapha's own label skincare products such as Body Wash, which has the long title: 'Rapha, Summer Embrocation, Baume Chauffant, Warming Body Balm. Performance skincare' (see Fig. 11.7). The copy on the packaging gives further details:

> Rapha Performance Skincare products are designed to protect your skin against the elements and the wear and tear of riding. A highly effective

**Fig. 11.7** [left] Rapha Body Wash (2017) (© Rapha—reproduced with permission)

summer embrocation for warmer conditions. Contains warming agents Wintergreen and Capiscum as well as Menthol and Arnica to help revive and comfort the skin. The unique fragrance is inspired by aromatic plants and herbs found on the slopes of Mount Ventoux. (Rapha 2017o)

The combination of this evocative description (using the language of sensorial marketing) plus the monochromatic design of the packaging gives the impression that the product is aimed at both sexes. This acknowledges that *all* cyclists need functional products that soothe and sensorial products that recall positive memories. Mont Ventoux is a mythical mountain, viewed by most riders as one of the hardest climbs in Europe and often included as an iconic challenge in the Tour de France. For the price of £20, Rapha have attempted to imbue their

**Fig. 11.8** Photograph of cyclist on Mont Ventoux, beside packaging of Rapha Body Wash showing same landscape (2017) (© Rapha—photographed with permission)

body wash with that magnetic feeling of elite summit success (Fig. 11.8) by utilizing a photograph of the landscape, a textual description and aromatic scent that taps into the experience.

The Soho Clubhouse retail space is connected to a similarly sized café which again displays goods imbued with cultural significance. A strip of pennant flags (the decoration at Pro races) hangs suspended from metal utility pipes above and a shiny metal bar, panini maker and Italian coffee machine add to the industrial chic ambiance that attracts 'hipster' clientele. A daily latte with heart-shaped froth art served in Rapha coffee cups is complementary to RCC members and many who come in do flash membership cards in exchange for their caffeine. The low café tables are glass display cases and these contain cycling related ephemera such as Ordnance Survey maps showing the terrain of classic climbs. A large screen situated behind the bar streams digital footage of international racing. These multi-layered elements all enforce the impression of Rapha as an adventurous European lifestyle brand, fueled by passion, adrenaline and a sense of adventure for the sport of cycling (see Fig. 11.9).

For the customer who likes immersion in luxury shelter and complementary sustenance, this highly designed, culturally loaded environment must provide a reassuringly elitist atmosphere. The Rapha bricks-and-mortar store offers an immersive experience, clearly fulfilling all five key experience–design principles that Pine and Gilmore (1998) define: theme the experience; harmonize impressions with positive cues;

**Fig. 11.9**  A coffee on glass display table containing paper map in Rapha's Soho Clubhouse, London (2017) (© Rapha—photographed with permission)

eliminate negative cues; mix in memorabilia; and engage all five senses (pp. 102–104). For the casual or hungry visitor, this shelter provides gastronomic, multi-sensory sustenance; a space to sit and consume, to walk around and enjoy. We know *that* and *how* this is a luxury shelter that provides sustenance as it is consumer indulgence at its zenith, supplying accessible, affordable glocal culture and high quality, promotional, storied experiences as part of packaged 'shoppertailing' or 'entertailing'.

## Conclusion

In this study, critical textual analysis of Rapha's goods, services and environments using Berry's (1994) basic categories of luxury goods has determined that we know *that* and *how* Rapha is a luxury lifestyle brand. It has shown that Rapha qualifies as a luxury brand through charting the socio-cultural indicators, refined qualities and culturally-loaded and materialised story strands that flow through the textual fabrics of its branded clothing, leisure offerings, Clubhouses (shelter) and cafés (sustenance). It has been discussed that luxury is manifest when pre-existing simple necessities and basic fundamental needs are fully met, and indulgence in the higher realms of esteem building and self-actualisation through material goods or experiences are attained. Therefore, if we believe its founder and CEO Simon Mottram's intentions, to '…take them [millions of cyclists] by the hand, and take them on the most amazing journey through cycling', then putting cycling itself at the heart of motivational self-actualization places Rapha's brand offerings in the role of agents, as satellite accoutrements through which the luxurious experience is achieved. Add to this the knowledge of Rapha's internal tagline 'glory through suffering' (Mottram 2017), then Rapha's luxurious goods are glorified packaging showcasing physical suffering, ultimately showing how Rapha's success is to dress the sport of cycling in the finest fabrics while telling tales of a luxurious experience.

This examination of Rapha altogether reveals how it has woven a 'red thread' of storied luxury throughout its brand world—its 'storyworld' (Abbott 2008)—and that these stories are activated with coherence through its material goods, texts and environments. Rapha utilises the history and myths of cycling as much as its contemporary scene to energise its audience and uses nuanced, value-based stories that rely on socio-cultural taste that speaks to a certain clientele. Rapha's textual and visual stories showcase themes of luxurious adventure, rarefied travel and a philosophy of leisure, and this rich story content is personally validated by Mottram, who claims Rapha's uniqueness in its field:

> So there are so many ways that we have been first, which I think is so important to the success of the company. Critically, urban wear, what we now call city clothing – we did that in 2005, when only a couple of other brands were even thinking about it. We were the first to do … story-based product. Nobody was doing story-based product, which is crazy as it is a sport full of stories. (Mottram 2017)

It is in this manner that Rapha is remarkable and distinctive in the marketplace, namely by critically introducing style to cycling, supported by an experiential luxury lifestyle portfolio that is built around stories. It is possible therefore to conclude that Rapha's storytelling is wholly integrated within its offerings where the stories act as a promotional call-to-action, successfully influencing and mobilising an increasing global audience in search of authentic, opti-channel brand connection and luxurious experiences that resonate in this new Age of You.

# References

Abbott, H. Porter, 2008. *The Cambridge Introduction to Narrative*. 2nd ed. Cambridge: Cambridge University Press.

Barthes, Roland. 1957. *Mythologies*. Translated from French by R. Howard and A. Lavers, 2013. New York: Hill and Wang.

Berry, Christopher J. 1994. *The Idea of Luxury: A Conceptual and Historical Investigation*. Cambridge: Cambridge University Press.

Bull, Andy. 2013. *Brand Journalism*. Oxon: Routledge.

BOF Team. 2017. "Building a Luxury Group Isn't Easy." *Business of Fashion*, 28 April. https://www.businessoffashion.com/articles/this-week-in-fashion/building-a-luxury-group-isnt-easy. Accessed on 1 June 2017.

Bourdieu, Pierre. [1979] 1996. *Distinction: A Social Critique of the Judgement of Taste*. London: Routledge.

Business of Fashion and McKinsey & Company. 2016. "The State of Fashion 2017." https://images.businessoffashion.com/site/uploads/2016/11/The_State_of_Fashion_2017.pdf. Accessed on 5 April 2017.

Butz, David, and Kathryn Besio. 2009. "Autoethnography." *Geography Compass* 3 (5): 1660–1674.

De Barnier, Virginie, Sandrine Falcy, and Pierre Valette-Florence. 2012. "Do Consumers Perceive Three Levels of Luxury? A Comparison of Accessible, Intermediate and Inaccessible Luxury Brands." *Journal of Brand Management* 19 (7): 623–636.

Evans, Dave, and Jake McKee. 2010. *Social Media Marketing: The Next Generation of Business Engagement*. Indianapolis: Wiley.

Evrard, Yves, and Elyette Roux. 2005. *Culture vs Luxury: The Paradoxes of Democratisation*. Puyricard: CEROG.

Gould, Stephen J. 1991. "The Self-Manipulation of My Pervasive, Perceived Vital Energy Through Product Use: An Introspective-Praxis Perspective." *Journal of Consumer Research* 18 (2): 194–207. http://www.academia.edu/7533291/The_Self-Manipulation_of_My_Pervasive_Perceived_Vital_Energy_through_Product_Use_An_Introspective-Praxis_Perspective. Accessed on 20 August 2017.

Google. 2017. Available at https://www.google.co.uk/search?q=rapha&oq=rapha&aqs=chrome..69i57j69i60l5.2458j0j7&sourceid=chrome&ie=UTF-8. Accessed on 4 July 2017.

Investing. 2017. "Currency Converter." *Investing.com* [Online]. https://uk.investing.com/currencies/gbp-usd-converter. Accessed on 3 July 2017.

Jones, Steve. 1999. "Studying the Net." In *Doing Internet Research: Critical Issues and Methods for Examining the Net*, edited by Steve Jones, 1–27. London: Sage.

Kapferer, Jean-Noël. 1997. "Managing Luxury Brands." *Journal of Brand Management* 4 (4): 251–259.

Kapferer, Jean-Noël, and Vincent Bastien. 2012. *The Luxury Strategy: Break the Rules of Marketing to Build Luxury Brands*. London: Kogan Page.

Lakhani, Dave. 2008. *Subliminal Persuasion: Influence and Marketing Secrets They Don't Want You to Know*. New Jersey: Wiley.

Lindsey, Joe. 2017. "Rapha Bought by Walmart Heirs; Here's How the Brand Might Change." *Bicycling*. http://www.bicycling.com/bikes-gear/rapha-bought-by-walmart-heirs-heres-how-the-brand-might-change. Accessed on 17 August 2017.

Marion, Gilles. 2000. Objets et marques de luxe. In *Le Luxe*, edited by O. Assouly, 293–317. Paris: Regard.

Merriam-Webster. 2017. "Athleisure." https://www.merriam-webster.com/dictionary/athleisure. Accessed on 4 July 2017.

Mottram, Simon. 2017. "D&AD President's Lecture," London, 11 January.

Ng, E. 2016. "Condé Nast Future Luxury 2016 Key Takeaways' Report." *WGSN*. Published on: 27 April 2016. http://library.northumbria.ac.uk/home. Accessed on 27 June 2017.

Oxford University Press. 2017a. *Oxford Dictionaries*. https://en.oxforddictionaries.com/definition/emporium. Accessed on 24 September 2017.

Oxford University Press. 2017b. *Oxford Dictionaries*. London: Oxford University Press. https://en.oxforddictionaries.com/definition/premium. Accessed on 4 July 2017.

Oxford University Press. 2017c. *Oxford Dictionaries*. London: Oxford University Press. https://en.oxforddictionaries.com/definition/chapter. Accessed on 5 July 2017.

Pine II, B. Joseph, and James H. Gilmore. 2007. *Authenticity: What Consumers Really Want*. Available at https://books.google.co.uk/books?hl=en&lr=&id=VpTSBgAAQBAJ&oi=fnd&pg=PP1&dq=authenticity+what+consumers+really+want&ots=45OsHP4Wnz&sig=SYBgk1yBcXrUc Sb_2iUw1rkqAZc#v=onepage&q=authenticity%20what%20consumers%20really%20want&f=false. Accessed on 19 August 2017.

Pine II, B. Joseph, and James H. Gilmore. 1998. "Welcome to the Experience Economy." *Harvard Business Review*, July–August 1998, 97–105. Boston, MA: Harvard Business School Publishing.

Rapha. 2017a. "01 Company." Rapha. http://pages.rapha.cc/about-rapha/company. Accessed on 5 July 2017.

Rapha. 2017b. "Flyweight." Rapha. https://www.rapha.cc/it/en/shop/flyweight/category/flyweight-collection. Accessed on 11 July 2017.

Rapha. 2017c. "Brevet Collection." Rapha. https://www.rapha.cc/it/en/shop/brevet/category/brevet. Accessed on 24 September 2017.

Rapha. 2017d. "Classic." Rapha. https://www.rapha.cc/it/en/shop/classics-/category/trainingandracing. Accessed on 24 September 2017.

Rapha. 2017e. "Classic Jersey II." Rapha. https://www.rapha.cc/gb/en/shop/classic-jersey-ii/product/CLJ04. Accessed on 3 July 2017.

Rapha. 2017f. "City." Rapha. https://www.rapha.cc/it/en/shop/city/category/cityriding. Accessed on 3 July 2017.

Rapha. 2017g. "Premium Denim—Slim." Rapha. https://www.rapha.cc/gb/en/shop/premium-denim—slim/product/DJO01. Accessed on 3 July 2017.

Rapha. 2017h. "RCC Membership—New Member." Rapha. https://www.rapha.cc/gb/en/shop/-rcc-membership—new-member/product/RCM04XX. Accessed on 6 July 2017.

Rapha. 2017i. "Membership 2017." Rapha. https://www.rapha.cc/it/en/rcc/membership. Accessed on 24 September 2017.

Rapha. 2017j. "RCC Terms & Conditions." Rapha. http://pages.rapha.cc/rcc-terms-conditions. Accessed on 4 July 2017.

Rapha. 2017k. "RCC Chapters." Rapha. https://www.rapha.cc/gb/en/rcc/chapters. Accessed on 4 July 2017.

Rapha. 2017l. "RCC Chapters London." Rapha. https://www.rapha.cc/gb/en/rcc/chapters#rccldn. Accessed on 5 July 2017.

Rapha. 2017m. "London Soho." Rapha. https://www.rapha.cc/it/en/club-houses/londonsoho. Accessed on 6 July 2017.

Rapha. 2017n. "United States RCC Summit Boulder." Rapha. https://www.rapha.cc/gb/en/shop/rcc-summit-boulder/travel/T1770. Accessed on 5 July 2017.

Rapha. 2017o. "Body Wash." London: Rapha.

Reed-Danahay, Deborah. 1997. "Introduction." In *Auto/Ethnography: Rewriting the Self and the Social*, edited by D. Reed-Danahay, 1–20. Oxford: Berg.

Ritzer, George. 2006. *McDonaldization: The Reader*. 2nd ed. Thousand Oaks, CA: Pine Forge Press.

Roberts, Joanne, and John Armitage. 2016. "Knowing Luxury: From Socio-cultural Value to Market Price?" In *Critical Luxury Studies: Art, Design, Media*, Ch. 2. Edinburgh: Edinburgh University Press.

Robins, Rebecca. 2015. *What Is Luxury in the Age of You* [pdf]. Interbrand. http://interbrand.com/views/what-is-luxury-in-the-age-of-you. Accessed on 20 August 2017.

Rocamora, Agnès. 2016. "Online Luxury: Geographies of Production and Consumption and the Louis Vuitton Website." In *Critical Luxury Studies: Art, Design, Media*, edited by J. Armitage and J. Roberts, 199–220. Edinburgh: Edinburgh University Press.

Sheehan, Brian. 2010. *Online Marketing*. Lausanne: AVA Publishing.

Sherman, Lauren. 2016. "Is the New Luxury a Better You?" *Business of Fashion*, 5 May 2016. https://www.businessoffashion.com/articles/intelligence/are-luxury-brands-ready-for-the-transformation-economy-wellness-health-direct-vision. Accessed on 17 August 2017.

Simmons, Annette. 2006. *The Story Factor: Inspiration, Influence and Persuasion Through the Art of Storytelling*. Cambridge, MA: Perseus Books.

Tesseras, Lucy. 2015. "Four Trends Changing the Definition of Luxury." *Marketing Week*, 30 September. https://www.marketingweek. com/2015/09/30/four-trends-changing-the-definition-of-luxury/?no-cache=true&adfesuccess=1. Accessed on 30 August 2017.

Vogelaar, Rijn. 2009. *The Superpromoter: The Power of Enthusiasm*. Translated from Dutch by P. De Wolff, 2011. Hampshire: Palgrave Macmillan.

Wood, Zoe. 2017. "Cycling Fashion Outfit Rapha Plots Route into the Fast Lane." *The Guardian*, 2 May 2017. Available at https://www.theguardian. com/business/2017/may/01/rapha-the-brand-thats-making-cycling-into-a-lifestyle. Accessed on 4 May 2017.

Woodside, Arch G. 2004. "Advancing from Subjective to Confirmatory Personal Introspection in Consumer Research." *Journal of Psychology and Marketing* [e-journal] 21 (12): 987–1010. http://dx.doi.org/10.1002/mar.20034.

# Author Index

© The Editor(s) (if applicable) and The Author(s), under exclusive
license to Springer Nature Switzerland AG 2020
I. Cantista and T. Sádaba (eds.), *Understanding Luxury Fashion*,
Palgrave Advances in Luxury, https://doi.org/10.1007/978-3-030-25654-8

# Subject Index

Mass consumption 71, 72, 80, 82
Masstige 82
Materials 89, 91, 95, 96, 98, 100,
102, 103, 105, 109, 111, 114,
222, 224, 233, 235–239
Membership 243, 254–257, 266
Millennials 148, 149, 151–153, 155,
157–169
Modern(ity) 180, 184, 187, 191,
198, 223, 229–231, 237, 238
Movement 90, 110, 111

Nationalism 76
Natural dyes 104, 105
Neocraft 99, 111, 115
New 224, 231, 235
new aesthetic 229
new design 223
renewal 229

Omega 205, 206, 209–213, 215–218
Omega Ultraman 206, 210, 214

Perfumes 151, 153, 158, 163, 166,
169
history of perfumes 149
Post 206, 210, 212
Prada 130, 132, 133, 138
Premium 246, 247, 250, 252, 253
Products 222, 223, 225–230,
236–238
Promotion 247, 248, 261, 268, 269

Quality 65

Rapha 243–269
Rapha Cycling Club (RCC) branches
243–269
Religion 65, 71
buddhism 64
catholicism 73, 74
confucianism 68
Retail 221, 226, 239, 243, 244, 246,
262, 263, 266
luxury retail 186, 189
online retailing 176, 178
Riders 245, 253–256, 258, 259,
263, 265

Selfish 74, 75
Self-narrative 246
Shelter 244, 262, 267
"Shoppertailing" 268
Social and cultural pressure 68, 79,
80
Social inequality 73, 74
Social media 150, 153, 163, 167,
169
Social networks 10, 207, 209–211,
213, 215, 217
Space 221, 223, 228, 231, 233–238
Spain 227–229, 231
Speedy Tuesday 206, 209–218
Sport 244, 245, 254, 263, 266, 268,
269
Status 68, 71, 80, 82

Lightning Source UK Ltd.
Milton Keynes UK
UKHW05201220120
357447UK00009B/78